The Hausa of Nigeria

Frank A. Salamone

University Press of America,® Inc.
Lanham • Boulder • New York • Toronto • Plymouth, UK

Copyright © 2010 by
University Press of America,® Inc.
4501 Forbes Boulevard
Suite 200
Lanham, Maryland 20706
UPA Acquisitions Department (301) 459-3366

Estover Road
Plymouth PL6 7PY
United Kingdom

Library of Congress Control Number: 2009936243
ISBN: 978-0-7618-4724-3 (paperback : alk. paper)
eISBN: 978-0-7618-4725-0

This book is dedicated to my wife Virginia. She allowed me to conduct fieldwork in Nigeria over a long period of time and through many personal disappointments. Through it all she stuck with me and encouraged me to carry on. I also dedicate this work to all my children who shared me with the field and my studies. Of course, the Nigerian people have contributed to my work over the years, and some still are there for me, aiding my understanding.

There's nothing that makes you so aware of the improvisation of human existence as a song unfinished. Or an old address book. Carson McCullers

Contents

Tables

Acknowledgments

There are many people responsible for any success I may have had. I have named my wife and children as well as the people of Nigeria. My mentor and friend Charles Frantz pointed the way for me and has always aided my work. SUNY-Buffalo supported my early fieldwork. Iona College has been generous in its aid over the years. The Fulbright Program chose me for a stretch in Nigeria at the University of Ibadan. Other government agencies have helped fund my research. The Dominican missionaries have been indispensable to my work over the years. Two Josephs, Riin and Miangu, were friends and helpers. Father Henry Yanju and his brother Edward helped me greatly as did Olu Moloye and Kunle Adamoso. There are too many more to name. Thanks to all.

Introduction—Wrestling with Identity: From Newbie to Elder

In 1990, I returned to Yauri in Nigeria's northwestern area. I had been there on many previous occasions. Many people whom I had known over a twenty-year period came to greet me. Among them was Sule Mamman, whom I had first met when he was in his early teens in 1970. I had seen Sule numerous times since. He and his cousin, Aliyu, had worked for me in the summer of 1972 for three months. I had described him in *Gods and Goods in Africa* (1974) as a Hausa Huck Finn. By 1990, unfortunately, drugs and drink had taken their toll on him.

When Sule first came to greet me he was barely able to stand and his perfect Hausa speech was marred by his drunken slurring of words. After a short time, I ended the conversation and said goodbye as politely as I could. The next day Sule returned to apologize to me, so he said. He invited me to accompany him to the market along the Niger River. Our entrance must have been a source of great amusement as we took motorcycle taxis, rather ungracefully riding on the back. Stumbling off the cycle, I followed Sule into the market where he promised to show me "something special." Alas, it was one bit more of his attempts to see whether I was wise enough to stay out of trouble, as the presence of naked Kamberi virgins attested.

INTRODUCTION

Anthropology's basic boundary marker from other social sciences has been fieldwork and the culture concept developed through it. Fieldwork has a romantic aura, one that has clung to it despite almost innumerable books and articles detailing its inner workings from almost every conceivable

angle. Certainly, movies, TV programs, and novels have wielded more influence over the imagination of the public than all the dry, technical tomes
academics have produced. Moreover, let us be honest, we have reveled in
Susan Sontag's (1963) characterization of the heroic anthropologist.

> The anthropologist is thus not only the mourner of the old world of the
> primitives but its custodian as well. Living among the shadows, struggling to
> distinguish the archaic from the pseudoarchaic, he acts out a heroic, diligent
> and complex modern pessimism.

Assuredly, there have been those like James Boon (1975) who have
bridled at the characterization, at least as Sontag applied it to Levi-Strauss,
but in our secret hearts do we not really at times allow ourselves the hidden pleasure of seeing ourselves as the heroes of our own fantasies "in the
field"? Who among us has not enchanted and bored our students with tales
of our work in the field, typically featuring ourselves in some heroic role?
   Certainly, there are heroic aspects to the anthropological endeavor, even
if they may not be exactly as Sontag described them. There are dangers in
fieldwork, psychological as well as physical, and we measure ourselves by
how well we survived them. There are also ambiguities we must face almost
daily. Learning how to cope with these imponderables teaches us a good
deal about our lives. In dealing with the young men whom I discuss – Sule,
Matthew, Jacob, Jude, and others – I discovered aspects of myself I truly
did not know I had. In spite of some troubling revelations and experiences,
such as the subsequent murders of two of my friends in the field, resulting
from their threat to the Islamic rulers of their areas, the experiences were
worth the pain and not all was pain, of course. There were many happy occasions. Never again does an anthropologist, I believe, feel so intently as in
the field, for it is not only our rite of passage but our life, as Sontag notes.
   It is not my intention to poke easy fun at others and myself. Rather, it is
my purpose to examine just what it is about long-term fieldwork, which so
captivates our own imaginations and contributes to the overall anthropological vision. For it does, in fact, do that. Edith Turner's moving opening to
her article (1997) "There Are No Peripheries to Humanity: Northern Alaska
Nuclear Dumping and the Inupiat s Search for Redress" reemphasizes and
expands my point.

> Victor Turner had a great respect for fieldwork. He believed rightly that anthro-
> pologists should supply a primary source of valid material for other readers,
> as literal as possible—a source that would be available whatever the interpre-
> tation and discussion that followed (personal communication). In the era of
> globalization, the need for fieldwork still holds and is even greater for the very
> reason that societies are no longer stable. When evaluating what an individual
> actually says, it is no longer assumed that his or her words represent what

the society says. Now, the *drift* of a social situation, recognized by the people themselves and the ethnographer to be revolving in a general way around the society's "Archimedean point," is as near as we can get (95).

Sulika and Robben (2007) indicate the continuing centrality of field-work in the anthropological paradigm. Indeed, they, along with Keesing and Strathern (1998: 8-9), view the cultural anthropologist as a humanist torn between basic dualities inherent in its position at the juncture where scientific and humanistic interests intersect. Out of the struggle between allegiance to each of these dualities and the marginal position in which fieldwork inevitably puts the ethnographer emerges our sense of identity both professional and individual.

Arthur P. Cohen (2007) notes that the very process of fieldwork forces us to ask ourselves, echoing the very question we hear repeatedly in fieldwork, who we are. Cohen asserts that a major part of ethnography and thus anthropology itself is revealed in the way we answer that question. Moreover, as I heard from my earliest days in anthropology many years ago, ethnography is autobiography. In what now seems an age ago, one of my colleagues pointed out to me that my description of the Gungawa was a dead on self-portrait of myself. I was stunned to hear it and even resisted it. However, that comment not only stopped me in my tracks, for I had not viewed myself in that light, but it has stayed with me to the present. Although it was not entirely true, there was enough truth to give me pause about how much one reveals through ethnographic writing. Of course, this should not be surprising. Cohen (110) notes that we use the self to discover others and vice-versa. We define ourselves in fieldwork against those whom we study. After all, there is probably no other experience in our lives so intense, so conducive to reflexive musing, and so all-encompassing to the young selves we were upon first encountering it, then fieldwork.

When we add the element of long-term return to the same location, we have only deepened that sense of reflexivity. At different stages of our lives, as we become different people and assume different identities, we have tested our sense of self in a similar setting. We have grown older, alas, and so have our friends in the field. They see us as the same but different and we do likewise. This social psychological aspect of fieldwork cries out for additional investigation. Toward that end, I offer the following reflections.

LOCATION, DUKAWA AND KAMBERI

The Dukawa (Hune) and the closely allied Kamberi, with whom they have a joking relationship, inhabit an area of northwestern Nigeria best described as a tropical savanna. Each group is found in a number of states in what was under British colonialism ruled as Northern Nigeria. Their language belongs to the Niger–Congo language family, Benue–Congo branch, Plateau Division. The center of the Plateau Division is 10^0 North Latitude and 10° East Longitude.

The majority of the Dukawa's 30,000 population are in Shanga District of Yauri Division and Rijau District of Kontagora Division. Both districts were in the old Sokoto State and adjoin each other. I will concentrate on Dukawa practices in Shanga District, although practices in Rijau do not vary much. Neither do practices diverge greatly in new areas into which the Dukawa have moved within the last decade or so.

Although small, Yauri Emirate, coterminous with Yauri Division, is noted for its ethnic heterogeneity. Shangawa, Gungawa, Lopawa, as well as Kamberi and Dukawa, consider themselves indigenous to the area. The ruling Hausa and Cattle Fulani are not considered indigenous. The ruling class is Hausa, not Hausa–Fulani as in many other areas of the North. The British, during their occupation, encouraged numerous other groups to migrate to Yauri, further increasing its ethnic diversity.

In such pluralistic situations, identity markers become quite significant. Given the Dukawa concern for equality, internally and externally, their resistance to Hausa and British control is quite understandable. A pivotal part of that resistance has been the preservation of religious practices in the face of pressure to convert to Islam. When armed resistance became impossible under British opposition, the Dukawa took to the bush and sought isolation from day-to-day contact. Such isolation has itself become increasingly difficult in the post–colonial world. Religion, therefore, is forming a last line of defense in the effort to sustain a separate ethnic and, consequently, political identity.

It is necessary to clarify what I mean by "tradition." I agree with Hobswam and Ranger (1983) that people "invent" traditions to suit their needs and that the search for a primordial collection of traditions in a living group is nonsense. Ethnic identities come and go according to their usefulness to a set of people engaged in a network of social interactions. Therefore, by tradition I mean an attitude of mind rather than a pristine chronological period somehow preceding any outside contact. This approach obviates the need to ascertain that a practice be of a certain age before it can somehow be considered "traditional," for if a people themselves have accepted a practice as an integral part of their "customary" way of life, then for them it is traditional. In conformity with Dukawa views, I have accepted the period just before the colonial period as their "traditional period."

During that period, and into the present, Dukawa social organization is acephalous, or multi-centric, an organization in conformity with their high regard for egalitarianism. They live in extended family compounds in which property is freely shared. Each member of the extended family (*dengi*) is allowed sufficient free land to support his nuclear family.

Dukawa egalitarianism carries over into relationships between the sexes. Even though there is a sexual division of labor, women keep their earnings from their crops (shea nuts, for example) and from the indigenous alcoholic beverages they brew (*giya* and *barukatu*) and then sell to their husbands and their friends. Moreover, the culturally preferred form of marriage includes the performance of bride service (*gormu*) for a woman, whom a man has chosen, with her consent, to be his wife.

Indeed, *gormu* provides a royal road for understanding Dukawa core values. A man forms great ties with his age-mates during the seven year period of bride service. The team goes from farm to farm, working on their future fathers-in-law's farms. During its work, team members are allowed no conversation. They may sing only in Dukanci, their native tongue. Specifically, they sing the *gormu* song of the young man who is performing the bride service. These gormu songs identify the men throughout their lives. At each important event in a man's life, he and his mates sing his *wakar gormu* ("wedding song"). Finally, it is sung for the last time at his *bikin mutuwa*. No man is allowed to use another man's song, for each man must compose his own *wakar gormu*, expounding his own virtues to his father-in-law and wife (Salamone 1982 and 1978).

After the completion of *gormu*, divorce is rare, but possible. The most common motive for divorce is adultery. Both men and women are cautioned against the offense. The Dukawa, however, differentially define the practice for each sex. For women adultery consists of any extra-marital liaison. Because polygyny is allowed for Dukawa males, adultery is defined for them as sex with another's wife, including those who have begun *gormu*.

The Dukawa regard adultery as more serious than murder because it strikes at the very cornerstone of their social structure and cultural identity, the family. In fact, an adulterer's own family will abandon him. His actions have brought shame on the *dengi*, and they quickly pay the compensation due the aggrieved husband. They may parade the adulterer around naked in public, his ear cut like a dog's, whose behavior his sexual excess resembles.

The injured husband is left to deal with his wife. His treatment depends on a number of factors, including his love and affection, her remorse, the number of children she has produced and his own nature, among others. A husband could take an unrepentant woman to the *kugom njir*, a high priest who is head of the major religious cult. Here the Dukawa bring supernatural force to bear to right the imbalance in society. Men have poisoned their unrepentant wives here and attributed the death to God.

Similarly, incest strikes at the core of the family. It is defined as intercourse within the *dengi*. The *dengi* consists of all descendants, whether in the male, female, or mixed line, from the great–grandparents. Only God can punish those who commit incest because no *dengi* member may harm another one. The offense concerns only *dengi* members. There is a hint that, just as in "God's" punishment of an unrepentant wife, human agency may help "God" along. No Dukawa, however, would openly admit to that possibility.

Because the Dukawa perceive the family as the institution that best defines themselves and protects their cultural identity, any attack on the family is a danger to Dukawa culture itself. No one can defend the offenders, for the offense is literally beyond defense, it attacks the very concept of culture itself.

Finally, the entire complex of inheritance rules stresses the unity of the family. All full brothers, and sometimes even all *dengi* members, work their farms communally. It is a rare Dukawa who enjoys being alone. Both male and female work is conducted in teams. If a man dies without any living sons, land goes to the *dengi* and to his *gormu*–mates. With their consent, widows are inherited by one of the deceased's junior brothers. A woman has a shame–avoidance relationship with her father–in–law; therefore sexual relations with a man's senior brother would be the equivalent of incest because a wife regards a man's senior brothers as the equivalent of his father.

The entire complex of inheritance rules stresses the unity of the family, its cooperative nature, and the need to maintain alliances with other families. As in every other egalitarian system, there is a real danger of centrifugal forces. Thus, anything working against the family which is the very bedrock of alliances and values central to the maintenance and persistence of Dukawa identity is combated ferociously, including the use of supernatural means and the intervention of the dead.

However, in order to understand the Dukawa in Yauri it is essential to have knowledge of the Kamberi as well. Moreover, the ties between the two groups illuminate the overall situation in the area. Interestingly, the Kamberi and Dukawa share an origin myth. Both ethnic groups claim descent from Kisra, a Persian, who led resistance in Mecca against Muhammad. The Dukawa claim descent from Kisra's son Dukkayanusu while the Kamberi assert succession from another son, Lata. More mundane linguistic evidence strongly suggests that the Dukawa, Kamberi, and Gungawa (Reshe) came from the area around Jos in Nigeria.

The Kamberi and Dukawa share a history of military alliance in addition to a common origin myth, linguistic affinity, and a simIler migration pattern. They also share a joking relationship or one of privileged familiarity. Cementing that relationship is the fact that each has a unique twist on an otherwise common salvation myth. Simply put, the group in question has lost all its members to an enemy save one remaining member who is left to die a horrible death. The enemy has submerged this man in the mud, leaving only his shoulder and head exposed. Because he belongs to a people who shave their heads, there is nothing for his rescuers to do but wait patiently for his hair to grow and feed him until that time comes. Finally, when his hair grows long his rescuers pull him from the ground by his hair. They give him a wife, establishing a blood tie between the groups.

The Dukawa claim it was the Kamberi who was the buried man while the Kamberi assert they rescued a Dukawa from burial. The Dukawa point to the shaved heads of Kamberi today. The Kamberi shave all but the top of their heads, leaving a long hairlock their lest they be buried again. The Kamberi laugh when they hear this story, claiming that they always shaved their heads, leaving a long hairlock on top. They state that they rescued a Hune from being buried alive. The reversibility of the story and their humorous argument is part of the joke itself. I have tested it out on members of both ethnic groups and was pleased with the laughs and good feeling it engendered. The fact that I knew the joke gained me goodwill with both groups.

Whatever the function and meaning of the origin myth, the fact is that the Kamberi arrived in Yauri a good deal before the Dukawa. There is significant evidence that by the fourteenth century the Kamberi were entrenched in the area and were Yauri's first rulers. The Dukawa came later. By the sixteenth century they were settled in the area. The two languages are similar, suggesting that the groups have never lost contact long enough for their languages to diverge. They are not, however, mutually intelligible as one study states (Gunn and Conant 1960). Regardless of their similarities, each group has stressed different aspects of its cultural values in order to survive over the years. These differences are clearly related to historical factors.

The Kamberi ruled in Yauri for a considerable period of time. The Dukawa were powerful but independent allies. As such, they enjoyed an independent position within the kingdom. As Hausaized rulers began to encroach on the state, the Kamberi were more exposed to attack than the Dukawa. Undeniably, as Balogun (1970) indicates, the nineteenth century civil wars were stimulated by Fulani expansion. In these wars Kamberi lost up to half their population. They fled from their cities and retreated to the bush, changing their lineage based social structure under the pressures and calamities of warfare. They had lost their capacity to respond to attack militarily. The Dukawa, on the other hand, had not lived in frontier settlements which required constant military preparedness while offering natural protection from mounted horsemen. Their shallow kin system, moreover, did not require further shrinking in order to meet new conditions. Nor, unlike the Kamberi's, did it need to become transformed into a sept organization. In fact, as I learned from the Hausaized Kamberi Sule Mamman, whom I discuss later, Kamberi who become Muslim very quickly re-establish their old kinship organization. Kamberi folktales, likewise, as well as their myths clearly demonstrate Kamberi bias for patrilineality and patrilocality.

Conversely, the Dukawa did not retreat to the bush. They remained in the bush. Thus, they maintained small households. They did not return to them. The never had lineages to lose. Their patrileterally-based households, depending on strong fathers to hold independent sons and quarrelling daughters-in-law in line proved both effective and viable under pressure. Hatred of Yauri's Hausaized rulers and their Fulani overlords stimulated Dukawa independence. Although some Dukawa have become Muslims and moved to settlements in more recent times, the vast majority have not. Those Dukawa who do convert to Islam for various reasons, mainly economic, do not pass as Hausa as many Kamberi or Gungawa do.

HAUSA-DUKAWA RELATIONS

The Hausa are the dominant group in Yauri. The Hausa–Dukawa history is marked by bitterness and mutual hostility. The Dukawa, whom the Hausa classify as "pagans" (arna), became victims of the internal slave trade which Hausa and Fulani raiders organized. Yauri's relative isolation prompted the Dukawa to choose it as a place of refuge. Because of Islam's association with slave–raiding, the Dukawa resisted any attempts at Islamic conversion. They interpreted any such pressure as hostile intrusion. Islam and its adherents, especially the Hausa and Fulani, still remain the antithesis of the Dukawa image of the good life.

In the various wars that mark Yauri's history over centuries, the Dukawa allied themselves with the Kamberi against Hausa, Fulani, and other Islamic forces. They continued their resistance into the nineteenth century against the most powerful threat posed to their continued existence, that of Ngwamse and his son Ibrahim, Fulani slave raiders centered in the nearby Kontagora emirate. As a defense, the Dukawa first strengthened their major towns, Iri and Duku. Continued pressure from Ngwamse and his son, however, forced them to begin to disperse. Their Kamberi allies who chose to stand and fight rather than flee suffered terrible losses. These losses were such that they the Kamberi eventually sought refuge in marginal bush areas (*daji*). The losses were so great, moreover, that they led to significant social structural and adaptational changes (Adamu, personal communication).

In order to escape conversion or its alternative, enslavement, the Dukawa moved further into Yauri's frontier area, Shanga District. The independent Fulani raider, Sambo, further stimulated their dispersal through his conquest of Rijau District in Yauri and his removal of that district from Yauri's control. Sambo's actions served to intensify the Dukawa's self–definition as not only non–Muslim but also anti–Islamic.

Under the Pax Britannica, Dukawa–Hausa relationships deteriorated. The British were able to force the Dukawa to do things the Hausa and Fulani were not; namely, to pay taxes. Taxes, moreover, were to be paid in coin, forcing people to enter the money economy, strengthening the central government. Such strengthening made it virtually impossible for any group to escape its control through flight. Because the Dukawa continued to struggle against British control as they had Hausa suzerainty, the British deemed them "truculent" and barbarians (A.D.O. Yauri to Resident, Kontagora: NANK: K6099, Vol.II, letter dated Oct.6, 1917).

In 1913, the Dukawa were in armed rebellion against British tax collectors. In 1914, ninety–six Dukawa fled to the nearby town of Koko, but the British found them and arrested them for non–payment of taxes. Both armed resistance and flight proved useless against British power, and British power was allied with the ruling Hausa. This alliance further reinforced Dukawa self–perception as "outsiders" who must rely on themselves for survival. Their Kamberi allies had been forced to adapt an accommodating posture of apparent docility to survive. They reinforced their servility through supplying wives to other ethnic groups while receiving none in return. The Dukawa pitied and despised their friends for their behavior while resolving to distinguish themselves from it through independent action.

To strengthen their ability to act independently the Dukawa used the opportunities the Pax Britannica afforded to disperse even further than they had from their centralized settlements of Iri and Duku to decentralized dwellings. These independent, self–sufficient settlements consisted of isolated extended family compounds, usually established a mile or more from similar communities. Quite rightly, the British perceived these settlements as Dukawa attempts to avoid taxes and escape their "civilizing" influence as well as that of the British Muslim allies. Consequently, the British misunderstood the Dukawa as the following passage reveals ". . . they had no chiefs of their own so have never recognized authority . . . Their headmen are usually harmless old dotards left in the town apparently to look after the graves of their ancestors." (A.D.O. Yauri to Resident, Kontagora: NANK: K6099, Vol.II, letter dated Oct.6, 1917). These "harmless old dotards" were, in fact, the most powerful priests, the *kugom njir*, of the Dukawa.

British misperception of Dukawa authority patterns cost Yauri a large section of land and split the Dukawa population between Yauri and Kontagora. (See NANK: K6099, Vol. II.) Those Dukawa who remained in Yauri tended to be more conservative than those who came under Kontagora's domain. They believed that they would be better able to maintain their old way of life in Yauri's bush area. Indeed, the majority of the approximately 3,000 Dukawa who remained in Yauri were actually elders and, therefore, most in touch with tradition (Adamu, personal communication).

IN THE FIELD

For a recent attempt to synthesize the two approaches within a single theoretical framework, see McKay (1982). Salamone (1982: 475) applies network theory to a particular ethnographic case to try and show that it can provide "a unifying framework for the integration of social structural and cognitive approaches to ethnicity." Barth (1984) suggests that David Cohen's (1977) concept of "moving contexts" might help us to refine our understanding of the complex interplay of "structural" and "cultural" aspects of ethnicity. Bentley (1987) makes an interesting attempt to integrate the two approaches -- both of which he seems to consider equally valid — by blending them with Pierre Bourdieu's theory of practice and the concept of habitus. Comaroff (1987: 319) seeks to show that ethnicity must be "understood to exist as a set of relations, a product of specifiable historical forces and processes rather than a primordial 'given'." (Bilby The remaking of the Aluku: culture, politics, and Maroon ethnicity in French South America p. 121).

When I first went to Yauri, there were no paved roads at all. Today there is a major highway connecting it with every urban center in Nigeria of any importance. Those young men who were children and adolescents in 1970 are members of Nigeria's important middle generation today, the age group coming into power or in power for a bit of time. These young men spent much of their formative years at the Catholic mission station, which the American Catholic priests of the Dominican order ran into the late 1980s before handing over to Nigerian priests. These youngsters viewed a model of change and modernization which profoundly influenced their lives. I have been able to observe Sule Mamman and Matthew Bello at various stages of their lives and seen changes in their lives in comparison with other young men in Yauri.

I first met Sule and Matthew in 1970. I had taken an exploratory trip to Nigeria, courtesy of a SUNY-Buffalo fund. My doctoral course work was finished and I had finally passed statistics. The Nigerian Civil War was over and it was easier to travel in Nigeria. I was not sure exactly what I was going to do. But armed with the assurance and stupidity of youth, I ventured forth.

I had an introduction to an English scholar at Ahmadu Bello University as well as an open invitation from the Bishop of Sokoto and some other American missionaries who had studied Hausa in a summer institute at Duquesne University. There was money in my pocket, an American passport and a return ticket in my wallet and I was young, healthy, and thin. There was no doubt in my mind, at least none that I would acknowledge, that I would conquer the world.

The old Pan-Am route along the West Coast of Africa was grueling but to my virgin eyes exciting and romance-laden. Each stop brought me to a new country and new people. Liberia, Ghana – the countries rolled by. In

Ghana I was allowed in the airport, intrigued by the James Bond ads for a dress shirt. The security guard and I exchanged pleasantries until I had to re-board. Things seemed to be going well, and I continued on my way with a warm feeling that all was going to go according to plan. Of course, there was as yet no definite plan of action but I am a jazz fan and improvisation around a sketch of the melody is all that is needed.

In those days the Lagos airport was not the nightmare it is today. Once I braved the outdoor passport desk, reaching over, around, and through the crowd clustered there, I want on to gather my luggage and clear customs. That word now has a double meaning, one fading into another. One piece of advice given me was to keep smiling and not lose my cool. So I gladly sacrificed a few pairs of socks to the agent to get through customs. It was still a novelty, playing anthropologist. Well, as Amiri Baraka said in his talk at the University of Connecticut to open the conference at the Harlem Renaissance (March 27, 2008), the young are allowed stupidities. I was no more an anthropologist than a baby pounding on a computer is a novelist. However, with practice we might gain some facility in our endeavors.

After a night at the Airport Hotel in Lagos and a swim in a pool whose very algae appeared exotic, I went back to the airport to journey on to Kano. The Nigerian Airways plan landed at Jos where the police briefly arrested me. There was a ban on taking pictures at the airport. A Nigerian officer on the plane had encouraged me to take a photo of the flowers, which I had admired. Almost immediately a police officer politely approached me. He asked for my camera, which I handed over. There was a brief conversation between the military officer and the police. The cop made a call to the tower, gave me my camera, and went on. The military officer said that I should not take any more pictures at the airport, smiled, shook my hand and left. I still am puzzled about the entire incident.

I spent a few days in Kano wondering what to do, a common condition for me in the field. A young man named Dan Ladi (Wednesday's Child) approached me and asked if I wanted a tour of Kano. I was hesitant but he seemed harmless so I agreed. It wasn't much of a tour, mainly consisting of walking through his compound but meeting his family was fun and a good introduction to some Hausa customs and traditions. There is that double-edged word again. The cost of passing this custom station was not much and the return was great. Dan Ladi did take me to see some museums and mosques and give me his version of Kano's history, which gave me an insight into how a twenty-something young man interpreted his legacy. He was a good conversationalist, enjoyed practicing his English and gave me some tips on speaking Hausa. It was also fun to bargain with him when he wanted to purchase a pair of my Levis, then a rare commodity. His offer of going into a joint business was interesting but not one I was eager to pursue. Later I learned that Dan Ladi had a reputation as a "loveable rascal," according to the missionaries. He was harmless and worth the admission for his entertainment.

It was time to move on and I managed to get a ride with an English businessman who put me up for a night, somewhat reluctantly but noblesse oblige, and drove me to Zaria where I was to reconnoiter with an ex-priest who was to put me up for a few days. So I went to Ahmadu Bello University in Zaria. When I arrived, I discovered that my contact had left. However, he left word with his steward to take care of me for a few days. Once more I mulled over my options. I had contacted my missionary friends from the Duquesne University classes before leaving for Nigeria. It seemed no one was going to meet me. However, I still had my cock-eyed optimism that all would be well.

God takes care of fools and children. I was a bit of both. So one day there was a knock on the door. A tall American man whom I had never seen was smiling and told me he was Father Justice and was going to take me to the bishop's house in Sokoto. Bishop Dempsey had received my letters and would be glad to have me visit. So we went on the road again, this time to Sokoto. While there I was reunited with my old friend Father Ceslaus Prazan, Father Ces to all.

He had been at the Duquesne Summer Institute. Ces had always been amusing and it was good to see him again. He was on local leave in Sokoto and entertained people with all the strange characters who hung around the mission in a place he called Yelwa. Ces was quite a story teller, for these characters emerged fully rounded as members of a novel. Among this cast of characters was a young boy who was quite unlike other Hausa boys, according to Ces, Sule was tough, could play baseball and was not afraid to catch a hardball coming at him at a high speed. At the time, I filed him away in my mind as someone whom I would like to meet but paid no more attention to him than I did to the simple-minded man Ces called Zake, lion, for his strength.

Ces and others urged me to follow-up on my interest in seeing Yelwa, a town he described as being about one-mile short of the end of the earth. He knew that an aspiring anthropologist would be intrigued with a place, which was in his words "unspoiled" yet by civilization. Of course, I later discovered quite the opposite was true but as Amiri Baraka says the young are entitle to and forgiven their stupidities. Thus, I eagerly accepted a ride back to Yelwa with an English banker who ran a branch of Barkley's in Yelwa.

The roads in 1970 were still red laterite paths for much of the trip from Sokoto to Yauri, the emirate in which Yelwa town is found. Thus, it was inevitable that we arrived in Yelwa covered in red dust, every pore of our body chocked with the substance. We looked like actors poorly made up for roles in a stage production. Father Peter Ottilio, the priest in charge of the mission, greeted us with his innate good humor and later told me I looked like a waif, bedraggled, chocking, and in dire need of food and water. Instead of water, he provided a cold Star beer, still the best beer I have ever tasted. He also provided food, drink, companionship and invaluable information and access to sources.

Two of those sources proved to be Sule and Matthew. Sule was introduced to me as a Hausa, whose father was a village head. Matthew, at that time going by his Dukawa (Hune) name of Matchew, was the exact opposite of Sule in many ways. Where Sule was sophisticated and a town dweller, Matthew dwelt in the bush. He was lean and tall while Sule was shorter and more muscular. Matthew was quieter than Sule and at that time did not speak English. Sule dressed in Western clothes, mainly hand-me-downs from the mission. Matthew was wrapped in a towel and had his teeth filed in the Dukawa fashion, one of the reasons the British termed his people savage and truculent. Matthew was doing his bride service, *gormu*, while Sule was still in school. The mission station, however, had influenced both young men. Over the years, I noted major changes in their lives, mainly as a result of this mission contact. But at this time I had no idea of these changes. Sule and Matthew were only part of a complex and bewildering mosaic of sights and sounds, images and colors floating in the humid air.

Sule had taken to following me around, reminding me of one of my own sons. He was never afraid to correct my Hausa. Indeed, he was proud of his reputation for speaking proper Hausa in an area often ridiculed for its back woods or bush accent. Sule was always curious about things, although he later teased me about my curiosity about all things happening in the area. He said I was like a Fulani, always inquiring about why people did things and what they meant. Sule, himself, watched and puzzled out everything in his view. I was better able to understand his uniqueness through observing him in contrast with his cousin, Aliyu, a meeker and quieter young man. When they argued as cousins will, Sule would grow weary of trying to explain things to Aliyu and begin pounding him with closed fists, not a common means of assault in the area. I would generally have the job of peacemaker. Fortunately, Sule usually stopped when I stepped in verbally.

When I ended my first short trip, I knew that my original half-formed dissertation plan would never be feasible. I wrote it up as a short paper. Rather, I would study religious and ethnic change in Yauri Emirate. As an ABD in history who wrote "like a goddamn anthropologist", I was comfortable in archives, especially those that gave me an opportunity to visit London. As an aspiring "goddamn anthropologist" I was happy to be in the field. Chuck Frantz, my dissertation director, gave me valuable guidance in shaping my study and plan of attack. Others helped me along at SUNY-Buffalo, too many to mention. At the time I read voraciously about Nigerian history and ethnology.

In 1972, I returned to Nigeria via London. I did my archival work in the British Museum, met some British anthropologists who were of help, especially H.S. Morris. Stephen Morris introduced me to a number of important people. Barbara Ward, his wife, was a kindly, scholarly woman, a fine anthropologist as well. My head was swirling as was my student's, Barbara Caiazza, now Barbara Barrington, who came along as an assistant and to gather her own information. Barbara made valuable contributions to the work and was able to work with women as well as men and provide a different and relevant perspective.

One of the interesting results of Barbara's presence was the opportunity to view many of the cast of characters in Yauri in a new light as they interacted with her. Father Peter was still Father Peter. His integrity is a basic part of his personality. In Flip Wilson's words, "What you see is what you get." Others, however, showed other aspects of their personalities. One priest became rather lecherous. I admit I did not notice this fact until Barbara called it to my attention. My self-absorption in the field has its downside. It was not the first time I had missed danger to Barbara. It was, sadly, not the last time I neglected someone in the field, leading me to conclude that my research trips should be conducted alone where I am the only one I need worry about.

Barbara's rapport with women was a marvel. She would get the other side of the story, showing that culture is not monolithic but has many shades and interpretations. The women's take on cultural reality differed in significant ways from the men's, leading me to a more nuanced view of not only what was happening, why it was happening but its many meanings. Additionally, Barbara's presence gave me an opportunity to view Sule, his cousin Aliyu, and Matthew in a new light; namely, as they altered their interactions because of her presence.

In their eyes, I was the head of a household, living in the old ADA's home. It may have been falling down but it served as a good storage place to put what few material goods we had. There was a table and chairs, cabinets, and other assorted chests of drawers, and not a few scorpions and scavengers. Things also became more settled as the mission's old cook came out of retirement to earn money for a wristwatch. Out of pity he cooked three meals a day, instead of the one for which I had hired him. The household had grown in size and importance with his addition, for Baba Kuku, the cook, had a fine reputation and assumed control of Sule and Aliyu who had moved into the house.

On subsequent trips I lived in various other places, a secondary school house with an Irish school teacher. His reputation increased greatly when I bought fresh Nile fish and eggs from the wife of the chief fisherman, the Sarkin Serakawa. He had been eating beans for breakfast and whatever else might be lying around. On another trip I stayed at the mission stations.

Subsequently, I made flying trips to Yauri while in other parts of Nigeria, teaching at Jos and Ibadan. My wife was with me while I was at Jos. Father Peter had moved to Ibadan, and we visited the old mission together with a young man who was working with me, a member of a group related to the Dukawa, the Dakarkari. The point is that each of these trips changed the way people perceived me while I noted changes in their life statuses and circumstances.

Sule and Matthew had not lived up to their early promises. Indeed, on one occasion Sule had come to visit me while I was living in the school. There was another young man, a soldier, with him. We had some Star beer and cigarettes. Sule offered me some pot, which I politely refused. He and the soldier smoked what they said was pot, and Sule offered me a hit off his joint. Again, I politely refused. Not too long after that incident, Sule showed up at the mission station. He said that he had to see me. I agreed.

He offered me many apologies for trying to get me into trouble. It appears that the military government had decided to entrap me. Once again military intelligence proved an oxymoron; for I not only did not inhale I did not puff either. The local government knew Sule had worked for me in the past and that I trusted him. Since I was an American, they figured, I smoked pot. I didn't, and that fact probably saved me from having a different tale to tell.

But the saddest tale I know of Sule was his descent into drunkenness and promiscuity. On my last trip to Yauri in 1990, Sule came calling again. He wanted to apologize, again, for his being very drunk and embarrassing me. I told him there was no reason to apologize to me. However, he wanted to show me something in the market. So we hired motorcycle cabs to take us the mile to the market from the mission. Sule stopped to point out the naked Kamberi young women. Because they were virgins, he said, they were naked. I knew it was unusual for Kamberi women to come into town totally uncovered. Sule indicated that this was a corner of the market only for Kamberi. Since he was a Muslim Kamberi passing as a Hausa, he was able to go among the "pagan" Kamberi.

Sule may have been able to do so but the Kamberi who are supposed to be shy and meek, a stereotype they consciously perpetuate but one at odds with their basic self-image, were not happy to see me in that area. I averted my eyes, apologized, and asked Sule if he were trying another of his dangerous pranks on me. We moved on and I am not sure what the point of that little prank was. Whatever it may have been, I emerged higher in his favor. We entered the middle of the market and met his relatives.

Some of them told a tale they had spun in the past, "Sule is useless (*banza*)." Well, the word *banza* has a stronger meaning, more like "bastard" but more in the sense of a wastrel in this case. Only his mother and grandparents could understand my soft spot for him. They had thanked me in the past for watching out for him. Indeed, one of the major sorrows of fieldwork is being able to predict the sad lives of some of the people we meet, lives that could have been happier and more productive. Perhaps, we have contributed to their heartrending fates simply through being far more privileged than they and holding out an example of a better live.

Certainly, Matthew's life also had more than a tinge of poignant failure. Matthew had begun to do bride service (*gormu)* for a woman of his choice. However, his older brother died. She was considered an asset to Matthew's group. Under the laws of the junior levirate, Matthew inherited his brother's widow. Normally, this marriage would pose no problem. Matthew would be able to marry his brother's widow and the wife for whom he was doing bride service. There was a complication, nevertheless, because Matthew had begun to take steps toward conversion to Catholicism. To make his group (*dengi*) happy as well as the missionaries, he had to choose his brother's widow. Choosing not to marry a woman whom his *dengi* wanted would anger them. Choosing to marry two women would be a bar to his becoming Catholic. Thus, Matthew married his brother's widow, left the wife for whom he was doing bride service, and became a Catholic.

Unfortunately, Matthew was never happily married. He was not promiscuous but his wife, Mary, was not beautiful according to Dukawa standards. Matthew considered her a bit "slow" and old-fashioned. The longer Matthew worked for the mission station, the unhappier he became. He moved to the town from the bush and happily went to other towns to work for the mission station. Matthew began to dress in the Yoruba style while his English improved greatly. For a time Matthew worked for me gathering information.

Indeed, he was quite good, caught on to the purpose of ethnography, and knew who had what information among the Kamberi. Matthew was particularly interested in religion, for which the Kamberi are famous in Yauri. Of course, he often rushed in where wise men fear to go. For example, the Kamberi keep snakes in snake houses. These are used for divination and other religious purposes – at times for snake handling to show the power of the priest. Matthew almost got both of us killed by reaching into one such house he believed was empty. There were snakes in the house as well as in the vines near the house. If the snakes didn't get us, outraged Kamberi might have. However, they appeared more amused than angry at us. The field does teach person humility!

Matthew eventually secured a job teaching in government schools, putting his mission training to use. However, his family life, as Father Peter reported it to me, was never really happy. Matthew also took to drinking, the curse of the Dukawa, who had a reputation for heavy drinking in any case. Matthew was frequently away from his family, frequently hanging out with Europeans and Americans. He seemed caught between past and future, marginalized – and to me an immensely sad figure with great talent who was never going to be happy. When the American priests left Yauri, handing the mission over to Nigerian priests, Matthew returned to the bush and farming. His story takes on for me an example of a medieval cautionary tale.

For me it is reinforced by a parallel tale that of someone who considered converting to Catholicism and then became a Muslim. For Dukawa becoming Muslim is the ultimate rejection of basic Dukawa values. Jude Bako and his son were special favorites at the Catholic mission center in Yauri. The head of the mission made great efforts in behalf of his family. Unlike Matthew, Jude had completed his gormu and was an accomplished hunter. The missionaries put great hope in Jude's being the means for convincing other Hune that there was nothing basically incompatible with being a Catholic and Dukawa. They sent Jude to the university after teaching him to drive a truck to support himself.

However, Jude's father had become a Muslim by this time. Gossips attributed his conversion to the numerous occasions on which he had been judged guilty of adultery. Islamic conversion gave him a legal right to four wives and as many concubines as he could afford. It also led to his becoming the Muslim headman of a Dukawa settlement across the Niger River from his own home village, the location of his embarrassment.

Jude withstood pressures to become a Muslim until he dropped out of the university. He had been the first of his people to attend a university and the pressure may well have proved too great. Upon returning to Yauri in 1984 he resumed his old position with the local authority. The withdrawal of the American Catholic priests, left Jude stranded. To keep his job with the local authority he had to become a Muslim.

The example of the Kamberi adaptation to changing times is also instructive of how people maneuver in the complex reality of life. People have to adapt their behavior to the social and cultural realities they face. Although the Kamberi adopted a front stage demeanor of docility, it was a presentation of self they hate. Those Kamberi who have become Muslims generally occupy respected positions in Yauri as head masters, government officials, and successful professionals of all sorts. When I asked a Kamberi head master about his being mistaken for a Hausa, he laughed and said that he never told people he was a Hausa and was not responsible for their errors. He still went to the bush to attend traditional religious services out of respect for his family. However, he said, he stood a little apart so that any Muslims who might be around would not consider him to be still a believer in the old ways. I might be mistaken but I think I saw a conspiratorial twinkle in his eyes and in his smile.

Much of what I have written about Yauri and its environs has been grounded in my experience with real people and real time. Indeed, much of what I have written about others has also been grounded in my experiences in Yauri. Because of that experience questions of the meaning of culture, identity, determinism, and social organization and structure are more than academic puzzles. They are the very puzzles of life itself, fraught with moral and, yes, spiritual meaning. My attempts to solve these puzzles led directly to my life's work; namely, trying to sort out questions of identity and meaning.

CONCLUSION

There is of course no single meaning to our work. Each of us brings a particular person, ourselves, to our work. So much of the last fifty years has been concerned with the baggage we bring to our work. Indeed, Papa Franz Boas was ahead in this aspect as in so many others. He looked carefully at our subjectivity and how it influenced our understanding. He anticipated so many "modern" movements, including reflexivity, as to stagger at least my mind. One of my abiding concerns is that in a quest for novelty the important lessons of the past will be lost. The fear of being out of date coupled with the need to find something new plagues graduate students in anthropology as in other areas. It is an understandable concern. However, the danger that accompanies it is that, as Margaret Mead warned, of reinventing the wheel. Often, the new version of that wheel is not as good as the one that already exists.

However, my recent focus has become sharper as the recent use of ethnic politics as an excuse for genocide has become more in vogue. The dangers of stressing ethnic identity have become more of a concern. Recent extensions of ethnic identity to include those living outside of a nation's borders seem to cultural group membership and me dangerous because their motivation is exclude residents from full political participation. The metaphor of blood seems sadly apt. What is cultural is being trumpeted as something innate and the "folk" can be called home to extirpate the aliens.

Bilby (1990) notes "Salamone (1982: 475) applies network theory to a particular ethnographic case to try and show that it can provide 'a unifying framework for the integration of social structural and cognitive approaches to ethnicity.' "He places this discussion within the context of situationalists versus primordialists in the theoretical analysis of ethnicity. Situationalists, as the name implies, view ethnicity as emerging within certain contexts to gain political ends while primordialists take a more ascriptive viewpoint. Bilby sees me as one who tries to reconcile the two positions along with Barth, David Cohen and Comaroff among others. Not bad company, indeed, in which to find oneself. Each of those whom Bilby mentions has an adherence to long-term fieldwork, coming back physically and intellectually to a particular case.

In reflecting on my field experiences in Yauri, I have noted how often I have come back to the youngsters whom I watched grow into men. Sule, Matthew, and Jude were more than just interesting subjects. They were to greater or lesser degree friends – mine and the priests at the mission station. Interestingly, the order of friendship was the opposite for the mission head and me. For him, Jude was closest, followed by Matthew and then Sule. My friendships went in reverse order. Jude left Catholicism to become a Muslim. He later began to seek reconciliation with the mission to the distrust of all but one of the missionaries. Matthew has never left Catholicism while Sule, a nominal Muslim claims to be a secret Catholic. Matthew and Sule have had serious drinking problems. Sule lost his police job because of his drinking problem. Matthew has had marital problems because of his wife abuse while drinking. Jude has kept his drinking to culturally approved standards. Interestingly, each of these men is marginal in significant ways to his own group and has had problems adjusting to modern Nigerian life.

Early on, I had noted that I was concerned with ethnicity in the broader sense of identity (Salamone and Swanson 1979: 181). The reason for my concern was my disquiet with the manner in which I saw Sule, Matthew, and Jude, too, struggle with the meaning of their lives as they tried on various identities and combinations of identities, seeking to find one which would better their life chances and happiness. Ethnography is not an abstract exercise, at least not at root. Rather it is based on flesh and blood people whose human struggles to make sense of the lives they lead offer us some glimpse into the meaning of the human condition. I am convinced that only when our own lives somehow connect with those who live the ethnographies we sketch do these narratives make any contribution at all to human understanding. Sadly, many of us have been too fearful of revealing the manner in which these ethnographies link up with our own lives lest we expose ourselves in embarrassing ways as being too human to be appropriately scientific or detached to understand those whose lives we report, no matter how abstract they may be. However, I submit that we cannot understand other humans and their lives unless we find that fragile and often embarrassing connection and thereby bare ourselves as "only" human. Indeed, ethnography *is*, at least in part, autobiography.

1

Hausa States

INTRODUCTION

There are about 50 million Hausa speakers in West Africa, primarily in Northern Nigeria and southern Niger. The variation among these 50 million people is great. A common language masks great variation from community to community, a variation made greater by the process of "becoming Hausa" in which minority groups change their ethnic identities to gain various privileges reserved to the ruling class. Unsurprisingly, the Islam of many Hausa groups is quite syncretic.

The Hausa, then, are usually considered to be comprised of the Hausa-speaking, Muslim population of Northern Nigeria and the adjacent areas of Niger, who have traditionally been organized into large, centralized states. In fact, they include these people and many others who are not Muslim but have some semblance of a generalized Hausa culture. Originally, the name "Hausa" referred only to the language of the Habe people of Northern Nigeria. These people were organized into seven independent but interrelated states called Biram, Daura, Kano, Katsina, Gobir, Rano, and Zazzau or Zaria.

The Fulani, or Fulbe, conquered these states and the seven other "illegitimate" Hausa states early in the nineteenth century. Under the leadership of Usman dan Fodio, the Fulani waged a jihad or Muslim "holy war" against the Habe, whom they accused of being lax in the practice of Islam. The Fulbe established the Sokoto Caliphate, ultimately incorporating fifteen states or emirates, into the Caliphate. Fulani rulers replaced Habe ones. The overthrown dynasties of two Habe states, Zaria and Katsina, established the new states of Abuja and Maradi. A third new Habe state was founded at Argungu. These three states preserved Habe customs, virtually unchanged

1

by Fulani customs. The Fulani rulers of the conquered Habe states became "Hausaized," becoming sedentary Town Fulani, rather than the Pastoral Fulani of the jihad. They took Habe wives, spoke the Hausa language, and took on other customs of the conquered people.

The term Hausa became even more extensive, referring to the original Habe population, the Town Fulani, the mixed population in the Hausa states, and other groups in the area, such as Tuareg, Kanuri, Gungawa, and others who have accepted Hausa language and culture. The term also includes "pagan" Hausa-speakers, the Maguzawa.

The Hausa of Nigeria are chiefly found in the provinces of Kano, Katsina, Sokoto, and Zaria, with a population about six to eight million. When one adds other Hausa speakers in Niger and communities in Ghana and throughout West Africa, the figure is about 50 million. The Hausa language is a branch of the Chad group of the Afro-Asiatic language family, serving as a lingua franca in West Africa.

Almost all Hausa farm at least part-time and the Maguzawa are full-time farmers. Muslim Hausa are also at least part-time occupational specialists. Agriculture is scheduled around the May-October rainy season with millet, maize, Guinea corn, and rice supplying the bulk of the diet. However, peanuts, cowpeas, sweet potatoes, cotton, sugarcane, bamboo, tobacco, cassava, and other root crops are also grown. Hausa also raise livestock including horses, donkeys, goats, sheep, and poultry.

The Hausa are famous for their markets and trading. The market system is quite complex, working on three and four day cycles. Large urban centers, such as Kano and Sokoto have daily markets. These markets are vital links in the state and even international area, lining units together in a cash economy. There are various market officials, male and female, who serve to keep peace and settle disputes. These officials follow the traditional Hausa pattern of ranked hierarchy.

SOCIAL ORGANIZATION

Muslim Hausa social organization is characterized by a complex system of stratification, based on occupation, wealth, birth, and patron-client ties. The Hausa tend to rank all specialties in a hierarchal and hereditary system. Inheritance is by primogeniture. The Hausa prize wealth and use it to form patronage links. However, wealth also brings with it the burden of great responsibility. The patron-client relationship binds all Hausa men to some extent.

The Maguzawa are organized into small villages comprised of exogamous patrilineal kin. Conversely, Muslim Hausa local organization is somewhat more complex. The compound, made up of a man, his wife or wives, and their children is the smallest social unit. Other family members, clients, and their families may also inhabit the compound. Therefore, patrilocal extended families or joint fraternal families often inhabit a compound. The *mai-gida*, or male head of the family, rules the compound. The compound forms a joint agricultural unit. Occupational specialties, however, are at the discretion of the individual.

As Muslims, each Hausa male may have four wives and as many concubines as he can support. Divorce is a common fact of life, and women often act in such a manner as to prod their husband into divorcing them, for the life of unmarried women is less restrictive than that of a married one. In conformity with the Muslim Hausa principle of hierarchy, wives are ranked in the order of their marriages. The Hausa prefer cousin marriage on either side, although patrileteral parallel cousin marriage in the Fulani style has greater prestige than any other form of marriage. Among the elite, women tend to be secluded and purdah is a sign of status among them. Among all Hausa respect and avoidance tend to be the rule. Division of labor is a basic principle. Men are responsible for agriculture, collecting activities, marketing, sewing, laundry, building repairs, and transport. Women cook, owing their husbands one cooked meal a day, clean house, take care of children, pursue their craft specialties, and sometimes engage in trade.

The Hausa pride themselves on being a "civilized" people with strong urban roots. They display a genius for organization. Their wards have a village organization, which is under the leadership of the village head. Formerly, there would be a titled official in the capital who held clusters of villages in fief. The emir would be the overall ruler of the particular state, which comprised a number of clusters of villages. British rule which was consolidated about the beginning of the Twentieth Century changed the system in a number of ways, providing greater power to emirs and local Muslim officials.

ISLAM AND ORGANIZATION

Islam has been part of Hausa life since the Sixteenth Century, but the Fulani jihad gave it predominance in Hausa life. The British then strengthened Islam even further in their policy of indirect rule. Both the Fulani and the British encouraged strict adherence to the basic beliefs and practices of Islam—pilgrimages, daily prayer, attendance at mosque ceremonies, adherence to Islamic law, and the stress on Quaranic learning, and alms giving.

A good deal of business is conducted with handshakes and one's word. To repeat, the system of markets, traders, and families binds together the various parts of the state and subsequently the state itself is bound to outside units. For example, village markets in rural areas meet periodically, on three or four day cycles. These markets are tied to those in larger settlements that have daily markets. In turn, the larger markets are bound to a still larger

central market in the regional capital. Officials tied similarly to the central
authority govern each of these markets.

Similarly, all Muslim Hausa social organization is stratified. Occupation,
wealth, and patron-client relationships play a part in the system but birth is
at its root. Family is a key factor, perhaps the key factor in the hierarchical
ladder. Sons are expected to follow their father's occupation and his wishes.
Society, in theory and ideally, is held together by filial loyalty. The patron-
client relationship is patterned on the father-son relationship and loyalty
to the Sultan and emirs, indeed to all officials, is that of family members
to one's father.

Although less complex in social organization than Muslim Hausa, the
Maguzawa are also organized along patrilineal lines. Their villages are
composed of exogamous patrilineal kin. Both Muslim and "pagan" Hausa
form their organizations around male figures. The Maguzawa, however, retain greater privileges for women freer to go out in public, usually exposing
their breasts with no reproach. The Maguzawa do not hold to wife-seclusion in any circumstance. For the Muslim Hausa wife-seclusion is an ideal
and put into practice by those who can afford it. It helps distinguish them
from their neighbors and serves as an ethnic boundary marker. Moreover,
patrilateral kinship provides the fulcrum on which marriage alliances are
formed, with men generally seeking marriage with their patrilateral parallel
cousins, further emphasizing the male tie.

Men serve as household heads and are responsible for agriculture, collecting activities, marketing, sewing, laundry, building repairs, and transportation. Women are responsible for cooking, house cleaning, childcare, and also
follow craft specialties and carry on trade, often through young daughters.
Women are expected to be modest and to stay within the household unless
accompanied by male family members or older post-menopausal women.

Historically, the Hausa and Hausa-Fulani ruled over local tribes, appointing village heads. These local communities were held as fiefs to feudal
lords. Again, this system emphasized male rule and a particular image of
masculinity in which calmness and male solidarity were essential. The subject tribes often were not Muslim and their women were allowed greater
freedoms. Therefore, control of Hausa women was essential in structuring
ethnic relations and maintaining ethnic boundaries. Hausa position within
the social structure and the cultural landscape determined gender relationships and cultural definitions.

BRITISH RULE AND CHANGES IN THE SYSTEM

British colonial rule, beginning in the early twentieth century, made
changes in the overall system. In general, however, the British system of

indirect rule simply strengthened the central authority while pretending to rule through local rulers. The British relied heavily on their Hausa-Fulani allies to maintain control of Northern Nigeria. In Niger, the French made no pretext of indirect rule and simply centralized the system openly. The result was a greater emphasis on male rule as personified in the dual mandate of colonial and native authorities.

Finally, the Hausa became more identified with Islam under colonial rule. The British found it necessary to strengthen Muslim leaders who were their allies vis-à-vis "pagans" who sought to resist the imposition of colonial rule or Hausa hegemony. The British perpetrated the fiction that Northern Nigeria was mainly Islamic. The truth was different in 1900. Allegiance to the West African Fulani Islamic ethos of male dominance helped unite Hausa and distinguish them from surrounding "pagan" peoples such as the Gungawa, Kamberi, and others. (See Greenberg 1947, Michael Smith 1955, Salamone 1998. 1993, 1985 for various accounts of material in this section.)

HAUSA ISLAMIC PRACTICES

Given the landscape in which the Hausa exist, the Islam of many Hausa groups is syncretic. Faulkingham (1975) notes that the Muslim and "pagan" Hausa in the southern Niger village he studied believed in the same spirits. Both believed in the same origin myth for these spirits as well. According to the myth, Allah called Adama ("the woman" and Adamu ("the man") to Him and bade them to bring all their children. They hid some of their children. Allah asked them where their children were. They said that they had brought all their children to Him. He then told them that the hidden children would belong to the spirit world. Faulkingham states that these spirits explain everything; the primary efficacy belongs to spirits.

The Hausa, therefore, share in the common Nigerian practice of maintaining systems of belief with ancient roots in the area alongside the universal religions of Islam or Christianity. These beliefs combine family spirits with relations to the primordial spirits of a particular site, providing supernatural sanction to the relationship between claims on resources. Indigenous theology links dead ancestors to the spirits of place in a union that protects claims and relationships to the land. Spirits of place include trees, rock outcroppings, a river, snakes, and other animals and objects. Rituals and prayers dedicated to the spirits of family and place reinforce loyalty to communal virtues and the authority of the elders in defending ancient beliefs and practices. In return for these prayers and rituals, the spirits offer their adherents protection from misfortune, adjudication, and divination through seers, or shamans. Evil is appropriately punished, for shamans or diviners work with the spirits to ensure good and counteract evil.

The continuation of traditional religious rituals and beliefs among the Hausa is not incompatible with counting oneself as a Muslim, for among the Hausa, individual participation in Islam varies according to a number of variables, including wealth and power. The more wealth and power one has, the greater the strict adherence to Islam. Furthermore, traditional Hausa religion, which the Maguzawa ("pagan" or "traditional Hausa," who are considered "people of magic") continue to practice, attracts a number of Muslim Hausa at one time or another.

This religion is spirit-centered. Following Islamic Hausa hierarchical principles, the spirits form hierarchies of good and evil. Sacrificial offerings and spirit possession are prominent characteristics of the worship. This family-centered religion has a number of diviners who serve as curers. Moreover, the majority of Muslim Hausa, who participate in the spirit possession cult, or Bori cult, are women and members of the lower classes.

Mallamai, or mallams, are men of Quaranic learning who teach the faith and often serve as healers. They have prestige befitting their learning and sanctity. Those mallams who are highly ranked serve in state-level offices combining religious and secular powers.

Despite the propaganda of some Islamic groups in Nigeria, how much any Muslim participates in Islam varies greatly according to ones wealth and power. Furthermore, the Maguzawa continue to follow traditional Hausa religious practices, oriented around a variety of good and bad spirits and involving sacrificial offerings to the spirits and spirit possession. In addition to family rituals, there are specialists who are diviners and who also prescribe cures for illnesses. Muslim Hausa participate in spirit possession cults, the *bori* cult, many of whose members are women and members of the lower strata of marginalized people. This cult incorporates many of the traditional Habe religious beliefs and practices.

The Hausa, therefore, share in the common Nigerian practice of maintaining systems of belief with ancient roots in the area alongside the universal religions of Islam or Christianity. These beliefs combine family spirits with relations to the primordial spirits of a particular site, providing supernatural sanction to the relationship between claims on resources. Indigenous theology linked dead ancestors to the spirits of place in a union that protected claims and relationships to the land. Spirits of place included trees, rock outcroppings, a river, snakes, and other animals and objects. Rituals and prayers the spirits of family and place reinforced loyalty to communal virtues and the authority of the elders in defending ancient beliefs and practices. In return for these prayers and rituals, the spirits offered their adherents protection from misfortune, adjudication, and divination through seers, or shamans. Evil would be appropriately punished. Shamans or diviners would work with the spirits to ensure good and counteract evil.

CONCLUSION

The Hausa have played a significant role in Nigerian history. They currently form one of the three major ethnic groups in Nigeria along with the Igbo and Yoruba. They have controlled post-colonial Nigeria for much of its period of independence and exert a strong influence on its current politics. The Muslim-Christian split is mainly between the Hausa-Fulani and their allies and the rest of Nigeria. Their insistence on imposing Muslim law on residents of their states within the Federal Union has led to a number of crises.

Islam has been a rallying cry for their cultural way of life and a means of ethnic identity. The combustible mix of religion and identity has forced Nigeria to confront ways to balance these dynamic forces in the midst of creating and maintaining a workable multicultural nation. It is a problem that will be with it for a long time.

2

Hausa Shamans

INTRODUCTION

Most references on the Hausa would lead the reader to believe that the Hausa are strong Muslims and, therefore, have no shamans. The careful reader might find that there is a group of non-Muslim Hausa, named Maguzawa, who have retained earlier practices, which Muslim Hausa regard as "pagan." Such a view would greatly distort the reality that a careful observer experiences on the ground. As noted in Chapter One, there are about 50 million Hausa speakers in West Africa, primarily in Northern Nigeria and southern Niger. The variation among these 50 million people is great. A common language masks great variation from community to community, a variation made greater by the process of "becoming Hausa" in which minority groups change their ethnic identities to gain various privileges reserved to the ruling class. Unsurprisingly, the Islam of many Hausa groups is quite syncretic, combining various Islamic practices with diverse traditional ones.

As we have seen, the Hausa, then, are usually considered to be comprised of the Hausa-speaking, Muslim population of Northern Nigeria and the adjacent areas of Niger, which have traditionally been organized into large, centralized states. In fact, they include these people and many others who are not Muslim but have some semblance of a generalized Hausa culture. Originally, the name "Hausa" referred only to the language of the Habe people of Northern Nigeria. These people were organized into seven independent but interrelated states called Biram, Daura, Kano, Katsina, Gobir, Rano, and Zazzau or Zaria.

The Fulani, or Fulbe, conquered these states and the seven other "illegitimate" Hausa states early in the nineteenth century. Under the leadership of Usman dan Fodio, the Fulani waged a jihad or Muslim "holy war" against the Habe, whom they accused of being lax in the practice of Islam. The Fulbe established the Sokoto Caliphate, ultimately incorporating fifteen states or emirates, into the Caliphate. Fulani rulers replaced Habe ones.

ISLAM AND TRADITIONAL RELIGION

Among the Hausa, individual participation in Islam varies according to a number of variables, including wealth and power. The more wealth and power one has, the greater the strict adherence to Islam. Furthermore, traditional Hausa religion, which the Maguzawa continue to practice, attracts a number of Muslim Hausa at one time or another. This religion is spirit-centered. The spirits form hierarchies of good and evil. Sacrificial offerings and spirit possession are prominent characteristics of the worship. This family centered religion has a number of diviners who serve as curers. The majority of Muslim Hausa, who participate in the spirit possession cult, or Bori cult, are women and members of the lower classes.

Jacqueline Nicolas (1967) states that most members of the spirit possession cult are women and prostitutes. In other words, they are socially marginal people. Michael Onwuejeogwu (1969) argues that Bori cults have homogeneity of organization and meaning throughout Hausaland. Moreover, they are, in his opinion, vestiges of Habe religion. Faulkingham (1975) disagrees with these findings, noting that there is more diversity in Hausaland than Nicolas and Onwuejeogwu grant. Muslims and *arna* (pagan) believe in the same spirits but Muslims claim that they do not need to perform rituals to these spirits. In fact, many do perform them, depending on the occasion and consult the bori doctor for aid.

The Hierarchy of Spirits (adapted from Faulkingham 1975, p. 13)

Allah
Mala'iku—angels
Annabawa—prophets
Rafani—the bookkeepers
Aljanu—close spirits
A. Directional spirits
B. Specifically evil spirits
1. Local
2. Elsewhere
C. Mushe spirits—soldiers
D. Inheritable spirits (Bori)

The participation of women in the bori cult among the Muslim Hausa is not necessarily a sign of their lack of power. Kabir (N.D.) states that the status of women in early Hausa society was rather high. In his words, they were "not confined." The interacted freely with men, marrying at a later age than is now common among the Muslim Hausa. They were able to own their own farms. They were also important members of the Bori cult. Furthermore, they had a significant role in domestic and clan religious rituals. Interestingly, some Hausa groups had matrilineal inheritance and it was not uncommon for elite women to be queens or titleholders. The famous warrior queen Amina was but one of many famous Hausa queens. The Hausa even had a title for women in charge of the bori, *Bori Magadjiya*.

THE BORI DOCTOR AMONG THE GUNGAWA

Just as Faulkingham and Last shed light on the Hausa expression of the Bori through examining its practice in related groups with ties to earlier pre-Islamic Hausa religion, so, too, I wish to shed light on the Hausa practice through examining a shaman among the Gungawa, a people who have traditionally "become Hausa" over time (Salamone 1975). The uneasy relationship between the Bori doctor of the Gungawa and the official Islamic power structure, including those mallams (Hausa religious practitioners) who practice medicine and also deal with spirits finds echoes in the writings of others who have studied the Bori cult. Some hint of the "original" Bori can be found among these minority people among the Hausa as well as insight into the process of adaptation that marks Bori among the Hausa.

Among Gungawa, real power is masked in modesty, for the naked display of power is culturally condemned. Those people who possess power among the Gungawa are those who least appear to do so. Moreover, they must deny their influence. The truly powerful tend to make the least display of their power, dressing more simply than other Gungawa and living more modestly than those who seem to have power do. There is, additionally, a gentleness and benign humor among the truly powerful. This gentle quality is true of religious as well as political leaders.

Medicine and those who practice it are held in high repute among Gungawa. Indeed, people from other ethnic groups come great distances to receive care from Gungawa doctors. The Gungawa are also noted for the skill of their Bori practitioners. Just as people confuse the Bori of the Maguzawa and rural Hausa who may be non-Muslims with the Hausa spirit possession cult, so, too, do people confuse the Bori of the Gungawa with that of surrounding Hausa. Interestingly, many, if not most, of the surrounding "Hausa" have Gungawa and other "pagan" ancestors.

Gungawa doctors do not cause any spirits to possess people. They do, however, talk to the spirits on behalf of their clients and convey their responses. It is also important to note that spirits does not possess them and that the spirits do not speak through them. The client can hear the spirits as well as the Bori shaman, although perhaps more faintly. The spirits do tend to speak in an oracular fashion, demanding interpretation.

The Gungawa Bori doctor is a benign trickster. Jugun Hella, whom I knew well, was a man who emphasized his large belly, one he made to appear larger to draw laughs. Jugun Hella enjoyed making people laugh and wore his green robe, a sign of office, loosely draped and purposely "sloppy." At the same time he displayed his wrestling scars, a reminder of his early athletic prowess. Bori sought to draw people to him, cloaking his religious potency behind a shield of humor. He perceived his role as drawing all people to him, not simply Gungawa, but also Christians, Muslims, and people of all ethnic groups.

There is deep significance in Bori's statement that he never talks to Allah because Allah is too far away. He says he believes in him but that Allah is too far away for the everyday problems of people. Therefore, belief in an otiose (distant) god is relatively emotionless, bloodless, and abstract. The spirit intermediaries are playful creatures who aid people in their approach to the sacred or whose bedevilment of people through adversity causes them to seek refuge in the sacred.

The Bori shaman, Jugun Hella, was open to all religions and quite knowledgeable about them. However, he was a threat to the Muslim power in the area. The mallams who saw him as a competitor were delighted when someone poisoned him in a fashion reserved for witches. At the time, people were reluctant to discuss his death. However, the finger of suspicion pointed to the ruling powers as being behind his murder. It is a situation that underscores the tension between Bori practitioners of any kind and the Mallam healers. (See Abdalla 1991.)

SHAMANS IN HAUSALAND

Diviners, or shamans, foretell the future and deal with personal problems. They fit into the scheme of religious specialists, a scheme that includes priests and magicians. The boundary among the categories is a shifting one at best. Diviners continue to play an important part in determining the causes of luck, both good and bad fortune. This includes the nature and cause of disease. Among the Hausa it is necessary to point that many of the Muslim holy men are themselves types of diviners who make amulets, which include decoctions of the ink in which pious texts have been written. They also manipulate sand patterns or use the stars to tell the future.

There is some discussion of males who attend Bori rituals as being homosexuals. The Bori rituals among the Hausa appear to be rituals of inversion, and among the Hausa homosexuality is considered an inversion of
appropriate male heterosexuality. The Bori cult is widely understood as
being a refuge from the strongly patriarchal ideal of Hausa Islam. Thus both
women and effeminate males find some respite there. It is important to
remember that although the Bori cult may be a "survival" from pre-Islamic
Hausa religion, it differs among the Muslim Hausa from that which is practiced among related peoples, such as the Gungawa, or among non-Muslim
Hausa, such as the Maguzawa. It has a different meaning for these Hausa.
Thus, when Besmer (1983) states that the spirit rides the possessed and
that this is somehow a symbol of homosexuality, it does not mean that it
has the same meaning for the Maguzawa, Gungawa, or other non-Muslim
groups who have the Bori cult. Among the Muslim Hausa homosexual
transvestites, or *Yan Dauda*, play a prominent role. Dauda, a praise name
for any *Galadima*, or ranked title, here specifically refers to the Prince, a *bori*
spirit who is a handsome young man.

These *Yan Dauda* sell various foods at ceremonies, mainly luxury foods
such as fried chicken, and serve as pimps for prostitutes. Women who attend Hausa Bori rituals are deemed to be prostitutes. Rene Pittin (1983)
lists three activities for Yan Dauda: procuring, cooking, and prostitution.
She argues that there is a close tie between prostitutes and Yan Dauda.
Moreover, the Yan Dauda in combining male and female roles mediates between men and women, occupying an ambiguous category. Living among
the prostitutes further provides a disguise for men seeking homosexual
activity. Protection and discretion are provided through this arrangement.
Certainly, the Bori cult provides a niche open to marginal people of all
kinds, not simply women or homosexuals. Butchers, night-soil workers,
musicians, and poor farmers are welcome there. Mentally disturbed people
of all classes similarly seek refuge among the Bori devotees.

Murray Last notes that among the group of rural Hausa non-Muslims,
whom he studied, there is an inherited obligation to appease particular
spirits. For some, this obligation is to become a member of the Yan bori.
Certain physical ailment may plague the chosen person. A headache is a
common ailment. The diviner whose aid the beleaguered individual seeks
will interpret the sign as a call to the *Yan bori*. This group is headed a Shaman who is invested in that position by the *sarki's* (emir's) younger sister.

CONCLUSION

There is a great deal of continuity between traditional Habe religion and
"folk" religion among the Muslim Hausa. In many ways, the mallams and

the various *bori* leaders are in a kind of complementary opposition. Although the mallams see "pagan" *bori* doctors and cult *bori* leaders, male and female, as threats to their position, they also appear generally powerless to stop them and profess belief in the same spirits as those honored by *bori* devotees. Their interpretation, certainly, is at least subtly different but the mallams know that many Muslim Hausa consult these shamanic healers when their own magical practices fail.

Jugun Hella, the *bori* priest whom I knew best stated that he was more powerful than all the other healers in Nigeria, for their people came to him to consult his spirits. He was ecumenical in his practice, turning no one in need away and asking no money in return for the use of his gift. In a day, when the *bori* has often become cheap TV entertainment, as Faulkingham indicates, there is still behind all the versions of the *bori* this simple humanistic boast and ethos of Jugun Hella. The power to heal is given by a higher power and is sacred in itself.

No matter how much current *bori* practice has changed to survive in an increasingly fundamentalist Muslim Hausa world, it still provides glimpses into the powerful source from which it came. It is a link with other forms of *bori*, which Lewis has shown stretch throughout a wide swath of Africa and the New World, and even now into Arabia with the ease of travel for the Pilgrimage. The pull of old spirits whose existence is rooted in the nature of the people themselves is compelling, and one people often find irresistible.

3

Up Close and Personal in the Field

On one or two occasions "in the field," I have felt in the presence of some sort of power or presence that I sensed I could not readily explain—or explain away. In my published papers, especially in my early years, I tended to gloss over these incidents, assuming the appropriate professorial distance from them. As I aged in the profession, I occasionally talked about these events in a half-joking manner, probing my colleagues somewhat indirectly to discern whether they, too, had experienced something beyond the ordinary in the midst of their work.

Many, it seems, had. Their stories varied from the truly incomprehensible to the somewhat charming. The former, I admit, I still view with more than a modicum of skepticism. The latter intrigue me and I, at least, *wish* them to be true. My own brush with the unusual falls into the category of things I *wish* to be true.

Bori was a boka, a traditional doctor, among the Gungawa people in Northwestern Nigeria. The Gungawa, or island-people, lived among the islands of the Niger River before their forced resettlement in the 1960s. The bori priest/doctor was a charismatic leader of great power who had to earn his position through his wisdom, skill, and diplomacy. He had to be the epitome of Gungawa culture, a living embodiment of all they deemed good.

When I met Jugun Hella, the bori in the 1970s, he was already famous throughout Nigeria for his ability to communicate with spirits, heal the insane, predict the future, and intercede with political and spiritual forces that threatened his people. To me, however, Bori appeared as a likeable clown who made us all laugh rather than a powerful figure about whom stories were told far and wide in Nigeria and its neighboring countries.

He simply appeared one day when I was visiting a resettlement village, making my rounds with Father Peter Ottilio, a missionary priest from New Orleans. Pete had regaled me with stories of Bori and I was anxious to meet him. Out of the corner of my eye, I saw a figure clad all in green loom up in the distance. Laughter preceded his approach and seemed to lift him up as he walked directly up to me.

I had to laugh at his antics as he wrestled with the youth, told jokes, pretended to steal items and acted the fool. Only later did I realize that because he was so powerful, he had to draw people to him with humor else they would be afraid to approach him. My inexperience manifested itself in my judging him by surface appearances. Bori seemed innocent and harmless. He was friendly and so I condescended to be friendly in return. That he was so tolerant of me, in retrospect, appears quite amazing and even amusing.

Gradually, however, I began to get not quite an eerie feeling but a strange one, nonetheless. Bori always seemed to know when I was approaching him. I tried to rationalize it by the fact that my walk, not my footwear, was different from his people. He also seemed to know what I wanted before I spoke to him. Again I explained his behavior in the acceptable fashion, reckoning him as a skilled psychologist.

Bori, however, went beyond the usual fortune teller tricks of discerning what people want to know. He was able to tell me my worries and desires without my articulating them. At first, I suspected him of simply repeating what Pete had told him about me or what he deduced from that knowledge. Pete is also a great trickster, and he and Bori were not above collaborating on elaborate schemes.

Pete, however, denied such hijinks. He didn't know me well enough at that time. Besides, some of the things Bori revealed were beyond Pete's ken at that time. Pete, also, had some eerie experiences with Bori from time to time. I later discovered that all the "European" who had met Bori had some tale or other to tell about him.

Later, I learned much more about Bori, the "divine fool," whose power frightened the Muslim rulers of his area so much that they poisoned him. They attempted to besmirch his reputation through accusing him of witchcraft. Although they did not succeed, they did frighten his villagers to the extent that no one would talk of him when I returned at his invitation to study with him only to discover that he had been killed. Even the missionaries, at first, tried to convince me that there had been no person named Bori.

Eventually, they relented when I asked for him by name not title. His death had frightened him and only after some years and more visits would they speak to me freely once again of my old friend. Meanwhile, I often remember Bori and his gentle power, his humor that drew people to him and allowed them to benefit from his gifts to heal and predict the future. I cannot explain how Bori knew my secret thoughts and even foretold what I would do. Perhaps, my memory is becoming more selective as I age. Perhaps, my imagination is romanticizing an old man whom I liked and took time to teach me whatever I wanted to know about himself and his people. Or, just perhaps, there may be more in heaven than in all my scientific philosophy!

4

Colonialism and the Creation of Ethnic Identity

Colonialism had profound effects on world history, including the creation of numerous ethnic identities in the colonized world. Africa's ethnic problems, for example, can be traced directly to its colonial encounter. This work examines the concept of ethnicity and the manner in which colonialism consciously and unconsciously created ethnic identities in order to aid in the control and administration of colonial holdings in Africa. Nigeria has been no exception to this process and the creation of Hausa and other Nigerian ethnicities has great importance to our understanding of current problems in Nigeria and Hausa culture in particular. The lessons derived from this exercise have much to offer in the areas of theory and practice in the current world scene as well.

Colonial societies are noteworthy for subsuming several different ethnic groups under an imposed foreign government, both allowing and requiring these groups to interact on many levels with one another. The enforced peace that the colonial power's superior force ensures further facilitates movement and interaction of peoples over large areas. Because social groups as well as individuals define their identities in situations of opposition and contrast with others, this increased contact with others stimulates and exacerbates the creation and development of identities with which to structure social interaction. These identities enable people to perform culture in their daily lives through the use of symbols, as Victor Turner and Richard Schenkman (1985) indicate.

By their nature, symbols not only point to what they represent, but also somehow become inextricably bound up with its meaning. Thus, the broken shards of pottery that each member of ancient Greek groups carried around both symbolized the group and were somehow part of it, for when the group reunited each member's piece of pottery fit with the others to reconstruct the whole. By extension, then, identity symbols are more than convenient signs of group membership, they somehow become part of each member's own personal identity, however arbitrary the original selection of symbols may have been. Through innumerable reenactments of performance rituals establishing one's identity, whether with other group members to distinguish the group from other groups or in interactions with group members to establish one's claim to group membership, a person internalizes these symbols, consciously or otherwise. If consciously, the individual may have a way feeling of humor as toward an old friend whose foibles are known. If unconsciously, then the symbol may be accepted without question as right and proper. I believe that most group members have a mixture of feelings, and it is this combination of awareness and out-of-awareness regarding what constitutes their identity performance that makes these performances so interesting and significant.

Since individually and in groups we have a range of identities open to us it is our interpretation and definition of any given situation that prompts us to choose one identity over another from those available to us. Of course, the range of accessible identities is finite but it is large. Moreover, it is only in light of the social identities of others that we can define our own identities. In other words, "we" are who "they" are not. There is no "us" without a "them". The major question, of course, is to what degree this difference is tolerated, respected, or ignored. The answer depends on a number of factors: racial differences, religious beliefs and practices, occupational opposition or complementarily, relations of equality or subordination, and so on. Colonialism consciously and unconsciously encouraged each of these factors.

Each group, for example, uses its identity to control certain social, economic, and political resources. Since these groups do not have equal access to the desired resources, ethnic stratification occurs and Furnival's plural society comes into existence. In fact, colonial societies favor one group over another, further encouraging an unequal balance of power. British colonial society was no different.

COLONIAL SOCIETY

By definition, colonial society is composed of an expatriate ruling class and a subordinated indigenous class. Of course each of these classes is comprised of a number of layers. Expatriates, for example, were made of rulers, civil servants, missionaries, temporary workers, merchants, assorted businessmen, wives, and even visiting academics. Settler colonies had further distinctions. These expatriates formed a dissimilar group who often disagreed, coming from different social classes in Europe.

Similarly, lumping together subjected colonial peoples confuses attempts to understand the colonial scene. There were differences in ranking among favored and less favored people in the colonial system. Colonial reality virtually demanded that those in power, the expatriate ruling class, work with favored indigenous people over less favored ones. In the British system that was the underlying meaning of Indirect Rule.

In Nigeria, Ghana, and other British colonies under Indirect Rule expatriates over represented the upper middle class in Britain. In social class origins and value, they presented a false and outdated side of British culture. Unsurprisingly, they structured their contacts with indigenous peoples along carefully pre-selected routes. They valued, for example, proper aristocratic behavior, favoring those groups, such as the Fulani, whom they considered more refined in demeanor and noble in tradition.

The tenets of indirect rule required local financial support for all local governmental functions, including education. Additionally, in Nigeria at least, the British found it useful to posit an innate hostility between Islam and Christianity, between Western and Islamic education and practices and significantly between democracy and adherence to tradition.

THE BRITISH TAKEOVER OF NIGERIA

Heussler's (1968) The *British in Northern Nigeria* is, perhaps, the best single source dealing with the establishment and evolution of British rule in Northern Nigeria. It has the added virtue of dealing with the expatriate section of colonial society in a manner that sheds light on its members' motivations and actions. Heussler manages to recreate the colonial milieu in his work, enabling the reader to empathize with the historical characters and situations depicted.

In 1900, when she assumed formal responsibility for Northern Nigeria, Britain's knowledge and experience of the area were remarkably slight. A handful of British nationals had had extensive trading experience in the new Protectorate's southerly regions along the Niger and Benue and a few had made brief excursions into the northern parts on various missions, commercial, religious, scholarly, and political.

There were, therefore, three major categories of people with knowledge and interests in the north- politicians, missionaries, and merchants. Politicians wished to keep rivals out of Nigeria. In the northern regions that essentially meant the French. Missionaries desired to convert "pagans" and Muslims to Christianity. In addition, they were filled with less clearly defined goals. Their desire, however, to keep the French out of the north was very clear. Similarly, merchants were interested in carrying on trade in a congenial atmosphere. Consequently, they feared and opposed French expansion into the northern areas of Nigeria. Whatever differences existed among members of these groups, they were united in their resolve to keep the French out of the north. Therefore, however reluctantly, the British assumed administrative responsibility for Northern Nigeria in 1900.They were determined to rule with a minimum number of Europeans and cost. That goal led to the promulgation of policies which often conflicted with the desires of missionaries and merchants, whose members had preceded British administrators to the north and, to a great extent, created the circumstances which required their presence there.

The role of Sir George Goldie (1846-1925) in the annexation process has been well-documented (Flint, 1960) and it is with some justice that he is termed "the founder of Nigeria." Certainly few people originally shared his perception that British annexation of land along the Niger River was indispensable to commerce's security. He came to that conclusion in 1877, a time when imperialism was unpopular in the United Kingdom. Shortly before, in 1868 the British had removed their consular official from the Niger in response to a June 1865 resolution of the House of Commons calling for an end to British involvement in West Africa.

Lack of governmental and popular support for his opinions did not prevent Goldie from capitalizing on his organizational abilities or from creating circumstances which forced the government's hand. Goldie's first steps were to eliminate the cut-throat competition among trading companies that had led to the stagnation of trade. In Goldie's eyes competition had forestalled the advance of trade to the upper Niger regions where the Muslim empires were. It was Goldie's ultimate aim to secure control of the entire Niger Valley for Great Britain. At the time, there were foreign powers from Senegal to the Nile Valley.

He understood that such a situation could not long exist. Therefore, he moved rapidly and by 1879 had formed the United African Company, the first of a series of amalgamations for trading companies Goldie organized, which he hoped to use for imperialistic purposes. His attempts to receive a charter, however, were failures for either economic or political reasons. Germany's entry into the colonial sweep- stakes in 1884, however, altered the situation.

Goldie's timely purchase of two French Niger trading companies enabled Great Britain to state at the West African Conference in Berlin (1884-1885) that she controlled the trade of the Niger Basin. By 1886 it had become obvious to Great Britain that Goldie's trading company could not equally compete with France and Germany. On behalf of a private company Goldie had been concluding treaties with local rulers while French and German agents were acting on behalf of their respective governments. Therefore, in July 1886 the British government chartered the Royal Niger Company.

Surprisingly, the company was given political powers without losing its economic privileges. It was nominally under the control of the office of the Secretary of State for the Colonies. In actual practice it carried out its directive to govern, preserve social order, and to protect the territory of treaty chiefs in relative autonomy. Its mandate gave the right to exercise authority over British subjects and foreigners in its territory. In effect, Goldie became the first British administrator of what was to become Northern Nigeria. Although he did not become the actual governor of the Royal Niger Company until 1895, he was its de facto ruler from its beginning. As such, he set the pattern for policies later followed by Lord Lugard, the first High Commissioner of Northern Nigeria. These policies included the elimination of slave raiding; religious tolerance, including the discouragement of missionary activity; and ruling through local rulers in conformity with "native laws and customs." In all but name, Goldie developed what Lugard later named "indirect rule" or the "dual mandate." That he and Lugard governed in a similar manner is not surprising. After all, Lugard served under Goldie in Nigeria in 1894. His race to Nikki in Borgu and the subsequent treaty he negotiated enabled the British to beat the French to the area.

Furthermore, his role in forming the West African Frontier Force was instrumental in keeping peace with France and bringing about the 1898 convention that together with that of 1893 with Germany ended the struggle for control of the Niger. Goldie had negotiated these treaties and Lugard was a trusted lieutenant. Additionally, however, the structural conditions under which these two men governed were virtually identical. They had to administer a vast area of about one-half million square miles with few trained personnel and little money. The area itself was composed of a large number of ethnic groups organized in a wide variety of political structures, ranging from large empires to households. Furthermore, slave raiding by the Fulani kingdoms on the southern "pagans" posed a major problem to the preservation of law and order and the peaceful propagation of trade.

When the British Government assumed formal control of Northern Nigeria on 1 January 1900, at Lokoja, it gave to Lugard all the problems that Goldie had attempted to overcome. In fact, it was primarily the result of Goldie's efforts that the British Government even recognized that problems existed. A major cause for that recognition was Goldie's defeat of the emirs of Nupe and Ilorin in 1897, a result of their persistent slave raiding. Fuller realization of the significance of the circumstances in Northern Nigeria led to British assumption of the political and territorial powers of the Royal Niger Company.

Goldie's policies resulted in an alliance between merchants and politicians. Although their interests were not identical, they coincided sufficiently enough to promote cooperation. Similarly, European missionaries had advocated a direct governmental role in protecting their interests. They had been upset with Goldie's separation of religion from politics and trade. There was little patience in the missionary community for his conciliatory gestures toward Muslim rulers. In fact, European missionaries attributed much of his anti-missionary attitude to his being a Jew. Bishop Samuel Crowther, however, was not so impatient. Crowther was a Yoruba Missionary who, unfortunately, became the focal point of an attack on African agents for the Church Mission Society (C.M.S.) by European missionaries. These attacks were led by' a group of missionaries who became known as the Sudan Party.

Members of the party were in favor of "pure, simple, primitive Christianity" presented through indigenous symbols (Owoh, 1971: 279). They believed in going directly to the people over the heads of their "despotic" Fulani rulers. To do so, they adopted the *tobe*, the traditional dress of the people, and spoke fluent Hausa. In that language they were eloquently outspoken on matters of religion, morals, and politics. Their presuppositions regarding the peaceful nature of non-Fulani and their readiness to accept Christianity added to their fervor. In fact, they believed that only the bigotry of their Fulani rulers prevented the Hausa from immediate conversion to Christianity.

They never understood that their adoption of the *tobe*, the Hausa robe, caused excitement among the populace because they thought the missionaries were converting to Islam. Owoh (ibid: 298) states, "The adoption of the *tobe* by European missionaries, then, was greeted with excitement by the local people because it brought the rich white missionaries within approachable distance." The failure of the members of the Sudan Party to live like Muslims, however, and the threat they posed to traditional Islamic teachers and the emirs created great political problems. Furthermore, the Sudan Party's opposition to African clergy had serious repercussions, with many Sierra Leoneans turning on the C.M.S. and condemning it to Hausa authorities. In addition, that policy split the northern and southern Nigerian churches for years.

Given both the manner in which the Sudan Party had conducted itself and its anti-Fulani stance, it is not surprising that Lugard and his successors were cautious in their relationships with missionaries. Circumstances forced them to rule through those very Islamic rulers whom the missionaries were condemning. Lugard desired to use as little force as possible in establishing British control. Missionaries posed a serious threat to his plans. He, however, was the son of missionaries and far from anti-missionary in his sentiments. Furthermore, he was quite aware of the contributions that voluntary agencies could make to the development of Northern Nigeria, and at a very small cost to the government. Such was the situation in 1903, the third year of Lugard's rust period of rule in Northern Nigeria, the year in which he defeated both Kano and Sokoto.

EARLY EXPATRIATE SOCIETY IN NORTHERN NIGERIA

There are a number of characteristics that distinguish expatriate societies from similar groups. Most obvious is the fact that expatriates come from another area, one that provides support, and one to which they ostensibly can return, sooner or later, when they finish their tour of duty. Indeed, "tour of duty" is quite an accurate description of expatriate perception of the definition of the situation- as Van Baal (1972: 87) makes clear in his own case. He went to the Netherlands East Indies because he believed was his moral duty to do so in order to serve mankind. Although further empirical work is necessary, it is probable that expatriates are not demographically or in value-orientation representative of their home areas. Thus, they tend to present a false and outdated version of their home societies to indigenous people. Furthermore, their contacts with those people are along pre-selected routes, congruent with their occupation of dominant power positions. Finally, although colonial officials, missionaries, indigenous staff, recognized representative of local people, servants, and the occasional anthropologist frequently differed bitterly, there were a number of instances in which overt disagreements were not tolerated, for each segment within the expatriate stratum had too much at stake in the preservation of the structure to endanger its maintenance.

The actual religious, demographic, and political situation into which the British came is important to an understanding of the patterns that they established. To put it concretely: without an understanding of the situation in which the British consolidated their rule it is impossible to understand the structure and functioning of the non-settler colonial society that Nigeria became.

In 1910 there were 338 Europeans in Northern Nigeria, 120 of who were merchants (Ajayi, Ab/p. *12/2:14*). In 1911 there were 678 Europeans in a population of 8,115,981. They constituted .00835 percent of the population, a figure that increased slightly in the census of 1921 to .01138 percent and to .01595 percent in 1931. The actual proportion of Europeans in the population in 1921 and 1931 was 1,168 of 10,259,993 and 1,825 of 11,434,924. Perhaps a more graphic illustration of the relative size of the two communities is given by a comparison of the number of Europeans and Nigerians per square mile. In 1911, there were .00265 Europeans per square mile compared with 31.74 Nigerians. In 1921 the figures were .00447 compared with 39.33. 1931's figures showed .0069958 to 40.58 (Brooke, 1933: 1). In short, the expatriate community was a face to face one, one that was both absolutely and relatively small.

Although Brooke (1933: 66) listed the north as essentially Islamic, the figures he gave for Sokoto cast doubt on his reliability in this matter. He reports, for example, only 126,505 "animists" among indigenous non-Hausa people in a population of 254,324 and 15,312 among a population of 1,106,649 Hausa. My own research (Salamone, 1974), centered on the Yauri region of Sokoto, and that of Barkow (1970), however, casts serious doubt on the accuracy of these figures. Much more probable is the analysis found in Trimingham's (Ab: P12/1:8:18-19) report to the CMS and MMS.

In it he stresses the rapidity of Islam's twentieth century expansion and the difference between Islam among the Kanuri, Yoruba, and Hausa. Among the Kanuri, Islam is deep and of long duration. Whereas it is a religion among the Yoruba, it is a civilization among the Hausa. The rapid spread of Islam in Hausaland, from 5 percent of the population in 1900 to 80 percent in 1950, resulted from British policy favoring Islam. After the British conquest, Islam was no longer viewed by the Hausa as the religion of the Fulani. Rather they viewed 1t as an alternate civilization, useful in opposition to western influence, and one honored by British policy.

One of the things to make clear is that until the British occupation Islam in West Africa was largely an aristocratic religion, professed by the ruling class who only attempted to impose it on their subjects in the early stages of the end of the 18th and beginning of the 19th centuries (Trimingham, Ab:P12/1:8:19). The distinction between sacred and secular, deeply imbedded in western culture, is antithetical to the Islamic state structure. Ironically, the Christian missionary has been one of the prime factors working toward distinguishing the two. That separation, which Trimingham (Ab: PI2/1:8:31) sums up as the "individual morality" of the missionary, is viewed by Muslims and non-Muslims in Northern Nigeria as a menace to societal stability.

The early situation, then, was one in which there were very few expatriates. Originally, almost half of these were traders, who had exercised quasi-political functions before the establishment of the protectorate. The miniscule forces of government officials were dependent on securing local cooperation for their efforts. Although missionaries could not cavalierly be excluded from the north, their work could be hindered, for they clearly presented a hindrance to the effective and smooth cooperation of Islamic officials. Given the face to face nature of the British community, much of the interaction takes on clear cut characteristics, typical of many of the societies which anthropologists are more accustomed to studying. In brief, conflicts clearly reveal underlying structural characteristics.

Thus, Rattray's (1934) hypothesis regarding indirect rule assumes added dimension when judged against Dr. Walter Miller's case history presented in the following section. Basically, Rattray (1934: 26.27) suggested

> . . . that, thirty or forty years ago, when the science of anthropology was still in its infancy, had the European conquerors of Northern Nigeria encountered such a state of society [that of West Africans] . . . they would have had neither

the knowledge, nor the means, nor the time to have comprehended it, and, in consequence, Indirect Rule, as we understand it would have been almost impossible of introduction. The complexity of a so-called 'primitive' tribal society would have been unintelligible to them, the intimately related social units would have seemed lacking in cohesion, nothing worthy of the name constitution or state would have been apparent. . . . It was inevitable . . . that the point of view, the only point of view, ever put forward to the British Government in those early days must have been that of this upper-ruling class-this alien aristocracy 'the Fulani, this foreign minority among the millions of inarticulate subjects over whom for a hundred years these invaders had wielded what was probably only a very nominal suzerainty.

In short, the end result of Indirect Rule was the strengthening of Fulani rule in a way predictable through the application of Smith's theory of the plural society. Indeed, Palmer's (1934: 37-48) response to Rattray is revealingly instructive. He accused Rattray of being pro-Hausa and anti-Fulani, concluding his attack by citing an un-named "learned member of the Nigerian Legislature" who complained "that he could never find out the difference between an Anthropologist and a Secretary for Native Affairs." Both, according to Palmer, were troublesome creatures who threaten a carefully balanced governing arrangement.

The point is that colonial society in Nigeria was quite complex. It was not a case of "the British" vs. "the Africans." Quite clearly neither "the British" nor "the Africans" formed a monolithic group. Rattray made explicit the alliance between colonial officials and Fulani elite. In addition, he demonstrated the simplified selective perception which enables the British to rule an area notable for its ethnographic complexity. Quite simply, British political officers accepted the Fulani's idealized version of political reality, one that those whom the Fulani conquered never accepted. Furthermore, because of its advantage in easing their rule, the British political corps solidified Fulani rule at the very time it was most in danger of collapsing.

Because of their personal contacts with indigenous peoples, missionaries, anthropologists, and secretaries for native affairs were in excellent positions to challenge this mutually convenient arrangement between Fulani and British colonial officers and its consequent distortion of reality. In turn, of course, missionaries, anthropologists, and secretaries for native affairs had perceptual biases of their own related to the interests and allegiances of their positions. As a consequence, competing versions of reality entered the colonial arena. Furthermore, although colonial officials had power to limit internal opposition, those whom they opposed frequently brought countervailing power to bear in Great Britain. It is, in fact, this extension of disputes and the resulting appeal to power ultimately residing in the metropolitan center that makes the concept of the "expatriate society" a useful tool.

THE HAUSALAND MISSION

It is simple to comprehend colonial policy regarding missionaries. The general picture has been presented in a number of places (Cf. Owoh, 1971: Crampton, 1967; Ayandele, 1966; and Galloway, 1960). The general pattern was composed of the following. First, there was the separation of politics from religion, a policy stemming from Goldie's days. Equally important, on the missionary side, was the "Sudan Party's" break with earlier missionary policy and its consequent downgrading of African missionaries. As a result of ignoring Crowther's policy, British missionaries began to emphasize individual conversions, rather than focusing on the community. This emphasis on the individual versus his community was one of the features of missionary activity that caused friction between missionary and administrator. Another characteristic was mission belief in the easy conversion of Hausa, leading to fierce mission/Fulani hostility.

Quite predictably each phase of mission/government interaction was one of disagreement and conflicting perceptions of their proper respective roles. Simply, missionaries believed that the government should help them to convert Muslims; the spread of British military power entailed the expansion of Christianity (Cf. Letter of Tugwell, Miller and Burgin to Lugard, 14 February 1901: CMS G3/A9/01). It was just that feeling, natural to the Fulani who had reached power via the *jihad* (holy war) that the British wished to combat, for it threatened to attack the core of the British-Fulani clientage relationship. At the same time, however, the British were honor bound to protect the missionaries, for, as Crampton (1967: 45) pointed out, an insult to one European was interpreted as an insult to all. Furthermore, although many officers were not themselves favorably disposed toward Christianity, and many members of the colonial secretariat were even anti-missionary Unitarians (Crampton, 1967: 55), Christianity was a symbol of the British Empire and many missionaries had powerful interests at home.

The correspondence of the Hausaland Mission from the year 1903 illustrates these generalizations in a specific case. In order to appreciate the importance of the Hausaland Mission to Northern Nigeria's social history it is necessary to provide a brief historical sketch of previous missionary work. More complete accounts are available in Ayandele (1966: 116.52) and Ajayi (1965), among others.

In 1855, T. J. Bowen, an American Southern Baptist, made the first serious missionary attempt to found a northern station at Ilorin. More promising, however, was the work of the Yoruba missionary, S. A. Crowther. Crowther's emphasis on community, rather than individual, conversion was less threatening to the emirs than efforts at individual conversion European missionaries favored so highly, an approach that ripped the convert from his or her traditional community. Proof of the efficacy of his method was the ease with which he obtained permission to open mission stations from allegedly anti-Christian Fulani emirs. In 1857 he opened stations at Lokoja, Egga, and Kipo Hill, all with the permission of Nupe emirs. Shortly thereafter Bida, Ilorin, and Gwandu granted permission for stations to be opened in their territories. The Fulani rulers did not merely tolerate these stations; they welcomed them.

Unfortunately, European missionaries undermined these promising early African efforts to convert the north. It was unfortunate because European efforts were predicated on an interpretation of reality that was as simplistic as that of most colonial officers. It erred, however, on the opposite side. European missionaries were strongly anti-Fulani and believed that the Hausa as distinct from their Fulani rulers were eager to embrace Christianity. They opposed Crowther's conciliatory policy and processed for the immediate conversion of northerners, in the process ignoring the Muslim emirs.

It is essential to note that those European missionaries were strongly imperialistic. Not only did they believe that the CMS should dispense with African agents, such as Crowther, but that it was the duty of Great Britain to protect missionaries and ease their conversion of Muslims and "pagans." At every opportunity, they attempted to force the government's hand on the issue. The pattern for colonial/missionary relations was set by G. W. Brooke's Sudan Party (1890-1892). That party was inspired by Gordon's anti-Mahdist campaign in the Sudan, and the fear that the Mahdi would rise in Nigeria. The CMS sent eleven Cambridge and Oxford graduates to Northern Nigeria, the largest single party they had ever sent to one area. The Sudan Party's attempt at cultural conversion failed miserably. Not only were their premises incorrect, but their protection against disease was tragically inadequate. They were intensely anti-Fulani and perpetuated the myth that all Hausa were nominal Muslims eagerly awaiting the liberation of Christianity, a myth that plagued missionary relationships with northern Nigerians for years.

The ultimate failure of the Sudan Party, ravished by illness and death, only spurred other missionary efforts. In 1891 a Hausa Association was formed in memory of J. A. Robinson of the Sudan Party. The real reason for its foundation was the conversion of Hausa. Goldie encouraged its foundation, for he had begun to appreciate that the government could use missionaries to build hospitals and promote education and other voluntary activities. Thus, Goldie helped establish that very pattern when he "gave" one hundred freed slaves to the missions for conversion, encouraging missionary belief that the "Sword of Steel" would go before the "Sword of Faith." The 1896 Bida War, in missionary eyes, became the precursor of what was to come. It was the immediate cause for the 1898 expedition of the Hausaland Mission to Hausa settlements in Tripoli, for added to missionary hatred of the Fulani and Islam, was their fear and hatred of French

Roman Catholics who were threatening to take over Northern Nigeria. One of the men in that party was Dr. Walter Miller, whose missionary career is itself a commentary on the development of British policy in Northern Nigeria.

Although Miller's endeavors were in many ways atypical of missionary work, and he personally was at least unique, it is for these reasons that his work is so important in exposing relationships within the expatriate community that otherwise remain implicit. Miller was one of those people who had a knack for forcing those who possess "potential" power into converting it to "actual" power, consequently easing its analysis.

Quite early Miller appreciated the importance of attempting to maintain close ties with the administration, ties which he hoped would facilitate his work, or at least allow him relative freedom in ignoring directives. His peculiar relationship with Lugard deserves a complete analysis, one beyond the scope of this work. As early as 1899, Miller was lavish in his praise of the new high commissioner, a non-Christian son of missionaries. In turn, Lugard was grateful for Miller's role in gaining the allegiance of Zaria in 1902, just two years after Miller's arrival. That allegiance allowed Lugard's man to defeat Abadie Nagwamanchi of Kontagora and to consolidate British control of the north. In turn, Lugard allowed Miller to establish a mission within Zaria itself.

1903 has been chosen as a period to describe relationships because it is the middle of Lugard's first rule, one in which what was to become fixed dogma was still fluid necessity. The mission community was entirely male, as Bargery's letters to the CMS director, Baylis, make clear. Bargery was requesting permission to marry and take his wife to the mission station. He had been in the northern mission two years and four months, a period equal to that of anyone else. His arguments in favor of marriage for missionaries and the assignment of women to the field are valuable in understanding the mission society of the early days. Personally, he argued, there was a danger of not returning to the field, for his future brother-in-law opposed his missionary work; his fiancée might lose her faith if left in that situation. More generally, there was a need for female nurses and doctors. A good deal of work could not be done in Nigeria's Islamic areas by men. Unless women were converted, much of the effort will be wasted. Significantly, Bargery suggested that the resident of Zaria's advice be asked.

The issue was the subject of a torrid debate and Miller sent a memo to the CMS which sheds light on day to day relations in the north. Briefly, arguments in favor of women in the missions were that there was a general peace, and the Mahdi presented no real problem. Furthermore, roads were improved, and whites were seen on every journey. As a result of the general peace and improved transportation, housing was more comfortable, for one could furnish the inside in European fashion while keeping the outside in the "native" style. Miller argued that there certainly was work for women to do. The hospital at Zungeru, for example, needed female nurses beyond the single one who worked there. Most importantly, women were needed to set an example for young children. He notes,

> The fearfully wicked character of all women, even to the little girls-they are ten times more immoral that [sic] the men-makes it impossible if we want the little lads who are about us to grow up healthy and clean to let them have anything to do with these women.

The need for a Christian home as an exemplar, led Miller to write that he favored mothers first over wives, an obvious slap at Bargery. That there was, however, a need to prove that married men were not homosexuals, Miller admitted. Furthermore, he grudgingly conceded that some good men might refuse to come to the mission field if their wives were left behind, but that might not be a real loss. There were some arguments against allowing any woman to come to the mission area. Mission life had a pioneer nature to it. Roads were bad from July to October. No schools were yet planned for the foreseeable future. Opposition to missionaries was still strong. Finally, the possibility of loneliness was great, for no band of lady workers was yet possible because of the necessity of offering them protection.

Finally, Miller offered the following regulations pending approval by the committee of the use of female missionaries. There should be at least four women, with reinforcements available. Each woman should be free of organic diseases, "Especially those peculiar to women." None should be under the age of 27 or 28, and at least one should be a "strapping old maid", who should be the group leader. No romances should be encouraged, nor should any publicity be given. Work would consist of elementary work, specifically "in the kindergarten style," and nursing and dispensing.

Quite obviously, Miller preferred unmarried clergy, and the parallels between early CMS stations and later Roman Catholic ones are quite suggestive. His authoritarian role is clearly evident in the virtual open rebellion he caused in 1903. The immediate point at issue was the binding nature of his instructions. These essentially would have given Miller absolute control over all missionaries and their households. Bargery led a successful opposition to his absolute rule.

In 1903 there was no permanent station. About fifty people attended services. All seven of the missionaries were university people. Preference for public school graduates with varsity training was a common British trait. The normal tour of duty was two and one-half years, followed by home leave. Relations with the government, which in 1903 meant Lugard, were carefully cultivated. In fact, Miller sent Lugard 19 pages of typed instructions in which he advocated changes in medical, moral and economic areas, with the use of force if needed. He complained of the hostility of government officials, and then he flatly stated that he was going to Kano and Katsina.

This upset Lugard, who wrote to Baylis on 5 September to comment on Miller's long memo. In the course of that response a number of important issues were addressed. First, he was not opposed to direct rule, but with the staff and money at his disposal, there was no alternative. Although he did not trust the Fulani, necessity dictated that he work through them. To that end officials familiar with Hausa and local customs were needed. Personally, he favored Christian missions, but progress must be made in conjunction with local conditions. This was not the time to anger the Fulani. In short, stay away from Kano and Katsina (Lugard to Baylis, 5 Sept., 1903, from Surrey). On 27 October he sent Baylis another letter warning that he would not support missionaries in Kano or Katsina with force. Missionaries should stick to pagan zones, for he had given his word to keep them out of Muslim territories. In point of fact, neither statement was true. Lugard had earlier rescued Miller's ill-fated expedition to Kano and would have done so again. Furthermore, he had not promised to keep missionaries out of Islamic areas.

Whereas Miller clearly wanted to work among Hausa only, his colleagues were perfectly willing and eager to go in pairs to villages of non-Hausa. Miller himself visited eight to twelve villages of non-Hausa in two tours of seven days each. In this work the missionaries were aided by their servants. Unfortunately, no one has yet analyzed the role of the young male servant in missionary work. Certainly, Miller was quite clear in his hopes that these young men, such as his Audu, would be catalysts in the coming Hausa conversion. Despite his close ties with Audu, Miller still believed in the fact of European superiority to the Hausa, a view he modified in his later life. In 1903, however, the highest praise he could give was that someone had acted "Almost like a white man" (Miller to Baylis, 11 June, 1903, CMS: G3 Ag/07/1903; Nos. 1-42, Reel Number 214).

Neither Miller nor Lugard, despite close ties, was lulled by the other's sincere friendship into misjudging his motives. Miller urged Baylis on 11 June to keep the distinction between the mission and the government clear. Any confusion in the peoples' minds between the two was detrimental. It must be stressed, however, that the relationship between missionaries and government was multiplex. Although missionaries might be a nuisance, they did perform valuable work at low cost to the government. For example, medical work figured quite prominently in the mission. Again and again, Druitt's medical skill is praised in letters. Lugard's letter to Hans Vischer, head of education for the Northern provinces (MSS British Empire S76: 11 January, 1914) discussed the complexity of missionary contributions in the field of education. At the beginning Lugard emphasized the lack of resources at the government's disposal. Missionaries were all too eager to fm the gap. The Ugandan experience, however, marred by Christian rivalry was held to be instructive. Therefore, a number of variables must be checked: the form of the missionary, the teacher, and the consent of the parents. Furthermore, spheres of influence should be established. A hint of a *quid pro quo* is found in Lugard's irritation that Islam was allowed into pagan areas where Christianity was excluded. More ironic is the fact that Palmer had invoked Lugard's Indirect Rule to keep missionaries out of areas where Lugard would have welcomed them. In offering a rare glimpse of his inner thoughts he wrote:

> . . . . purely secular Education divorced from Moral Instruction and from Religion among races who have not the tradition and the ethical standards which centuries of Christian teaching and environment have produced in Europe, infallibly produces a class of young men and women who lack reverence alike for their parents, their social superiors, their employers, or the Government. They lack self restraint and control, and they lack the foundation on which all the highest and best work in the world is based whether of public and civic usefulness, or of private incentive and effort.

Consequently, Lugard ordered moral education in the secondary schools. He further ordered contact with the Moral Education League in England and the securing of their publications. In addition, he asked that hours for optional religious education be certified, and that the spheres of influence for various religious missions be established (MSS Brit. Em s76).

The impetus given by Lugard's actions is clearly seen. In 1913 there were 38 mission stations in the Northern provinces. In 1917 there were more than 60, including churches in Kaduna, Zaria, and Jos (Secretary, N. P., to Private Secretary to H. E., Governor-General, 17 January 1918, MSS Brit. Em s76).

Lugard, however, did not remain in power long and those who replaced him continued the canonization of Indirect Rule. Their motives may well have been mixed, but as Ayandele (1967: 145-52) rightly argues, missionaries presented political problems and were quick to cause difficulties wherever they went. Miller's expedition to Kano in 1901 was a colossal blunder. Merchants were opposed to missionaries, moreover, because they denounced the liquor trade and the general comportment of merchants. Ayandele (ibid.) makes clear that the policy of men like Girouard and Temple was anti-missionary because, however much they admired Islamic culture, they were afraid of missionary exposure of their shortcomings.

Indirect Rulers had much to hide from the gaze of the British public through probable revelations by the missionaries to the British press. Many of the Residents were overbearing in their attitudes to the natives and condoned many acts of oppression by the chiefs and emirs. The officials were, in a missionary observer's view 'brave English officers, genial, good natured, but utterly ungodly, all living loose lives, all having women brought to them wherever they are.' Missionaries also felt that in the pacification of the territory much bloodshed that could have been avoided, the report of which never reached the Colonial Office, occurred. In places where missionaries were allowed to establish themselves many people who could not obtain redress for wrongs from Residents flocked to missionaries for 'advice' (ibid.: 151).

The missionary mentioned in the quotation was, of course, Miller and the implacable opposition he had to the slaughter of Nigerians, exemplified in the Hadeja campaign, earned him the hatred of numerous administrators. In short, under Percy Girouard what had been necessity for Lugard became policy.

The response that J. F. Matthews (MSS Afr s783, 27 July, 1924) gave to his brother, Basil Matthews's book *The Clash of Colour* (1926: London, Cargate Press) serves as a clear example of the attitude of colonial officers to outside criticism,

The difficulty with you righteously indignant ones is to put yourselves in our place, to visualize the enormous areas and distances involved, the fewness of communication facilities such as railroads, roads and telegraph wires and (most of all) the attitude and mentality of the inhabitants and the consequent difficulty of effect of one's action on the minds of Englishmen.

Matthews went on to bemoan the result of "half-baked education" on the wrong natives who then exploited their illiterate brothers. That hostile attitude toward those who let the side down was applied against missionaries, anthropologists, and others who publicly deviated from the office line. Although the American anthropologist Oberg worked in East Africa, his (Oberg, 1972: 77-78) comments apply to Northern Nigeria.

Nothing in my past had prepared me to live within barriers as rigid as those which separated Europeans and natives or to come to terms with the harsh punishment sometimes meted out to natives. . . . In retrospect it is easy to see how such conditions enforce conformity and limit the freedom of the anthropologist. . . . It was in Africa that I first encountered culture shock as a personal problem and, I might add, one which also troubled some of the British colonial officials. However, I had the problem of adjusting to two subcultures: that of British colonial officialdom and that of the native people of Ankole . . . . At the time the government station at Mbarara in the district of Ankole consisted of eight British officials. Life in the station was governed by strict routine. Office hours were from eight to one, then lunch and a siesta until four in the afternoon. I was soon informed that house visits during siesta hours were strictly taboo. At four most of the men and women went to the nine-hole golf-course . . . . My relations with the British officials were strained until I adapted myself to their three primary social interests, which were golf, hunting, and the sundowner circuit. . . . At a sundowner the quiet officiousness of the British was replaced by talkative friendliness.

The early colonial period in Nigeria reveals trends in expatriate society that became solidified during the Classic Period of Colonialism, the interwar era. A discussion of that era is well beyond the scope of this paper. Those interested, however, might study the problems faced by the Church of the Brethren in establishing missions in the Bura area in the 1920s (Edinburgh House, Box 271).

SUMMARY

Expatriate society in Northern Nigeria demands further analysis for a number of reasons. Chief among these is the fact that Northern Nigeria provided the prototype for indirect rule, a situation that originally developed from necessity as an *ad hoc* set of social relationships and then became transformed into a quasi-sacred cultural set of principles. These principles determined when, where, how, and with whom interactions could take place. Furthermore, Northern Nigeria had the reputation for being the locus of the best overseas administrators, and, therefore, of being another type of model. Finally, Northern Nigeria was not a settler colony. The number of expatriates was always small and the categories to which each expatriate belonged clearly delineated.

The British established colonial government in a sparsely settled area containing numerous minority ethnic groups. To govern this area they had few officers, fewer of whom were well-trained. They quickly formed an alliance with the ruling Fulani, whose views regarding political, social, and economic reality it was convenient to accept. Within the British ruling group there were people who threatened the fundamental perception of reality that justified Indirect Rule. While each group that differed from the dominant section of the British segment did so for different and at times antagonistic reasons, each shared the fact of support from the metropolitan area and could not simply be crushed or ignored.

Each category had its own reasons for being in Nigeria but all were subordinate to the cause of empire, for quite clearly no expatriate could be in Nigeria without the permission of the government. Therefore, while there were conflicts within the expatriate community, there were no disagreements regarding British right to rule. For example, while Miller quite openly argued that the cross should follow the sword, he never objected to the right of the sword to be where it was. Although the specifics of the operation of government might be questioned, the right to govern never was.

These arguments, however, were not quibbles. They were real conflicts, ones which determined patterns of interaction. Missionaries tended to view

the Fulani as "the enemy", frequently failing to distinguish between ruling
and cattle Fulani, while tending to idealize the Hausa. The British officers
did the opposite. The examples given in the body illustrate both "type" errors. The Hausa-Fulani alliances or the intricacies of the *jihad* tended to be
victims of ideological bias. Quite expectedly, the ruling elite of the British
and local authorities increasingly identified their causes, and missionaries
tended to identify with non-Fulani and non-Muslims.

Within the expatriate community arguments regarding means could be
carried outside Northern Nigeria. Examples are given that clearly show that
appeals to the governor could succeed. At the same time, one could always
appeal to London. The final success of the Church of the Brethren provides
a dear example of the impact metropolitan politics could have on policy in
the north. Furthermore, there were conflicts within each segment of expatriate society. The administrative services were no more monolithic than were
the missionaries. Again, while each presented a unified front toward other
segments, and all did so toward Nigerians, each was internally differenti-
ated. To those familiar with the work of Evans-Pritchard (1940), Gluckman
(1954), or Durkheim and Mauss (1963), this fact will not appear strange.
To many analysts, however, plural societies have been treated as rather
static entities whose members from constituent parts met in stereotypical
encounters.

What is being suggested is that a more dynamic perspective will prove
useful. Specifically, conflict within each segment demands analysis and is
as problematic as agreement. Over what issues will there be splits within
each constituent of each of the plural segments? Over which issue will there
be agreements? The use of the, Mahdi as a bogey-man illustrates the use of
appeal to 'a common enemy to compel unity in the face of opposition. At
root plural societies last because members of the ruling segment agree to
confine their disagreements within the plural framework.

They also last because alliances are formed across segments. The administration formed alliances with the old ruling elite, thereby changing a system
under the guise of preserving it. These alliances and those of the missionaries with enemies of the system were the results of differential perceptions of
reality, within and between each segment. A host of problems in this area
have only begun to be explored. In addition, the entire issue of ties to the
metropolitan areas and the outside world demand as much attention as
those of differential perceptions and patterns of interaction. This paper has
not explored that issue. Certainly, however, it has suggested that these ties
were of vital importance to events within Nigeria. Appeals to those outside
the north were frequent. Now it is vital to work out a typology of appeals,
frequency, and success of each.

Van den Bergh's (1973) insight, based on his research at the University
of Ibadan, that conflict within an elite segment is confined within reason-

able limits and works to preserve the system because of basic agreement on ultimate organizational goals, including its preservation, holds true for the colonial situation. Nevertheless, no one has taken the next logical step and described and analyzed the significant issue of the unexpected consequences of the struggle.

CONCLUSION

Primary among the criticisms that third-world scholars and "radical" social scientists have directed against applied social sciences in general and social anthropology in particular has been their alleged failures to study the colonial context in which much of its field work has been carried out (Cf. Asad, 1975; Lewis, 1973, for examples.) Although these critics usually exaggerate their arguments and typically do not prove that early scholars were either overt *or* covert racists, it is true, nonetheless, that social scientists have paid relatively little attention to the colonial milieu, Condominas's (1973) *pre-terrain*.

Social scientists have described Furnival's classic plural society, colonial society, in works of greater or lesser detail. They have failed to provide adequate descriptions, however, of the workings of colonial society in non-settler communities. Furthermore, these descriptions, with rare exceptions, tend to be outsiders' views which typically describe either the subordinate sections of the plural society or contact areas. Rarely does any social scientist analyze the dominant stratum. Indeed, it is rather suggestive that, on the whole, novelists such as Paul Theroux, Joyce Carey, and George Orwell have offered the best descriptions of expatriate societies, ones that compel emotional assent.

Therefore, this chapter concentrates on: (1) expatriates, especially missionaries and colonial officials; (2) those from indigenous society who were most likely to come into contact with them; (3) type situations of contact among members of different components within the expatriate segment and among members of different categories of expatriate society and indigenous people from various categories of that part of the plural society. These variables are studied in the Northern Nigerian context at the time of the establishment of colonial society in the early twentieth century. Such concentration eases identification of problematic areas and formulation of further hypotheses.

5

Indirect Rule and the Reinterpretation of Tradition: Abdullahi of Yauri

Radical social scientists and third-world scholars have accused traditional social scientists, especially social anthropologists, of failing to study the colonial milieu in which a majority of its field studies have been conducted (cf. Asad, 1975; Lewis, 1973 for examples). There are notable exceptions to that neglect. Among those exceptions are Morris's (1968) study of Asians in East Africa, Ajayi's (1965) study of missionaries in Nigeria, Beidelman's (1974) call to study up in which he uses a Weberian framework in order to understand expatriates in Africa, and Heussler's (1968) study of the British in Northern Nigeria (cf. also Oberg, 1972; Pitt, 1976; Jones, 1974; Reining, 1966; Salamone, 1974, 1977, and 1978; Savishinsky, 1972; Schapera, 1958; Stavenhagen, 1977, and Tonkinson, 1974 for a few such works).

Still, it remains true that social scientists have tended, by and large, to neglect the study of colonial society. This relative neglect entails both serious theoretical and methodological consequences for the social sciences, for it both narrows the range of societies in its comparative repertoire and masks a source of systematic bias. After all, expatriate societies are but one transform of plural societies, one possible manifestation of deeper underlying structural principles. Unfortunately, as Beidelman (1974: 235-36) correctly indicates, those segments of society closest to the anthropologist did not capture his or her wonder. Neither were they perceived as fit subjects for analysis.

Furthermore, when social scientists did turn to the study of colonial societies, even to expatriate segments of it, they tended to present an outsider's viewpoint. Consequently, studies of subordinate segments dominate the literature. Rarely do social scientists "study up" and, consequently, studies of super ordinate segments are scarce (cf. Salamone, 1977 and 1978 for references to studies of expatriate segments of colonial society). Even rarer, if not actually nonexistent, are studies of an indigenous ruler's perception of colonial reality.

As Fallers (1955) recognized long ago, any adequate understanding of colonialism's role in sociocultural change demands that social scientists investigate and analyze interactions among members of different segments of the colonial social structure as well as their understanding of the meaning of those transactions. Fallers (1955) provides an almost unique exception to the neglect of the point of view of indigenous rulers found even in studies of the super ordinate segment of colonial societies. That almost general neglect is only partially attributable to lack of data. It is primarily attributable to an unstated bias, namely the belief that local rulers were mere passive observers of the colonial scene.

It is clear that indigenous rulers far from being passive pawns of colonial administrators were in fact active participants in shaping colonial policy. That policy in Northern Nigeria takes on major importance because of the significance Northern Nigeria held for the rest of the colonies as the prototype for indirect rule. Additionally, Northern Nigeria had a reputation for -attracting the *crème de la crème* of the colonial administrative corps and, therefore, presenting a model for proper executive behavior.

Dorward (1974) discusses the inner workings of that model and its meaning for other areas-of Northern Nigeria. In brief, the only prestigious appointments were in the Hausa emirates. In contrast with the aristocratic Hausa-Fulani emirs, the egalitarian Tiv were a bit too rough-and-ready. Only Tiv who were willing to conform to British conceptions of what Hausa rulers should be were perceived as civilized. After all, what Dorward terms a working misunderstanding of Tiv political institutions had grown up in Nigeria.

Dorward (1974: 461) credits Charles Forbes Gordon's ethnographic work with laying the foundation for that working misunderstanding, one that has stubbornly persisted in the works of even trained anthropologists such as, the Bohannans. In that misunderstanding the Tiv are seen as having neither central political institutions, nor rulers. There are only segmentary lineages which exist only situationally. Therefore, in order for indirect rule and its consequent developmental benefits to have succeeded the Hausa-Fulani pattern of the emirates, the model for efficient and prestigious rule had to be imposed on those politically acephalous people. So low in prestige was a posting to Tivland that until 1931 only education officers sat for Tiv examinations. Learning Tiv was definitely not the road to advancement in the colonial service.

On a personal level, many British officials found the diffidence of the Hausa talakawa [commoners] more congenial to their own prestige and self-image than the rude egalitarianism of the Tiv. Besides, in the British horse-riding hierarchy, tsetse-infested Tivland was a low status posting. Prestige and promotion were to be found in the Hausa emirates (Dorward, 1974: 465).

There was another working misunderstanding taking place in Northern Nigeria. It took place in the Hausa emirates and occurred in relationships between British administrative officers and the indigenous emirs. It affected the other areas of Northern Nigeria, as Dorward makes clear, for the model that was imposed in acephalous areas was one based on a misunderstanding of traditional politics in the emirates.

The following theses will be examined in one emirate: (1) indigenous rulers were active participants in colonial rule; (2) colonial administrators misunderstood the traditional system and in so doing failed to preserve the old one and created a new one that was far more centralized than the old emirates had been; (3) the indigenous rulers reinterpreted the old system to their advantage and were active partners with administrative officers in the working misunderstanding that marked colonial rule; (4) and that contact between emirs and administrative officers was instrumental in leading to the emergence of the modern centralized Nigerian government. That process, furthermore, can be traced in interactions between individuals.

SETTING

In 1902 the British assumed control of Yauri from the Royal Niger Company (Cowper, 1970: 17). It is an understatement to say that it was in serious decline, for it had experienced a series of calamities in its recent past. There had been a tragic civil war and slave raids from Kontagora by the dread Ngwamanche and his successors. The consequences of warfare and slave-raiding were loss of lives, land, and morale. If the British had not intervened, Yauri, which had shrunk from about 17 thousand to 1,486 square miles, would have ceased to exist (cf. Adamu, 1970; Cowper, 1970: 17).

In 1904 Yauri became part of Kontagora Province, a polity it had once ruled and one that was merged in 1907 with Borgu. Even in the midst of that larger heterogeneous conglomerate Yauri's ethnic diversity was noteworthy. The *Gazetteer* of *the Kontagora Province* (Duff, 1970: 42) gives the following figures. In a population of about 35 thousand there were 7 thousand Kamberi, 16,200 Gungawa, 3,575 Yaurawa, 5 thousand Shangawa, 16 hundred Hausa and 1,150 Fulani. Although no Dukawa or Lopawa are mentioned, they were in Yauri and their numbers continued to grow. For various reasons, British administrative officers did not want them in Yauri and were tampering with traditional boundaries in order to keep them out (cf. Salamone, 1974 for a discussion).

In addition to being ethnically heterogeneous Yauri was also occupationally diverse. Table 1 (page 12) illustrates that diversity. It is significant that with less than 20 percent of its population Yauri had 50 percent of Kontagora's craftspeople. It lacked smelters, however, which was a result of British redistricting. Most of Kontagora's fishermen lived in Yauri, an important fact since dried fish provided a stable export for the area. Both occupational and ethnic heterogeneity were associated with Yauri's former position as the most highly organized state in the area. Yauri, moreover, was one of the *Hausa banza,* one of the seven "illegitimate" Hausa states. It was the last Hausa state on the east-west Niger trade route and the first on the west-east trade route. Furthermore, Yauri's islands served as a refuge area, for the Niger islands were relatively safe from the attacks of the Fulani cavalry.

British reimposition of order encouraged the growth of ethnic heterogeneity, for migration sharply increased into the area (Cowper, 1970: 17). Occupational heterogeneity also increased, for order meant that Yauri's ideal trade location could be maximally exploited. Its fertile, and largely empty lands, were also a prime attraction and open for easy settlement in the *Pax Britannica.* Of course, there was a price to pay for British law and order. That price was placing ultimate power in British hands. British rule halted further decline of Yauri but also recognized its dismemberment and even added to it slightly by deeding the Dukawa areas of Yauri, Rijau District, to Kontagora, even though they traditionally had been part of Yauri. British power meant British taxes and changes in the traditional power structure. It is important to point out very clearly that it did not mean the preservation of traditional political systems.

THE POLITICAL SITUATION

Following two illegal reigns, Abdullahi became emir, or sarki, of Yauri in 1923. Both reigns, those of Aliyu of Jabo (1915-23) and Jibilu (1904-15), resulted from ill-conceived British intervention in Yauri's political processes. In neither case did they even pretend to follow the major precept of indirect rule; namely, ruling through local authorities. Quite simply, in neither case did they consult the kingmakers and, in Aliyu's instance, they installed a person who was not only outside the legitimate Jerabawa dynasty, but who was also a Fulani from Jabo near Sokoto. The choice of any Fulani to rule Yauri would have been a grievous insult, for Yauri prided itself on maintaining its Hausa dynasty. During the *jihad'* of Usman dan Fodio in the nineteenth century, it had chosen a tributary status *(dhimmi)* in order to stave off Fulani conquest.

Choosing any Fulani, therefore, was an error. Aliyu, however, was not simply any Fulani. At the time of his succession all segments of Yauri society thoroughly despised him. Nevertheless, because the British thought highly of his use potential, J.C.O. Clarke, the administrative officer in charge of Yauri, rather cavalierly continued to defend him, even when Aliyu's faults became embarrassingly apparent to all.

Crowder (1973) presents the general outline of Aliyu's career and its relevance for the colonial history of Yauri and its neighbor, Borgu, quite starkly. The British, unequivocally, needed a person through whom they could govern what had been a difficult area to pacify. A major factor, clearly, in Aliyu's rise to power and his continuance as emir despite his unpopularity and corruption was his willingness to cooperate with Clarke in striking out against the major obstacle to Yauri's pacification, namely, the Dukawa whom the British customarily termed truculent (cf. NANK: SNP 16/K6066, I). Clarke and Aliyu simply transferred Dukawa towns and the 3,071 people in them to Rijau District, Kontagora Division, thus removing a source of opposition to both British rule and Aliyu's reign.

Aliyu's fall, as his rise, resulted from British assessment of their interests. Aliyu's unpopularity and blatant corruption had little, if anything, to do with his removal. In fact, even after the district officer for Yauri, L. Blake, issued a sweeping condemnation of the emir in 1918, the emir not only weathered the storm but remained in power until 1923 (Crowder, 1973: 108).

Only after Aliyu's actions caused an open rebellion in Borgu did the British sack him. His cruelty, unpopularity, and corruption counted for nothing. In spite of lip service paid to the preservation of traditions, even Lugard approved of certain of Aliyu's actions that violated traditions, such as the ceding of Rijau to Kontagora and the abortive merger of Borgu with Yauri, not to mention Aliyu's very appointment as emir. Finally, it was not murder, mendacity, cruelty, illegitimacy, or even gross malfeasance of office that led to his demise. It was the Gungawa's threat of mass migration that began to tip the scales against him. The Gungawa, "the most prosperous and enterprising of the Yauri tribes" (E. C. Duff NANK: Sok. Prof/ 150/ p/1918) were furious with Aliyu's stealing of tax funds. That coupled with Borgu's revolt toppled him from power and the government made him headman of the Sokoto works staff.

Although a legitimate local chief replaced Aliyu, the basic established pattern of interaction remained in force. The British continued to strengthen the government's power at the expense of local ethnic groups. In that aim, they used local rulers. Simply because he was a legitimate and popular ruler, Abdullahi was more suitable for their purposes than Aliyu had been. People were willing to allow a popular and legitimate ruler more leeway than a usurper. The deeper structural principles and relationships between British colonial officers and the emir, however, had not changed. In turn, Abdullahi sought to use the colonial situation to achieve his own objectives of obtaining the return of Rijau District and the strengthening of the emir's control over Yauri's many ethnic communities. He came close to achieving the first goal but did come close to victory. 'His second goal, however, was easily accomplished. The first goal, the return of Rijau, was almost gained with the aid of P. G. Harris. Ironically, when Harris was later promoted to Senior Resident, Sokoto, he opposed the transfer and kept -Abdullahi from achieving a goal the two of them had worked so hard to achieve.

Abdullahi recognized the changes colonialism was bringing to Yauri. Among those changes were the increase in the number and percent of Hausa in Yauri, the increase in the number of Gungawa who changed their' ethnic identity to Hausa (Salamone, 1975), the presence of increasing numbers of foreigners, and numerous other social, economic, and political changes. Primarily, colonialism distorted traditional power relationships. Developmental trajectories were distorted as were traditional avenues for redress of grievances. Even the very perspective from which scholars have viewed colonial reality has been colored as has the western perception -;'f traditional relationships (cf. Mabugunji, 1972; Dorward, 1974).

The study of one relationship in the setting described, then, should provide an opportunity to analyze the ways in which local authorities were active agents in the shaping of colonial reality and its consequent changes in traditional relationships. In the course of that examination the various theses can be tested and refined for additional scrutiny in other cases.

THE YAURI DAYBOOK AND ITS RELEVANCE TO THE UNDERSTANDING OF COLONIAL REALITY

Both P. G. Harris and Abdullahi were remarkable people. No one, unfortunately, has yet written a biography of either of them. Even a sketch, however, is sufficient to make the point.

Harris, born in Liverpool in 1894, was educated at St. Bees School, Cumberland. Until 1914 he studied law and passed his solicitor's examination upon completion of his studies. Then, with the beginning of the war, he joined the King's (Liverpool) Regiment. In 1916 he was appointed Lieutenant of the Infantry, Nigeria Regiments. In 1919 he joined the Nigerian Administrative Service as a Class IV administrative officer in Kano.

Promotions came in steady succession. After his Kano tenure, Harris served in the northern secretariat, then at Kabba and Niger. In 1935 he became secretary of the Northern Provinces and senior resident, Sokoto, in 1938. From 1940-43 he was consul-general at Douala, Cameroons. In 1944 he was appointed resident, a position he held at his death in 1945.

Harris fit the model of the well-rounded colonial administrator: intellectual achievements such as a solicitor's training, an anthropology diploma from the University of London in 1933, ethnological publications in scholarly journals, and membership in intellectual organizations; appropriate recreational activities of tennis, golf, music, and sketching; club memberships at the proper clubs in London; and a distinguished army career with sufficient duty in France. In sum, Harris projected an almost stereotypic image of the ideal administrator.

In a parallel fashion, Adbullahi fit the model of an extraordinarily capable chief, one saddled with a hopelessly inefficient native authority and a backwater emirate. Heussler (1968: 109) stated the situation quite succinctly:

In the administrative field the problem was the classic one in situations of relatively unfettered in benign autocracy: an able ruler, a hopeless N.A., a silent population. If the ruler was not restrained there would be irresponsibility. If he was disciplined too much he would become discouraged and obstructive. In either case the well-being of the Emirate depended on one man, and what would happen when he was gone: The D.O. trod a tightrope, gently restraining here, complimenting there, advising, urging forward, and counting on the new generation to supply future office-holders who would help and at the same time check the next chief.

Abdullahi was born in 1901 and educated in a western school, the Provincial School at Kano. Thereafter, he taught school at Birnin Kebbi and retained an active interest in western education until his death in 1955. When Aliyu was deposed in 1923, Abdullahi was a popular choice for emir. It is quite clear that the British regarded him as a model of what the new breed of emirs should be (Harris, 1938: 293). Until his death, in fact, Abdullahi was affectionately regarded by British administrators in Northern Nigeria {D.J.M. Muffett, personal communication). In that feeling, the common people of Yauri still concur.

Fortunately, the Yauri Day Book permits an opportunity to see the actual process of interaction that took place between an administrator and chief who were generally considered models for others to follow in the course of indirect rule. The period covered in the book, 17 May 1928 to 9 February 1931, in fact is one in which indirect rule had been firmly established and had not yet been seriously attacked. Therefore, it shows the features of the system in a self-confident stage of development, after the rhetoric attendant on its introduction and before the defensive apologies consequent after later attacks. Through analyzing the Yauri Day Book it is possible to isolate typical features of indirect rule in action in order to facilitate comparison with other case studies and thereby eventually develop general empirical propositions regarding its operation in contrast with the current situation in which rhetoric often replaces reason.

The day book is a record, or diary, of events in Yauri and actions taken regarding them by either Abdullahi or Harris. It is in reality more than that: it is a record of the interaction between representatives of two governing systems as they adjusted to one another. It is also the record of an indigenous ruler's perception of colonial reality. The comments each makes on the other's statements present in a point/counterpoint form a history of the development of their relationship and a telling commentary on its nature. Thus, while there is no doubt about the affection they held for each other, there is also no denying the fact that power was never far from either man's mind and the British held the ultimate sources of power.

Behind the facade of indirect rule, they exercised as direct a control over the people of Yauri as circumstances permitted. Their control reached down to the most minute of affairs. The emir of Yauri, furthermore, was clearly a collaborator in the extension of power. In fact, his superior grasp of the intricacies of Yauri's cultural, social, and political relationships enabled him to exert significant influence over British policy. Furthermore, British awareness of his popularity, integrity, and ability stimulated their decision to work through him in conformity with the philosophical principles of indirect rule. It was simply good politics to rule through Abdullahi. In turn, their policy strengthened Abdullahi's influence regarding the administration of both everyday matters and over subordinates, many of whom did not realize that frequently he was merely carrying out British decisions. Indeed the day book demonstrates rather persuasively that the colonial administration either made or approved virtually all decisions in Yauri.

Specific discussion of the contents of the day book from) 7 May to 31 December 1928, its first year, helps to clarify the situation. One hundred and sixty-four separate items were coded. The predominant issues were economic". Religion and ethnography were the least discussed matters. Other topics discussed were law and order, education, health, and relations with other rulers. Second only to economics in prominence, however, was the matter of proper relations between the emir and the administrative officer. Quite clearly, then, the major concerns of colonial administration were economics and prestige.

Care must be taken to point out explicitly that coding was carried out for the predominant content of an item. Thus, health, education, religion, or relationships with other rulers were frequently mentioned in other contexts. In fact, it is taken as a measure of their importance that such delicate matters were treated within the context of other affairs, a treatment in keeping with traditional Hausa practice.

What is so intriguing is that local rulers were equally aware of the same realities as colonial administrators and often used their specialized knowledge of economic relations to great political advantage. For example, during the famine of 1928 Abdullahi quickly prohibited the sale of guinea corn to foreigners as well as importation from them. On the feast of the *Idi he* exhorted farmers to continue in their work and save their corn because "No one knows the future." Furthermore, he threatened to confiscate any land that remained unused, and, therefore, unproductive for two years in succession.

Such actions were in conformity with the tenor of the colonial government's desire to help keep costs down while increasing revenues and help account for the preoccupation with economic matters found in the day book. In fact, the growing literature on power brokers helps put Abdullahi's actions in perspective. For example, Vincent (1977) and Vengroff (1975) discuss the active role of African chiefs in promoting change and eroding tradition. Vincent (1978) carries on the discussion in promoting an action perspective for change.

Certainly, Abdullahi's advice to Harris on how to solve problems in a way that would cause least friction provides supporting data for action, or power broker approaches to change. On occasion Abdullahi advised Harris to back down from a confrontation while providing him with knowledge that enabled him ultimately to save face and gain power. Thus, when local porters refused to transport loads from ships to shore at Yelwa, Yauri's capital, Abdullahi defended them and pointed out that the money offered them was less than their traditional pay.

On other occasions his knowledge of local patterns of behavior enabled the government to avoid conflict. When the Fulani sought to avoid taxes, therefore, he simply told the government what back roads they would take in order to avoid the collectors. There was no need then to drag anyone in and waste power by using it unnecessarily. The Fulani caught in the act of herding their cattle on back roads usually paid their taxes in a good-natured way, admitting they had been outsmarted at their game.

The relationship between the emir and administrative officer was a reciprocal one. The emir profited from it every bit as much as the administration. It is not surprising, therefore, to find the administrative officer counseling patience when the emir suspected subordinates of plotting against him. The emir, furthermore, frequently was pleased to let the British take responsibility for unpopular decisions. Thus, when the Dukawa refused to leave his emirate and to pay the stated tax rate of 4/6 for both men and women, instead of confronting them head-on he sought the district officer's advice and aid against the real culprit, the district head of Shanga, where the recalcitrant Dukawa lived.

There are other examples of the emir's letting the British pull his chestnuts from the fire. The point, however, is simple. Although the British quite clearly held power in Yauri and even openly ordered the emir about at times, the emir, in turn, knew quite well how to work the system to his advantage. He was not in any sense of the term a mere passive figurehead.

The complexity of the relationship between emir and district officer, perhaps, emerges in finer detail when some of the items listed in the category relationships are considered. Certainly, each sought to gain from their transactions. Their genuine fondness and respect for each other, however, precludes facile analysis. Obviously, some of the gifts and favors are attributable to courtesy of office. Not all of them, however, can be dismissed so easily. A number of favors, for example, touched on intimate matters, universally found in the domain of friendship. The emir, for instance, not only found the district officer a place to live but also looked into providing him with an adequate garden. Knowing of Harris' ethnographic interests, he took great care to provide him with appropriate informants. In turn, Harris displayed his friendship in a number of ways. He obtained "Yoruba phonograph records" for the emir, taught him to use a checking account, sent him lemons and bananas, and obtained medicine which the emir admitted to liking "too much."

Heussler (1968: 105) assesses the situation accurately:

> The experience of working together on common tasks could bring about a considerable intimacy and meeting of minds. Seeing each other daily, the Emir of Yauri and the local D.O. soon developed a close working relationship, discussing matters frankly and speaking openly with one another. Asked for his advice and preference on whether to start work on a new road or finish repairs on an old one first, the Emir stated his opinion clearly and gave reasons which the D.O. found acceptable.

More significant than specific claims in establishing their genuine friendship and respect is the tone of their written remarks to one another. That tone is always amiable, never testy. It was, in fact, frequently quite jocular. The following passage illustrates the point. Here are 95 cows and 16 sheep brought to me by a Cow Fulani who told me that he got these afterwards, therefore they are not included in my list to you (Yauri Day Book: 37-38). That was Abdullahi's way of teasing Harris about his interminable lists. In return, Harris could twit the emir from time to time. When Abdullahi sent him students to reprimand for not bringing their books home on their holidays, Harris responded, "I have seen the students. Maybe the books are coming in the mail."

In back of their genuine affection for each other there was always the clear realization that power lay in British hands, that requests for aid were simply orders in a polite form. The British understood as well as Abdullahi that his knowledge of affairs gave him a lever, one he used subtly but unmistakably. The emir's aid to Harris was certainly not altruistic, for by instructing him in local laws and customs and making him aware of Yauri's ethnic intricacies he sought to increase his own authority and legitimacy. Predictably, he came to associate his own interests with those of the British and in later life gave in to excesses of authoritarian rule.

The need for law and order dominates a good part of the material discussed. There was need for concern since the Native Authority police appear to have been rather inept judging from contemporary descriptions. Abdullahi was eager to raise their standards and wanted to do so immediately. He seems to have tried every possible method for doing so: exhortations to show endurance; engaging a former police officer to improve standards; placing that officer under surveillance and correcting him when his salute for the troops was not considered satisfactory.

The emir went beyond exhortations and had police jailed when the occasion warranted. Furthermore, he had people fired quite readily for failing to live up to high standards. More positively, his men were outfitted in the best available uniforms, which were chosen by the emir. In fact, his interest in police affairs extended to the smallest detail and he knew that the cost of replacing a whistle was 2 shillings. Any constable who lost one had to pay for its replacement.

The same meticulousness was applied to fields of health and education. Abdullahi's teaching career had instilled in him a desire to improve and spread education. He took great care to retain the services of a scholar whom he considered to be an excellent teacher to direct Yauri's education program. He exerted his considerable charm to soothe his injured ego when an enemy and rival of the teacher caused problems. At his command a third party was always present whenever the teacher and his enemy had dealings with each other.

So eager was Abdullahi for the spread of modem education that he had little patience with those students who refused to appreciate its benefits. Harris restrained his enthusiasm by pointing out that there was no need to force education on those too foolish to perceive its benefits. Many others would be glad to take their places. The emir showed his love for education in a number of ways. He took great care to ensure that textbooks and pocket money were available for scholars. So much did he value education that he had educational lists ready before they were requested!

Abdullahi was patient with requests for other types of lists, but he was never enthusiastic about preparing lists of births, deaths, immigration, emigration, diseases, economic trees (mahogany), census data, and so forth. If those lists were not sufficient, Harris wanted lists of former emirs, important historical events, and any other lists that would aid his ethnological work (cf. Harris, 1930, 1938).

There was one case that could have provided Harris with far more valuable ethnographic information than most of his lists, but he ignored it. Abdullahi politely referred to the value of the event, but Harris was too preoccupied with a possible assassination to understand what he was being told. The case involved a madman. Typically, an intelligent man had grown his hair long, slept in trees in the market, and publicly bewailed his fate. It was a traditional response to a modern problem, for the man was bewailing his fate at having to live under white domination. Harris was perturbed at the man's saying he cared not a whit for white man's rule. Furthermore, Harris's training was in the older school of British ethnology and not in the more advanced techniques and theories of social anthropology. Abdullahi tried to sooth his feelings:

> It is not Mallam Abande who did that thing; he is called 'Gado'. I have investigated this case thoroughly. It's true that he used to climb up a tree in order to spend the night there. Since the madness started to worry him he has never failed to sleep in a tree. I even learnt that the madness is increasing whereas Mallam Abande has been cured. I have sent a letter asking the people to tell us of their conditions (Yauri Day Book: 54).

Abdullahi did not mention in his reply the fact that the madman had threatened to kill the British, for it did not need to be referred to. The emir's role was to reassure Harris and an air of competent calm permeates the book. Religion does not receive much mention in the day book, but it is never far from the surface of any discussion. The few times that it is mentioned does shed light on its function in the colonial relationship. Thus, it is mentioned directly in the political context of registering people and aiding their pilgrimage to Mecca. Such mention underlines the fact that the British never forgot, nor were permitted to forget, that Islam was the north's official religion.

Finally, although there are only three direct mentions of relations with other Nigerian rulers they are sufficient to piece together the pattern of relationships. To the sultan of Sokoto, deference was due as was proper to the successor of Usman dan Fodio. Technically, the sultan was the political and religious overlord of all the faithful in the Hausa emirates. In fact the sultan only gave orders to emirs on matters of great concern to the British, such as the control of rinderpest. Relations with other emirs were based on the fact that they, too, were vassals of Sokoto but independent rulers in their own rights. Courtesy was the rule. Emirs cooperated with each other when such common efforts did not threaten their sovereignty and were mutually beneficial or at least perceived as such. Heussler (1968: 142-43) again sums up the matter well:

With inter-emirate warfare at an end, the idea of cooperating with neighbors was attractive. Financial or political motives were sometimes present, as when Gwandu and Yauri worked together to comer herdsmen who had always played emirates off against one another in evading payment of *Jangali*. Furthermore, in such matters as road building, control of rinderpest, or an antihopper campaign, forward-looking chiefs like Usumanu of Gwandu and Abdullahi of Yauri found themselves closer to a D.O. or a veterinarian than to their own people. Chiefs of this kind had to some extent left the world of tradition and would never go back.

CONCLUSIONS

The Yauri Day Book provides data which suggest the following conclusions. Although real power in the colonial period lay with the British, there was mutual acknowledgment that legitimacy lay with the emir. A number of incidents illustrate that the emir was an active participant in the political process, using the system to consolidate his power over subordinates and members of minority ethnic groups.

Rather than re-establishing traditional relationships, moreover, indirect rule reshaped political, social, and economic interactions in Yauri. Abdullahi contributed to that process by reinterpreting the meaning of traditions for the British. So successful was he in that endeavor that he became visibly upset when anyone suggested that the British be replaced by African administrative officers (Heussler, 1968: 144). The emir had become an ardent Anglophile and, more importantly, knew that his power would be reduced in any Nigerianization process. Quite simply, no African could accept his reinterpretation of traditional relationships.

Through such reinterpretation, he was able, it is true, to bring about more efficient and honest government than had been the norm in Yauri, at least during the previous hundred years. At the same time, however, subordinate ethnic groups, such as the Gungawa, Dukawa, Shangawa, Kamberi, and Lopawa discovered that they had less autonomy than previously. Abdullahi was able to achieve those aims because of his keen perception of colonial reality and his own competence, evidenced through his mastery of even the smallest details of colonial rule and especially in his perception of the inner workings of indirect rule.

Abdullahi, who was fascinated with modernization, perceived colonialism as a means toward dragging Yauri into the twentieth century. He used the British as much as they used him. Thus, he knew that if he himself adopted modern ways it would facilitate receipt of aid in bringing Yauri into the modern age. Therefore, his fascination with modern things should not be just looked at as an individual matter but as part of a wider social strategy. It eased contact with the British. He drove a Ford, smoked western cigarettes, had a checking account, owned western lamps and lampshades, listened to Yoruba records on his gramophone, and also sponsored educational reforms, built roads, fought rinderpest, and in numerous other ways sought to modernize his emirate. Finally, the friendship between emir and colonial officer set a pernicious pattern for future internal relationships in Nigeria. Even Abdullahi fell into the trap of using his position for personal gain and confusing his welfare with that of the emirate's. Additionally, it was in this period that modernization became confused with westernization. This paper suggests that investigation of the independence movement from the point of view of the relationship between local rulers and colonial administrative officers will prove quite enlightening.

Study of one brief period of colonial rule in one small emirate has sought to demonstrate that it is possible to discover an indigenous ruler's attitude toward colonialism. More importantly it has also sought to demonstrate that discovery of that attitude answers fundamental questions about the nature of colonialism and permits further comparative empirical investigation in other emirates that will increase the understanding of relationships between colonialism and modern day Nigeria.

6

Indirect Rule Continued

British colonial policies such as military force, anti-slavery legislation, taxes, commodification, and indirect rule all combined to change Northern Nigeria's rural social formation. For slave owners, who made up to a growing part of Northern Nigeria's social formation before colonial rule and who used slave labor on plantations, mining, leather works and textile production, the nature of transformation was two-fold. First, British colonial rule weakened the economic conditions of slave owners. Second, after weakening their economic base, British colonial rule transformed these slave owners into various class and non-class positions. The paper concludes that the transformation of former slave owners into these new class and non-class positions negatively affected their ability to accumulate wealth as they previously had. Therefore, they found it difficult to transform themselves to feudalists or capitalists. Colonial rule reduced them to positions of traders and administrators. In these positions they could not participate in productive economic activities until the end of colonial rule (Ferdnance 1998, 233).

It is essential to keep in mind that the expatriate community was absolutely and relatively small. In 1931, for example, there were 1825 expatriates in Northern Nigeria in a total population of 11, 434, 924, or .01595% of the population. This meant that there were .0069958 non-Nigerians per square mile compared with about 41 Nigerians (See Brooke 1931). It is no wonder that Kirke-Green refers to colonial officers as "the thin white line (ms)."

The presence of Islam among the Fulani and other northern peoples also helped define the overall situation. At the time of colonial rule, Islam was essentially a colonial religion. It had not yet seeped down to the common people. In truth, moreover, the rapid spread of Islam in the Hausa-Fulani area, from about 5% of the population to about 80% of it is a result of deliberate British colonial policy. Quite simple, the British did not possess the means to rule the vast area of Northern Nigeria directly. Consequently, they found it convenient to encourage the appeal of Islam and to rule through Muslim rulers "indirectly." The end result of Indirect Rule was the strengthening of a foreign group of conquerors, the Fulani, and the acceptance of their idealized version of political reality. It was, needless to say, a version which local people, the including the Hausa, rejected.

In addition, however, to being useful, the Fulani version of political reality coincided with the British ideology of Indirect Rule. In sum, the Fulani claimed to come from Arabia and to form aristocratic Islamic elite of scholars. When the Hausa rulers failed in their duty to uphold proper Islamic principles, they, under the leadership of Shehu Usman dan Fodio, waged a jihad and established a true Islamic state. That state, the Sokoto Caliphate, united a number of subordinate states under its rule in what had been the Hausa area of the North, plus other areas never under their rule. Thus, from 1804 until the British conquest of 1903, the Fulani reigned supreme in Northern Nigeria and their governmental structure was essentially that of a "purified" Hausa state. (See Hendrixson 1981, Dorward 1974, and Smith 1960.)

British colonial officers did not allow the facts to cloud their visions. They were armed with the evolutionary anthropology of their day and used its tenets where convenient to get on with the tasks of governing. That task of governing included the "pacification" of Northern Nigeria. In this task the Fulani version of reality suited their fancy and needs. British fancy posited people at various stages of development. So-called Hamitic peoples presumably were more advanced than various "Negroid" peoples, and Muslims were obviously closer to Christians than "pagans." Fulani claims to non-Negroid ancestry and their adherence to Islam allowed the British to categorize them as "true rulers" and natural allies of the British. (See Evans-Pritchard 1951 for a succinct summary of the prevalent ideology. Lugard 1906, 1919, and 1922 offer sources of his views on the Fulani.)

This British ideology had very real implications for the development of Fulani ethnicity. Interestingly, as Hendrixson (1981: 56) indicates "Prior to the beginning of the jihad in 1804, the category Fulani was not politically important for the Toronkawa," that branch of the Fulfulde speaking people who were in Nigeria. The Toronkawa, significantly, did not consider themselves Fulani. However, between 1804 and the British conquest of Sokoto the Toronkawa arrogated to themselves as a ruling elite and to those pastoralists who supported them the term "Fulani" (Hendrixson 1981: 45). Moreover, the British further consolidated the Fulani claims to provide a natural ruling aristocracy and to make that a current hallmark of their ethnic identity.

The Hausa-Fulani became models of civilization. The British, in fact, raised them above models. They made them partners in the spreading of high culture to the pagans. Those "pagans" who resisted British rule became "truculent" and "cannibals" in the literature (Dorward 1974: 459-60). Consequently, the spread of the Hamitic/Hausa-Fulani culture, including Islam was a positive stage in promoting cultural-evolutionary progress. It is not surprising, therefore, that in order to validate their hold on their favored position; Fulani began to stress tradition, defined in terms of religion, as an ethnic boundary marker in this period (Hendrixson 1981: 57). In fact, as Crowder (1964 In Markovitz 1971: 28) states

> . . . in the earliest interwar period many emirs and chiefs ruled as 'sole native authorities," a position which gave them for practical purposes more power than they had in pre-colonial days, where they were either subject to control by a council or liable to deposition if they became too unpopular. . . There was thus a minimal undermining of the traditional sources of authority. The main change for the Fulani Emirs of Northern Nigeria, for instance, was that they now owed allegiance to the British Government rather than to the Sultan of Sokoto . . .

Dorward agrees that Indirect Rule in Northern Nigeria provided the model for the rest of British rule in Africa and that it frequently increased the power of traditional rulers. Moreover, many of these "traditional" rulers were of rather recent origin. Dorward maintains that local rulers were active agents in strengthening their own power and hoodwinked political officers who were frequently willing dupes in the social construction of reality. The Fulani were masters of this particular colonial game and they cooperated with the British in the negotiation of Fulani ethnicity in Northern Nigeria.

There were, however, people within the British expatriate group who threatened the fundamental perception of reality that justified indirect rule and the negotiated definition of Fulani ethnicity. Among those who posed the greatest threat were missionaries. Missionaries had their own version of reality, one that did not view the Muslim Fulani as the natural rulers or Islam as a stage that would enhance so-called pagans. Colonial officers feared that missionary activity would rupture their tenuous alliance with Fulani rulers.

To bolster their own power British administrators created the official wisdom, that emirs opposed not only Christian missionaries but also Western education. In fact, some, but not all emirs opposed the fact that missionaries were the primary carriers of Western education to the North. Ubah (1976: 352) and Omatseye (1981) argue that emirs based their opposition to Western education on the seemingly inextricable link between it and missionaries. Ubah (1976: 363) is even of the opinion that the emirs would not have strongly resisted mission schools if colonial pressure had been brought to bear. He states "but the administration itself was timid, and the emirs did not hesitate to exploit this timidity." In fact, British op-position to missionaries in Islamic areas was far from timid and suggests that it was their perception of the North as Islamic that led them to keep missionaries out of the area for so long. That perception, moreover, was essential to the ideology that supported what Dorward (1974) terms the "working misunderstanding." The fact that missionaries in general actively opposed the façade of indirect rule did not find them many supporters in the Northern Nigerian administration.

It is relevant to recall that the sacred tenets of Indirect Rule required local financial support for all local governmental functions, including education. Since Western education was too expensive for local support and since missionaries were the only other feasible alternative for Western education, then the second tenet of Indirect Rule came into play, the presumed innate hostility between Islam and Christianity, and the definition of the North as Islamic except for the Middle Belt area, the area around the confluence of the Niger and Benue Rivers. The inherent logic of indirect rule demanded that missionaries be opposed even when they were the only feasible ve-hicles for education (Graham 1966:167-68). Abernathy (1971) and Push-kin (1971) have graphically discussed the disruptive effects of differential educational policies. In sum, even in "progressive" emirates the North was woefully behind the Southern part of Nigeria in every field of modern education. Its system of education was run by Southerners and expatriates.

It appears clear, then, that the Fulani or "Hausa-Fulani" as the British began to refer to the ruling elite of the old Hausa emirates had to redefine their identity in light of the new political situation that the British conquest brought to Northern Nigeria, indeed to Nigeria as a whole. The very uses of religious and traditional criteria as an ethnic device, as Hendrixson (1981) so nicely notes, is best understood as a response to their negotiations with the British and a means toward establishing themselves as "natural rulers" in the colonial evolutionary ideology. Their alliance with Hausa people has parallels elsewhere in Northern Nigeria in the alliance of "Hausa" peoples with those whom they have conquered in a strategy with a double purpose: to validate their claims to legitimacy and to recruit allies in that cause (Salamone 1973, 1975a, 1975b, 1980, 1982, and Salamone and Swanson 1979). The only difference is that they have hyphenated their new ethnic identity, Fulani, with that of the Hausa, in an effort to keep their alliance with the pastoral Fulani and to safeguard their claims to legitimacy as heirs and purifiers of the old Hausa tradition.

The response locked the Hausa-Fulani rulers into certain behaviors. They had to acquiesce in matters impinging on the ideological and economic essence of Indirect Rule. Thus, "real" Muslim emirs opposed missionaries and modern education. Local authorities had to collect taxes for British officials even in cases where there were no legitimate traditional bases for such actions. Although the Hausa-Fulani rulers received very real political benefits for their compliance in these transactions, there were also very real costs; namely, the resulting backwardness of the North in comparison with the rest of Nigeria and the reactionary requisites of being a Hausa-Fulani emir. Islam, which has often been a true modernizing agent, as for example under the Aga Khans, became a roadblock in Nigeria's development.

CONCLUSION

Throughout the colonial world colonial powers created situations that led to the emergence of new or newly defined ethnic groups. People reacted to the exigencies of the colonial situation through forming groups that protected their situations or that enabled them to seek a better position in the novel reality of colonial political, social, economic, and religious life. The Zulu and Sotho, for example, materialized from the conditions of British colonialism in South Africa. The Yoruba, a collection of warring and disparate peoples speaking related languages and sharing core traditions, found it expedient to shape a common identity to interact with other similar created identities in the colonial situation of Nigeria.

Ethnic identities are after all situational, as Ronald Cohen (1978: 388) has argued. ""Ethnicity is first and foremost situational . . . the interactive situation is a major determinant of the level of inclusiveness employed in labeling self and others." What Cohen states about ethnic identity is also true of other identities as well. Moreover, it is through interaction and symbols that shape the content and perception of interaction that identities are formed, established, and maintained.

A brief look at Goffman's view of how one establishes social identity helps clarify the issue. Social identity is closely allied to what he termed the "front" or "front stage." The front is "that part of the individual's performance which regularly functions in a general and fixed fashion to define the situation for those who observe the performance" (Goffman 1949, p. 22) The front has a "collective representation" and sets up an appropriate "setting," "appearance," and "manner" for the performance of the social role, such as regional identity, which the actor is performing. For consistency of interaction, the social actor must fill the role and communicate its meaning in a coherent manner.

It is here that Goffman discusses impression management, which is the way in which a social actor controls and communicates information via his or her performance. Because the actor is coherently playing a role, he or she becomes that role for the duration of the performance. Other social actors can fine tune their reactions accordingly. This dramatic realization is clearly seen in the performance of identity in colonial multiethnic situations.

Goffman indicates that social actors make a greater effort to perform an idealized version of the role through being more consistent in adhering to norms, mores, and laws of society than when alone. The audience has a great deal to do with consistency of performance. In other words, the other everywhere, helps shape the performance of people. The performer hides inconsistent beliefs and everyday behavior that does not conform with expectations while choosing to emphasize behavior consonant with the idealized image of the role.

But we can go beyond this profoundly simple fact. Social actors, no matter how cynical, like stage actors often inhabit their roles so completely that they become that role. We find people seeking to distinguish themselves, that is, their real selves, from their fronts or social selves. They may bring family pictures to work or play music they particularly like there, even if it is not what others may like. Whatever the means, there is an attempt to fight the capture of their innermost selves from their social fronts. But often anyway the two may merge. Perhaps, one has become so socialized that there is little difference between the two. Or there may be great reward in being thought one with pioneers whom people admire. The feedback process has a great deal to do with the overall process of identity formation and identification.

The colonial authority had culturally mummified "tradition" via historical acts of promulgation. Abner Cohen (1993), however, has drawn attention to another aspect that is more subversive. His work has been concerned with the powerful forces of culture, through music and dance performance, in mobilizing a popular awareness of underlying political and economic interests. In elaborating this theme in the present chapter, I wish to consider the extent to which the ebb and flow of tides of the popular expectation generated through dancing have a cosmic dimension.

Such performances may be considered as collective representations in a Durkheimian sense. They express and promote the growth of a certain confidence, a mutual credibility; a gathering will to succeed that is as relevant to understanding subversive popular movements as it is to understanding the dynamics of the market in the mainstream domain of economics. Cohen demonstrates how a group may reconstitute itself on different bases, how new identities are fore fronted to maintain cohesion, and how this new focus can become a basis for mobilization and transformation of the community. In his analysis of the Hausa community of Sabo, he argues cogently that the group reestablished its solidarity through its recognition of and adherence to a particular form of Islam, as the reference to ethnic solidarity became increasingly less viable.

Cohen demonstrates how a group may reconstitute itself on different bases, how new identities are fore fronted to maintain cohesion, and how this new focus can become a basis for mobilization and transformation of the community. In his analysis of the Hausa community of Sabo, he argues cogently that the group reestablished its solidarity through its recognition of and adherence to a particular form of Islam, as the reference to ethnic solidarity became increasingly less viable. Ethnic identity is a type of political identity. It is a means of mobilizing support to attain perceived goals, support which calls upon the principle of ethnicity, or presumed common descent (R. Cohen 1978). That it changes over time to suit various situations has been established in numerous places (Hendrixson 1981).

Although ethnic, and therefore, political identities are mutually negotiated, there are limits to the process. The British, for instance, possessed a colonial ideology based on evolutionary anthropology. That ideology was indeed, flexible but it was not totally malleable. When it could not be reinterpreted or adjusted, it forced rigid, even logical, compliance within the constructed boundaries of the defined realities. This compliance and Hausa-Fulani performance of their colonial influenced identity during the enactment of the colonial drama helped fix that identity during the postcolonial era and the ethnic conflicts of that period, a process we see reenacted within the boundaries of the former Soviet Union (Marker 2004).

During these periods of expansion, Western European and Soviet powers formed new colonial multiethnic provinces (e.g., Rhodesia, French Indonesia, German East Africa) and satellite states (e.g., Czechoslovakia, Yugoslavia). They did so with little regard for the people living in the newly controlled areas, or for existing geographic or cultural boundaries. Populations that had previously identified themselves as distinct, based on their cultural, ethnic, and/or religious heritage, were forced to unify under a single *national identity*. The new multiethnic colonial territories and Soviet states were maintained, upheld, and controlled through the use of violence, and through the implementation of imperialist policies. Certain populations were denied their political, economic, social, and *human rights*. Imperialist policies promoted ethnic rivalry by favoring one group above the others, distributed resources in an unequal manner, disallowed democratic governments, and prohibited local participation in governmental decisions and actions (Marker 2004).

Once the superior power of the colonial power was removed, the disparate ethnic groups began to struggle, often gruesomely, among themselves for the control of what the colonial powers had left. Too often genocidal struggles and outright greed marred the gains of the struggle for freedom from colonial oppression. Despite the frequent setbacks, however, there have been historic gains in places like South Africa and Ghana, for example, to find ways to overcome the identity politics fostered under colonial regimes. New realities can foster more productive group interaction than those promoted in the divide and rule politics of colonialism and neocolonialism. It is important that policies be developed in African states and throughout the world to encourage realities that help promote these benevolent new realities.

7

Religious Change in a Northern Nigerian Emirate

Colonialism and the Fulani jihad brought a number of changes to Nigeria. Not the least of these changes was the mixture of religion with politics. Both Islam and Christianity spread because of power struggles between European and Fulani interests. This approach takes into account what a number of scholars (Herskovits 1943: 394-402; Aquina 1967: 203-219; Guiart 1970: 122-138) have argued for; that is, a more processual approach to the phenomena of conversion. Such an approach stresses the active roles of the convert in responding to a proselytizing agent. Geertz (1968), for example, made the important observation that Islam is neither an independent variable nor a monolithic entity. His point is that it is idiosyncratic in every sociocultural system in which it is found and therefore cannot be used as an explanatory model in itself. Rather, Islam itself must be explained as part of a process of interaction which we can call Islamization.

The particulars of Islamization may vary because of local sociocultural elements, but the etic features used by all Muslims to distinguish themselves from non-Muslims are rather consistent and so allow comparisons to be made, which then allow us to separate sociosyncratic responses from more universal ones. Barkow (1970) offers a Nigerian example, the Hausa-Maguzawa relationship that aptly illustrates the advantage of this approach.

Like Islam, Christianity has a well-developed etic code of belief and behavior that in practice allows for great variation. Recent research (Sahay 1968) has indicated some ways in which this process occurs. In any event, it is clear that the convert is not a passive recipient of a prepackaged faith, as early acculturation theory tended to suggest. Rather, the convert chooses to identify himself as a Christian or a Muslim because of emically perceived advantages. Conversion is, emically at least, a very rational process. Whether the advantages in any particular case are real is a matter for further empirical research, as I have discussed at greater length elsewhere (1972). In fact, many of the disadvantages that may accrue from conversion result just because conversion is a process and not an event; that is. It takes place over a period of time and requires constant learning of "Christian" behavior. A convert often discovers after conversion that such behavior conflicts with internalized values or society's norms (Sahay 1968; Guiart 1970; Salamone 1972; Luzbetak 1970).

It is important to point out that Christianity is no more a monolithic entity than is Islam. It is also important to make clear that there is no "typical" convert or "typical" missionary approach, unless we are talking about stochastic relationships. Unfortunately, no one has yet supplied us with the data needed to produce these mathematical models. As a step toward gathering that data I would like to offer the following research approach and then to give an example of its application.

An important research strategy is first to discover what kind of people are learning what kind of Christianity. I grant that this should be stating the obvious, but the literature is filled with examples that prove that this is not an obvious statement (Heiss 1970: 49-53). Too often stereotypic views of missionaries replace solid empirical research. Therefore, solid analysis of the entire missionary situation and its ecological texture is sorely needed. Barkow (1970) has already indicated how an approach combining that of Le Vine and Barth (1970) can advance our understanding of cultural change. Such an approach emphasizes conversion as a process, in fact as a number of processes, rather than as an event. It has the further advantage of working out from the individual without sacrificing the overall framework.

The northern area of Nigeria provides a laboratory rich in ethnic diversity, an area that provides adequate data to illustrate the approach I suggest. Barkow has clearly analyzed, for example, methods used by two subcultures of the Hausa to distinguish themselves from one another. The minutest differences are overplayed and large similarities are ignored, in much the way Goffman (1959) predicted that groups attempting to preserve separate identities would behave. Groups which, at one level are etically similar, will, because of the differences in the environment, be emically different. The desire to preserve these differences may greatly influence the responses made to similar ecological change and the presence of Christian missionaries in an area is an ecological change of great importance. Groups, then, that appear to outsiders to be mere "variants" of one another are frequently to insiders "foreign" people, simply "not like us, at all."

This is exactly the case in Yauri Emirate, Nigeria, for the Dukawa and Gungawa. Harris (1930), among others has suggested that these "tribes" are subgroups of one another, but Gunn and Conant (1960: 10) point out incisively that the "traditional ability of the peoples of the middle Niger region to adjust to one another within larger political units may constitute their chief significance for Nigeria as a whole." If we dwell on the more sophisticated Barthian approach, we shall understand better how ethnic groups operate rather than be bogged down in outmoded theories of biological transference of culture. As Harris (1930) makes clear in his excellent detailed descriptive account of the Gungawa in Yauri, the Gungawa and Dukawa, whatever the truth of their common "origins" may be, have in Bateson's terminology a different ethos.

The above point has been, perhaps, somewhat labored, for I wish to show that the two groups I have chosen to discuss from the Yelwa area are indeed two distinct ethnic groups. That is important because part of my research strategy consists of studying the ways in which two different ethnic groups use ethnicity in exploiting different ecological niches in the same general area and how this then conditions their response to two variants of missionary influence. Unfortunately, in the past the tendency has been to forget the importance of differences among groups in an area as small as Yauri.

A number of other considerations may have justified such an approach in the past, but this can no longer be the case if we wish to avoid the pitfalls of both the grossly macrocosmic approach of too much social science and the microcosmic approach of our own past that too often ignored interaction between groups in a fruitless search for the "pure" structure unpolluted by "culture-contact." In the real world, as Barth and his disciples (1970) have so clearly shown, groups do interact and change because ethnic boundaries are permeable. It makes anthropological work complicated, but it also makes it much more interesting.

This paper presents a discussion concentrating on the advantages that conversion to Christianity might have for members of two particular ethnic groups as they see it. Insofar as possible, the total context of the missionary contact is at least sketched. The differential response of two groups in the same area to two different missionary strategies is presented, viz. that of the Gungawa to a United Mission Society (U.M.S.) approach and the Dukawa to a Dominican Catholic approach. To make the comparisons clearer only one aspect of the ethos of each group will be considered, that is values regarding women.

A logical next step would be to take the same ethnic group and discuss the responses of its members to two different religions as Ottenberg (1971: 231-260) does for the Igbo. In the Igbo case he found that the major variable operating was wealth-prestige. The Gungawa offer a case in Yauri of people choosing between Islam and Christianity.

YAURI DIVISION

Although not all Dukawa and Gungawa live in the Yauri Emirate, there
have been Dukawa and Gungawa there for at least 200 years (Harris 1930).
The people I am comparing live in two villages that have been in the Yauri
area for at least 200 years and show little difference from Dukawa and Gungawa outside the Yauri area, at least as described in the works of Gunn and
Conant (1960). Father Ceslaus Prazan, O.P., has done a great deal of ethnographic work among the Dukawa. His manuscript is currently in press,
and he has assured me that there are no significant differences between the
Dukawa I studied and those outside Yauri (personal communication). Insofar, then, as any segment of a larger group is typical of that group, the two
groups compared here are typical of Dukawa and Gungawa settlements.

Both the Dukawa and Gungawa fled to Yauri, long a haven for those
forced to seek refuge. Both seem to have come from the Kontagora region to
escape Fulani slave raids. If one believes the myths of origin, both are of the
same "stock" (Harris 1930: 291-321). Today, however, they are culturally
distinct ethnic groups who use their alleged genealogical ties as a means of
ordering their mutual relationships in the complex interethnic world that is
Yauri. Whatever the facts of their common cultural origin, each group has
become a distinct ethnic group by emphasizing different cultural traits and
values, values that have a high "survival" role in the complex Yauri world.
By first describing that world briefly and then focusing on one set of values,
responses to two groups of missionaries are made more clear.

Yauri is one of a number of emirates in what, under British rule, was
Northern Nigeria. More specifically it was part of Sokoto Province. Today it
is a small emirate and division in the Northwestern State of Nigeria. It has
an area of 1,306 square miles and is located along the Niger River. Its total
population is 72,000, or about 58 persons per square mile. Yelwa, population 8,000, is its largest city. Most of the inhabitants of Yelwa identify
themselves as Hausa and look down on the totally nonHausa rural inhabitants. Unlike other emirates, Yauri has no rural Hausa farmers, except for
Gungawa Muslims who identify themselves as "Hausa."

This scorn for the rural people enables the inhabitants of Yelwa town to
verify to themselves their own Hausa identity. This verification is necessary
in the face of the scorn shown to them by more sophisticated Hausa from
Katsina or Sokoto whom they encounter on their many trading expeditions
and who occasionally pass through Yauri. Barkow (1970) has done an
excellent job in describing the psycho-cultural processes involved in maintaining and establishing self-identification in striving to achieve a "more
perfect" ethnic identity.

In northern Zaria, Muslim Hausa (both rural and urban) and the pagan Hausa (the Maguzawa) established patterns of behavior that served

as boundary markers. Those in the lower-ranked groups, the rural Hausa and Maguzawa, borrowed behavior traits from the urban Hausa. The rural Hausa, however, were torn by events, for they feared identification with the pagan Maguzawa Hausa yet felt strong emotional pulls to the Maguzawa way of life. The Maguzawa served for the rural Hausa as living proof of their Hausa identities, for they were all that a good Hausa was not. They were pagans. They were drunks. Their women worked in the fields, etc. The Maguzawa played up to and exaggerated the stereotypes held of them by the Hausa.

The same process is at work in the Yauri area even though the ethnographic details are different. The minority groups in Yauri are not subgroups of the Hausa. They are separate groups. While in northern Zaria Barkow's three groups form part of a continuum on a scale measuring "Hausaness," at Yauri the situation is one of ethnic pluralism. At Yauri, the Hausa regard the pagan minority groups as inferior and emphasize their differences from them. Individuals may now and then pass as Hausa, but even after Islamic conversion it would be hard for groups to pass through the Hausa ethnic boundary in Yauri.

A full discussion of the reasons for this fact would fill a separate paper. In brief, the town Hausa need other ethnic groups to exploit the many ecological niches in Yauri. They fear that for themselves to do so would cost them their self-identification as true Hausa, an identification often endangered because of their alleged Kanuri and "mixed" Gungawa origins. To people in Katsina and Kano the inhabitants of Yelwa are bushmen or "hicks."

The majority of Yauri's peoples are, therefore, politically minority groups; that is, they have less access to power than do the ruling Hausa Fulani. The minority peoples live either in the bush, like the Dukawa, or on islands like many Gungawa. Decisions made in town are sent to the bush via representatives of the rulers. These representatives carry on all business in Hausa, the *lingua franca* of the area.

In a number of ways, the Hausa-Fulani impress on minority peoples their inferior status *vis-a-vis* themselves. Since the Hausa, by definition are Muslims, the minority people tend to identify Islam, Hausaness and power as interchangeable entities. All do not, however, perceive Islam as a means to power for themselves, for Islam has long been the religion of their oppressors. The fact that the current Emir is a wise and generous ruler means less to them than the fact that Muslims enslaved people and are still their tax collectors. The road to power in the Northwestern State of Nigeria is via Islam. The Yauri division is no exception to the general rule. Every member of the government is a Muslim. Every merchant of importance is a Muslim. In short, anyone of any real importance is a Muslim.

The recent political reforms, begun in 1970, curbed the power of the old native authority but not of Islam. They, in fact, strengthened it by bringing

Muslims from outside Yauri into the division to fill positions of power. The divisional secretary and executive officer, for example, are both Nupe from Kwara state. All the members of the government must attend the mosque regularly or else risk censure. Since the Emir of Yauri is the *de facto* spiritual leader of his emirate, such activities increase his religious prestige. Thus, the loss of political power to the newly constituted division has not led to a loss in religious power. Nor does it seem likely to do so since the government leaders in Yauri are eager to point out the Islamic basis for their rule.

It is in their interest that the pagan population of Yauri be given daily reminders of the power and prestige of Islam, for the larger the percentage of Muslims, they believe, the less will their power be questioned. While this may seem to contradict the earlier assertion that whole groups will find it difficult to cross ethnic barriers, it does not. The government leaders are generally from outside Yauri. Further, there was no assertion made that any conscious barriers were placed to the conversion of whole groups. It should be mentioned that the converts try to "pass" as Hausa, but the Hausa continue to refer to them by their original ethnic name.

Within this complex interplay of ethnic groups, the Dukawa and Gungawa must survive. Each group has chosen (in Barth's phraseology) to exploit a different ecological niche and has entered into symbiotic relationship with other groups. If Christianity or Islam has adaptive and exploitative potential it will be chosen to the degree to which it interacts with other elements of Dukawa and Gungawa life. The Dukawa, for example, have adapted to the area as horticulturalists who are also the best hunters and leather workers in the area. The primary work team for all these activities is male.

Moreover, all the male members of the work team are tied together primarily through having done bride service together. They are tied together in a relationship cemented by female links. Each man feels closest to those who have helped him perform his *gormu*, bride service. Those who have formed *gormu* teams hunt together and farm together. Logically, then, women are the external signs of male solidarity in Dukawa society and divorce is never permitted. Adultery is rare and Dukawa informants consider it a crime that strikes at the very fiber of Dukawa society. Anything, therefore, that might interfere with the organization of male work teams would be resisted, for it is through these work teams that the Dukawa defines himself *vis-a-vis* other ethnic groups (Salamone 1972).

For the Dukawa male, *gormu* service, a seven-to-eight-year project, functions as a rite of passage. It is never performed alone, but always with the assistance of one's age mates. Young work teams travel from place to place working on gardens in widely scattered parts of "Dukawaland." Such teams, obviously, perform many functions, not the least of which is tying the acephalous Dukawa together by affirming their ideals openly and facilitating communication and contact among the small compounds.

The Dominicans threaten the Dukawa ethos in a number of ways not at first patently obvious. Certainly, the Dominicans cannot help but admire the chastity of Dukawa women. They do realize the vital importance of the institution of *gormu* in cementing Dukawa ties. They have, however, alienated the Dukawa by insisting that potential converts adhere to the Catholic definition of marriage. By that they mean that no sexual intercourse is permissible before the performance of the exchange of vows.

While the missionaries have ingeniously patterned the Catholic ritual after the Dukawa ritual, they have failed to realize the importance of the Dukawa distinction between "having a wife" and "being married." Any young man doing *gormu* HAS a wife. He is not MARRIED, however, until the completion of his bride service. In fact, he will not complete his bride service until he is sure that his marriage is sexually satisfying, a fair precaution in a society that strongly prohibits adultery. Usually, he also demands proof of his wife's fertility before becoming fully married, another reasonable precaution in a society with a low incidence of polgyny for only 50 percent of the Dukawa in Yauri have more than one wife. To tamper with the institution of the *gormu* in any way threatens to change it significantly.

While the incidence of polygyny is low, it does exist and its most frequent type is leviratic. The levirate, as anthropologists have stressed for some time, serves a number of functions. It maintains alliances; it provides for widows and their children; it serves various religious purposes, etc. The Dukawa, like other people, consider it a secondary form of marriage, that is no one is expected to have only a wife obtained through the levirate. But Christianity forces one to have but a single wife. The convert, therefore, who has a wife, would have to refuse to honor his solemn obligation should the levirate situation present itself. The convert doing *gormu* and facing the necessity of the levirate would have to withdraw from Dukawa society since he would be forced to cancel his bride service contract lest he have two wives.

So long as the Catholic emphasis is on individual converts and demonstrable knowledge of the faith, the individual will learn, often after conversion that he is somehow "less" a member of his society than he was previously. If the advantages in remaining a convert are high enough, enough other members of one's society may become converts to effect changes in Christianity that will make the convert more comfortable. A wiser missionary approach among the Dukawa would be to emulate that used among the Gungawa.

Whatever their "ancestry" the Gungawa of Shabanda are today one people with a widely uniform culture, as the following quotation from Harris (1930: 291) makes clear:

> One would have expected to find much greater differences seeing that offshoots of several differing tribes—Shanga, Kamberi and Bussa—are to be found in the

islands, having been driven there during the raids from Kontagora in the 19th century. The position appears to be that whatever a man's tribe may have been, once he has joined the island community his children become islanders both in name and custom.

What Harris is describing, of course, is the cultural basis of "descent" and the formation of new ethnic-groups to adapt to new environments. The Gungawa are different in significant ways from any of the other ethnic groups from whom they draw their members. They are different because they must retain their distinct ethnic identity to exploit their particular niche in the wider milieu. The Gungawa are horticulturalists, and their onion farming is of major importance to non-Gungawa as are their fishing activities. Lately, Islam has begun to spread in Kwanji district, of which Shabanda is part.

Because Shabanda was not directly part of the Kainji Dam project, none of its people were forced to relocate, and traditional farming methods of shifting horticulture continue to be practiced. No part of Yauri, however, escaped the results of Kainji completely. One result of the dam was the opportunity to give frequent examples of Islamic power to resettled Gungawa, and most of the 44,000 people resettled were Gungawa. While these resettled Gungawa have been the prime targets of proselytizing efforts by Muslims, the strengthening of Islamic conversion methods has had a "spill-over" effect that is other groups are being preached to by well-trained *mallams*.

The *mallams* are trained through a government-sponsored agency, the Islamic Education Trust, founded in Nigeria by Sheik Ahmad Lemot and is affiliated with the International Islamic Education Trust centered in Mecca. Its main Nigerian office is in Sokoto. There, post-secondary school students are trained for three months to instruct local *mallams* in "modern methods" of conversion. These students are hired by the local authorities during their vacations to supervise in-service training for local *mallams*. The student assigned to Yauri, Musa Abarshi, has appointed a *mallam* to keep a constant watch on all other *mallams*. This *mallam*, Mallam Hamaidu, had been an Arabic teacher at the Gebbi Primary School, one mile from Shabanda. The choice was by design, not accident. Suffice it to say that the training is rigid; the *mallams* are tested carefully on their knowledge of Islam and methodology of conversion. The government supplies the *mallams* with motorcycles and permission to settle in the villages. Government approval is one key to their success. Another is the fact that the resettled Gungawa underwent a major ecological change.

They no longer live on islands or along the banks of the Niger. They find it difficult to irrigate their onion plants by traditional methods and find instead that they must irrigate them with Lister pumps avalleble only through the government. It is no surprise that while there were few Muslims on the islands there has been a tremendous increase in the number of Muslims since the resettlement was completed in 1968. The resettled Gungawa are finding it to their political and economic advantage to convert to Islam.

Those Gungawa who live in Shabanda have traditionally been renowned for their rapid acceptance of "modem methods." They have, in short, been willing to adapt to survive. In the present situation in Yauri it is not surprising to find the people of Shabanda living in peace with people who are remarkable for their "fearlessness of the Niger," and who supply a valuable source of needed protein to members of other ethnic groups.

While male work teams are the basis for the work organization, unlike the Dukawa situation, women and their chastity do not form the valuable tie linking men together. The Gungawa form their male work teams on a patrilineal-patrilocal basis, with a chain of authority highly articulated on a kinship basis from the most minor of officials to representatives of the Hausa emir.

The chastity or lack of it of Gungawa women only becomes important if a question of paternity should arise. No Gungawa family is willing to lose any potential members. A woman who leaves one of its members while pregnant or who appears pregnant shortly thereafter is a cause of concern, for there is danger that the child will be lost to the kinship group of the man she left. By prohibiting divorce and proclaiming the sanctity of the family, Christianity strengthens Gungawa social organization. It does so by reinforcing its underlying principles. The need for families to remain together was recognized by the first United Mission Society missionaries to the area in the early 1950's.

The approach used was that of converting entire families or large sections thereof. Since the Gungawa do not have either the *gormu* or the levirate and since polygyny is relatively rare, there was little to interfere with the HMS stress on monogamy. They do have a four-day bride service that a man and his young male kin perform immediately after his first marriage. But the lengthy service of the Dukawa is foreign to them. Gungawa bride service stresses the solidarity of the patrilineage and the acceptance by one's patrilineage of one's spouse. The emotional tie of the Dukawa is missing in the Gungawa service.

Furthermore, the Gungawa found much to gain from the HMS religion. From the first, the Gungawa preached the faith to other Gungawa. Indigenization was thus facilitated since one did not have the barrier of European presentation. Unlike the Dominicans' case with the Dukawa, outside ethnic groups were not brought in to preach as catechists. The Gungawa ran their own church in Shabanda. They have translated parts of the New Testament into Gunganci after first creating a written language.

The practical advantages of a written language for a trading people became readily apparent. The advantages of having some members practice the old faith and others practice Christianity seem readily apparent also. While Christianity continues to grow in Shabanda, a sizable number of people remain traditionalists in religion. Many families have both Baptist and traditionalist members and live in perfect harmony with another while some are Muslims, some are Christians, and some are traditionalists, for this reflects a rather wise adjustment to reality that enables people to maximize the opportunities available for each group. Outside Shabanda, the number of converts to Islam is increasing so rapidly (Rouer 1970) that if the rate continues almost all resettled Gungawa will become Muslims.

One interesting result of the Gungawa conversion to Islam in large numbers is the phenomenon of schismogenesis it presents. Outside Shabanda the newly converted Gungawa try to dissociate themselves as much as possible from the pagan Gungawa. In turn, pagan Gungawa mock them rather openly. Since the Hausa refuse to acknowledge these new Gungawa completely, one can predict that the Muslim Gungawa may form a separate ethnic group, exploiting a different ecological niche from pagan Gungawa and embracing radically different values. Shabanda, it must be stressed, is important because it offers a special setting for Islamic and Christian conversion, because it combines traditional and modern elements.

Its people travel the seven and one-half water miles to the Dominican hospital for preventive checkups while other ethnic groups will not travel there from down the road for serious illness. People from Shabanda send large numbers of students to institutions of higher learning. For example, ten young men were in universities and teacher training schools in 1970. No other minority group in Yauri had even one in an institution of higher learning. The elementary school on Shabanda is a major reason for the success of its young people. In its way Shabanda is a model of how change was able to come to the Gungawa without the major ecological wrenching consequent on forced resettlement.

SUMMARY

Individuals will become converts to those religious systems that enable them to better adapt to their ecological niches. The U.M.S. has aided the Gungawa of Shabanda by emphasizing the kinship bases of their authority structure and providing an easy access to literacy. Christianity has failed to make many converts among the Dukawa because of the dissonance between the value system of the Dominican missionaries and those values that bind Dukawa society together. The V.M.S. have striven for mass conversions in an effort to make the convert feel at ease in his new role. The Dominicans have treated the individual and thus isolated the convert and vitiated their chances for further conversion.

The D.M.S. first gained a foothold in Shabanda by reinforcing family ties. It did so in a way compatible with Gungawa society. That it has other advantages for the inhabitants of Shabanda became rather evident as time has passed. The converts learned of these advantages after conversion. But their successes served as positive feedback to other Gungawa who in about twenty years have made the island one of the major centers of Christianity in northern Nigeria.

The Dominicans, by stressing individual commitment and by cutting converts off from ties formed by the *gormu* complex, have tended to isolate their converts from their ethnic groups. It is granted that the Dominicans and V.M.S. faced different problems, but the Dominicans have failed to set up an indigenous clergy and have demanded a high initial knowledge of Christianity from Dukawa converts. As negative feedback is sent to the Dukawa system by converts, one can predict a low conversion rate, at least so long as the *gormu* complex remains adaptive for Dukawa social organization.

The recent resettlement of Gungawa consequent on the building of Kainji Dam has given impetus to an Islamic conversion movement. The resettled Gungawa, faced with adapting to a different ecological niche, have been turning to Islam for its greater economic and political advantages. The government-sponsored effort has made inroads at Shabanda. Finally, Shabanda with its Christians, Muslims and traditionalists provides a unique setting for the study of religious change in a more traditional Gungawa setting.

8

Competitive Conversion and Its Implications for Modernized Nigeria

INTRODUCTION

Competitive conversion exists when two or more proselytizing agencies seek to recruit members from the same population and membership in one organization mutually excludes that in any of the others. Competitive conversion logically can range from almost zero competition, where one agency successfully forbids and persecutes its competitors, to a situation of equality in competition. The practical effect of the competition is to increase the potential, or at least promised, benefits available to new members. Several factors help both to clarify any given situation and to construct a paradigm of competitive conversion situations.

Among these are: techniques of conversion, agents, types of converts, occasions of conversion, and changes in behavior of converts. In studying conversion sociologically, I follow SHIBUTANI and KWAN (1965) who hold that true conversion is rare and that people convert in order to obtain perceived situations.

Genuine conversions are rare occurrences; they usually involve serious disturbances in interpersonal relations over a long period of time, the lowering of one's level of self- esteem, a period of torment from a sense of worthlessness, and the sudden grasp of a new outlook that enables one to form a new self- conception. This type of conversion cannot be expected to take place on a large scale (Shibutan and Kwan 1965:80)

I do not deny the possibility of true conversion, only their frequency. As individual, not group phenomena, they are moreover the concern of the psychologist, not the social scientist. I am, therefore, concerned with group behavior in a recurring type situation, one I have labeled competitive conversion. The term "competitive conversion" is RONALD COHEN'S (personal communication) and labels a phenomenon many scholars have studied but never labeled (cf. EKECHI 1971 and SALAMONE 1976 for examples). The lack of naming is indicative of the need to direct attention to defining aspects of the phenomenon in order to facilitate comparison.

Controlled comparison is a major goal of this paper. A limited aspect of a wider problem is studied in one area and then compared with studies by other scholars along the same dimensions named on page one. Social and cultural hypotheses derived from the Yauri case are used to examine four other examples of competitive conversion in Nigeria. Finally, general hypotheses are offered for testing elsewhere.

Behavior is analyzed from a symbolic interactionist perspective. It is argued that each group seeks to define situation in a way that will give it an advantage seeking to maximize opportunities and minimize losses. Those proselytizing agencies that can convince potential converts that they offer greater benefits and fewer disadvantages will have greater success. This perspective places the study of conversion within the more general concern of identity studies, of self presentation. Therefore, I devote careful attention throughout and especially in the conclusion to these further implications.

YAURI AND ITS SITUATION

Yauri, located along the Niger River and away from large centers of population in Nigeria's northwestern savannah grasslands, has long been an ideal refuge. Its fertile islands and fishing waters, now spoiled by the Kainji Dam, provided sustenance for industrious peoples while separating them from the armies of Songhai Borgu, and the Sokoto Fulani Empire. Ruled by nominal Muslims since the eighteenth century, the overwhelming majority of its peoples until recent times were traditionalists (arna or pagans). In the early nineteenth century the Muslim Fulani, under Usman dan Fodio, forced a *dhimi* status on Yauri that of an infidel state allowed paying tribute in order to retain its non- Islamic customs. Furthermore, while ruled by Hausa and listed, as one of the Hausa states, the overwhelming majority of its population has been non- Hausa. Accordingly, it is considered one of the Hausa *banza* (the seven true Hausa states).

Yauri has an unusually heterogeneous ethnic population. Of its total population of about 120,000, the groups considered indigenous are the Kamberi (10,000), Dukawa (4,000), Gungawa (40,000), and the Shangawa (25,000). All other ethnic groups are, in a sense or another, strangers. That includes the ruling Hausa (20,000), Serakawa (1,000), and members from a number of different ethnic groups, who like the Yoruba and Midwestern-ers , have been attracted to Yauri during the colonial and post colonial period. In addition, most of the 10,000 soldiers and their families stationed in Yauri after 1972 are Christians from outside Yauri.

"Heterogeneous" also describes the religious situation. About half of Yauri's people are either openly or *de facto* traditionalists in religion. This includes the Dukawa, the Kamberi, and the Gungawa. The Shangawa and the ruling Hausa are Muslims. Although the Gungawa are still mainly traditionalists, when they change ethnic identity to Hausa, they also change their religion to Islam. (The rate of that change has increased significantly since the building of Kainji Dam, as has the consequent resettlement of Gungawa from riverine areas to mainland areas poorly suited to horticulture; see Salamone 1975 a) Also, a growing number of Kamberi to Ngaski District from the towns of Wara and Libata are becoming Muslims and are moving into professional jobs, such as teaching and governmental operations. There are very few Christians among the indigenous groups: about 100 Gungawa, 25 Dukawa and a few Kamberi. The only relatively successful community of indigenous Christians is that of the United Mission Society (officially the United Mission Church of Africa) found at Shabanda among the Gungawa (Salamone 1974 c and 1976).

In sum, Islam is associated with the politically dominant Hausa. Muslim Yoruba tend to occupy some of the economic positions once controlled by Christian Igbo. Christian Midwesterners and soldiers from non- Yauri ethnic group occupy most of the other economic positions in Yauri. Midwesterners who plan to remain in Yauri signify that desire through conversion to Islam. Many of the resettled Gungawa are using a traditional pattern and converting to Islam on the way to becoming Hausa.

SIMILARITIES BETWEEN
CATHOLIC AND INDIGENOUS NORMS

The Dominican missionary station at Yauri founded in 1959 is part of the Dominican network, itself part of the vast Catholic missionary network emanating from Rome. It cannot properly be understood apart from that fact. In common with other mission groups, especially other Dominicans, the group at Yauri shares a common heritage that must be applied to its situation. The heritage has been influenced in general by along religious competition with Islam. Specifically, it has been molded in Nigeria by the Dominicans' association since 1949 with the predominantly Igbo Catholics, whose opinions of Muslim Hausa are notoriously hostile. Their experiences with Igbo helped fashion Dominican conversion methods and techniques as well as attitudes as I discuss below in the section on approaches to conversion.

Cultural attitudes toward sex, marriage, drink, authority, local culture, and other sociocultural phenomena are remarkably uniform from one Dominican station to another. The Dominicans are unalterably opposed to anything that interferes with monogamous marriage. They are opposed to coitus except between married partners, whom they define more literally than even some of their fellow Catholic missionaries. They approve of a general division of labor, but do not like Islamic wife seclusion. The pattern of interaction between men and women have separate jobs to do, but mix freely in socially. Women have a say in choosing their marriage partners and have honorable, though distinct, occupations. Men should protect women, be masculine, but relatively democratic. The freedom if the Dominican sisters is a cause for comment in Yauri, but the Dominican men are relatively dominant and definitely in charge of the mission station. The Dominicans do not object to drinking or smoking. Moderation is also the explanatory term to describe Dominican views on gambling. The Dominicans are careful not to object to traditional nudity, Furthermore, they show open approval of many traditional cultural aspects, although like Muslims they believe that the best of these are precursors of what is found in their religion.

The principle of seniority is strongly approved by Dominicans. However, their belief in individual salvation fosters practices that are opposed to it. Finally, the Dominicans expect converts "to behave as Christians." Behaviorally, that means that converts will associate with other Catholics or those studying to be Catholics more than they will with others. It means plural marriages or divorce are forbidden, that participation I traditional religious rituals are prohibited, and that the convert will be in fact be more Catholic than Catholics in the United States and Europe.

This somewhat unreal situation is further reflected in the composition of the Dominican mission station. The structure of the station in 1972 was as follows: There were two American priests, one lay brother, and three sisters. The indigenous Nigerian personnel consisted of five catechists, only one of whom was from Yauri and one Yoruba woman who helped in Gungawa areas. Four of the catechists were from the North Central State and were Kafancan and Shendam. The personnel were generally young with only one sister and one catechist over fifty. Four of the five catechists were in their twenties, making them both strangers and rather young for religious specialists. Two of the three sisters are in their thirties, and none of these three American men was beyond his middle forties. One priest, in fact, was in his middle thirties. The Yoruba woman was in her forties.

The catechists and Yoruba woman were all married. None of the Dominicans was, of course, married since each had taken vows of celibacy. All speak Hausa. However, none spoke it as a first language. The degree of fluency varied from almost "native" level to elementary. While the indigenous personnel spoke Hausa fluently, all but one spoke it with accents of non-Yauri Hausa. The other, a Dukawa, spoke it as a second language. However, his work was essentially confined to other Dukawa.

In common with other Dominicans those at Yauri live in a manner that although modest by American standards is beyond the means of all but a few of the people. They are celibate, a fact difficult for even sophisticated people

Table 8.1. Comparison of Erickson's Stages of Development with Hausa Stages of Development

Erickson		Hausa		
		Stage		
Stage	Age	Male	Female	Age
Trust vs. mistrust	infancy (0-2)	karamin yaro	jariri	birth to 6
Autonomy vs. shame	toddlerhood (2-4)			
Initiative vs. guilt	early childhood (4-6)	saurayi	budurawa	marriage
Competence vs. inferiority	school age (6-12)	ango	amarya	marriage to 60
Identity vs. identity diffusion	adolescence (12-20)			
Intimacy vs. isolation	young adulthood (20-40)			
Generativity vs. stagnation	middle adulthood (40-60)			
Integrity vs. despair	old age (60+)	tsoho	tsohuwa	60+ to death

of Yauri to comprehend. The sisters control their own money and resources, a fact comprehensible to most. However, they also drive their own car and do not cook for men. They do not have children, nor are they either married or courtesans. Therefore, they occupy an anomalous category.

Even a brief overview of local values highlights areas of probable conflict and agreement between the Dominicans and member of local groups.

Although all groups indigenous to Yauri favor polygyny, the Dukawa alone do not allow their members to intermarry with members of any other group because they believe that marriage presents sufficient problems without compounding them by introducing cultural complication. Although culturally similer to the Dukawa in many ways, Kamberi have used their locally attributed "docility" (kirki) as a strategy to structure interactions in order to protect themselves from more powerful groups. The contribution of their women to ore powerful groups is a logical outgrowth of the practice, for they believe that men whose mothers are Kamberi tend to look favorably on Kamberi. Indeed, Kamberi women are highly prized as wives, for they are reputed to be more chaste and docile than any other women in Yauri and consequently, to be better mothers. Their sons seem, in fact, to be even more firmly dedicated to them than is common. Furthermore, that kindly disposition so extends to other Kamberi, proving the wisdom of the strategy.

In addition, Gungawa have a form of polyandry known as secondary marriage, a sign of constant male/female conflicts. Dukawa and Kamberi oppose any form of concubinage while Gungawa favor it. Each group in Yauri has a sexual division of labor. Each allows men and women to mix socially. However, if one were to construct a continuum of male/female relations, Kamberi women would rank "shyest" and Gungawa most "hostile." Dukawa have a rather free give and take.

Table 8.2. Stages of Moral Judgment (from Newman and Newman 1991:296)

Level 1: Pre-conventional
Stage 1: Judgments are based on whether behavior is rewarded or punished.
Stage 2: Judgments are based on whether the consequences result in benefits for self or loved ones.

Level 2: Conventional
Stage 3: Judgments are based on whether authorities approve or disapprove.
Stage 4: Judgments are based on whether the behavior upholds or violates the laws of society.

Level 3: Post-conventional
Stage 5: Judgments are based on preserving social contracts based on cooperative collaboration.
Stage 6: Judgments are based on ethical principles that apply across time and cultures.

While Dukawa values are not totally compatible with Christian values, they are compatible enough to ease their association with Dominican missionaries, for the missionaries do not object to nudity, drinking, smoking, free association of the sexes, or progressive marriage. The major problem between Dukawa and Dominican centers on the presence of the junior levirate and bride service (*gormu*) marriage among the Dukawa (See SALAMONE 1972). *Gormu* marriage, part of the Dukawa's self definition requires a man in the company of his age- mates to work a specific period of time for his wife's father. At set periods he receives greater rights to his wife. At the completion of the bride service and the performance of the appropriate rites, he is deemed married, and any children born during his bride service are members of his father's linage. The junior levirate requires a man's younger brother to marry his widow and raise his children if his widow is willing. The Dominicans can accept either of these practices but not both if polygyny results.

In contrast, Kamberi and Gungawa members have converted both to Islam and various forms of Christianity. There has been long-established pattern of ethnic change among the Gungawa (See Salamone 1975 a). Underlying the pattern is a cultural value for being pragmatic and seizing opportunities. Whenever Christianity has presented clear-cut advantages, Gungawa have become Christians, fitting the stereotype of the "man on the make." Kamberi who convert do so inevitably as a means of preserving their ethnic identity. Conversion affirms and preserves their ethnic identity.

SIMILARITIES BETWEEN
ISLAMIC AND INDIGENOUS NORMS

In a very real sense, each Muslim male is a missionary. However, this paper focuses specifically on that segment off the Islamic population that is institutionalized for missionary work on order to compete formally with Christian missionaries , the Islamic Education Trust (I.E.T) The I.E.T. founded in Mecca in 1972 by Sheik Aimed Lemot, replaced Jama'atu Nasril Islam, an organization that has found its work in Yauri reduced to supplying educational materials . Those who became I.E.T. members were convinced that the Jama'atu approach was too conservative. Therefore, the I.E.T began to work through local governments in order to organize local *Mallamai* (Islamic teachers) and to raise their standards in accord with its states purpose, the improvement of Islamic missionary efforts. To that end post-secondary school students receive training of "modern methods of conversion." In turn, during their vacation these young men work for local governments supervising "in service" training of local *Mallamai*, providing structural links between programs and the Sokoto headquarters. Furthermore, these students choose head *Mallamai* of local I.E.T.'s who are directly responsible to them. The student's absence for most of the year provides them with sufficient structural distance to serve as courts of appeal for settling local grievances.

Cultural attitudes pattern interactions of *Mallamai* and members of groups whom they seek to convert. Thus, the belief that Islam is essentially a man's religion, one that is conformity with human nature is used to attract male converts, who will insist on the conversion of their wives and children. The cultural ideal is for clear sex roles specificity, an ideal quickly approached as a man's wealth increases (Roder 1971). The specific model is that of Hausa Fulani male/female relationships (BARKOW 1971). Logically, entailed in the attitudes regarding male/female relationships is a strong double-standard exemplified in the Islamic view regarding non-martial coitus. Although both young men and women are expected to have pre-marital sexual knowledge, young women are also expected to be virgins at marriage.

In Yauri there is a strong Islamic condemnation of any behavior associated with traditional religious practices. Thus, drinking bottled beer is a high prestige item while drinking traditional beer is considered "pagan" behavior. Similarly, dancing and nudity are condemned because of their "pagan" associations.

For the orthodox Muslim human nature had never been lost and consequently has never been in need of redemption. It does need guidance, and the Qur'an provided it. Furthermore, man must work with his group in order to attain paradise. The idea of individual salvation strikes Muslim in Yauri as strange. Indeed, it strikes members of all groups in Yauri as strange, for only the mad draw off by themselves away from their fellows.

The I.E.T. trains its personnel to have an attitude of limited tolerance. This demonstrated clearly through Islamic attitudes regarding interethnic marriages. Any Muslim man may marry any non-Muslim woman. Since marriages in Yauri tend toward patrilocality, the woman will be surrounded by Islamic affines and she is usually easily socialized into the Islamic community. For the same reason, no Muslim woman may marry a "pagan" since she will be surrounded by traditionalists. The only exceptions are Muslim widows who may marry Gungawa men. These men however, are usually in the process of becoming Hausa (Salamone, 1975 a).

COMPARISON OF CHRISTIAN
AND ISLAMIC APPROACHES IN YAURI

The idea of a centralized mission agency in Islam is clearly an example of what KROEBER (1952) termed stimulus diffusion, for the structure of the

I.E.T has been clearly influenced by Christian missionary organizations. It is also certainly an effect Christian missionaries did not anticipate but one compatible with MILLER's (1970) hypothesis stating that the missionary is an unconscious agent of modernization.

The organization of the I.E.T. parallels not only that of Christian missionary organizations but also that of Islamic governments in Northern Nigeria, to which the I.E.T. is subordinate. Similarly, the cultural attitudes of the I.E.T. mirror those of the Islamic government. However, the I.E.T. has systemized these attitudes into a more coherent from than that usually found. In Yauri it has taken care to train *mallamai* to present a uniform and orthodox version of Islamic teachings. *Mallamai* must read and write Qu'ranic Arabic and undergo training to prepare them for their work. In turn, the I.E.T. certifies them, without that certification *mallamai* cannot preach publicly. This grassroots codification of Islam in innovative, for in the past such new codifications were associated with a *jihad*.

The government demonstrates its sensitivity to the way in which *mallamai* present themselves in a number of ways. Because local people suspect the motives of any unmarried people who come to live among them, no *mallamai* is either unmarried or under thirty years old, an age sufficient to command respect from Yauri's old people since by that age a man has at least one wife and several children. Furthermore, all of Yauri's Islamic missionaries present themselves as Hausa, Fulani, or Hausa-Fulani , members of group enjoying high prestige. Furthermore, the government id aware of the advantages that accrue from having *mallamai* live in a way simller to that of the people among whom they work. By living in the villages and farming, *mallamai* present a vivid model for the villagers. In addition, living in the villages enables them to ascertain which people have greatest influence and, therefore, which conversions will be most efficient.

The Dominicans do not share the advantages of Islamic missionaries. What they do have are skills desired by people in Yauri. Since it is impossible for foreign missionaries to remain in Islamic areas in Nigeria simply

Table 8.3. **Qualitative stereotypes in Yauri**

Group	Stereotypes
Hausa	merchants, composed
Fulani	warlike
Kamberi	gentle
Gungawa	helpful
Dukawa	fighters, craftsmen
Yoruba	civilized
Igbo	antisocial
Shangawa	wrestlers
Midwesterners	helpful
Europeans	civilized

Table 8.4.   **Ranking of Interethnic Marriage in Yauri Among Parents of Schoolchildren (n=121)**

Father's ethnic group:	Hausa	
Mother's ethnic group	Gungawa	11 = 9%
	Kamberi	7 = 6%
	Fulani	6 = 5%

as missionaries, the loss of the mission hospital to the government meant that the Dominicans had to find substantive skills or services desired by the indigenous people which they alone could supply. The schools provide this function.

Both the Dry Season and Vocational Schools are consciously innovative. Both have a number of religious and organizational goals in common: the presentation of the Dominicans in a favorable light in order to keep them in Nigeria, conversion of its students, etc. However, the more immediate aims of each school differ. Briefly, the Dry Season School aims at the conversion of the non-Hausa or newly-Hausa while the purpose of the Vocational School is to create an atmosphere in which the Dominicans can continue their conversion efforts. Therefore, the Vocational School recruits Hausa and Hausa-Fulani apprentices who will be indebted to the Dominicans for the benefits resulting from their education.

THE DRY SEASON SCHOOL

The model or template for the Dry Season School was set forth in a paper by one of the Dominican missionaries (Champlin s.d., but probably 1970). Although the overriding purpose of the Dry Season School in theory is religious, in practice all of the schools including the "model school" at Malumfashi which instructs catechists, do offer material comforts and benefits beyond the reach of those attending. These enticements are for the Dominican subordinate to their primary purpose of converting people through discovering their world views. However, they are aware of the benefits derivable from material enticements.

The Dry Season (ca November to May) is a logical time to conduct a school seeking to attract people who are not attending full-time schools because the Dry Season is culturally defined as a time to engage in activities other than farming.

In Yauri, the Dry Season School is a logical outgrowth of the day-to-day work of the Dominicans and their identification with the non-Hausa peoples. Daily the Dominicans attempt to do some teaching—counting, reading, writing, and speaking English- firmly establishing their association with learning. They openly tell the people that learning to count, read, and write will keep them from being cheated by tax collectors and merchants, implicitly understood to be Hausa.

The population of the Dry Season School varies, but there are about thirty students in attendance at any given time. All are male, most are Dukawa. The predominance of Dukawa at the mission station reinforced the local perception that the Dominicans "belong" to the Dukawa. Thus, the increasing willingness of Dukawa to attend the Dry Season School signals a growing Dukawa receptivity to baptism, given their belief that literacy and Christianity are casually related. The successful enrollment of Muslims , albeit those outside the mainstream of Yauri's Islamic society, would help dispel this notion, and the Dominicans believe increase the conversion rate among older Dukawa , for as of September 1972 only eleven Dukawa in a population of about 4,000 had been converted. Therefore, four Gungawa Muslims were specially recruited in an attempt to combat the stereotype. Similar recruitment among a fishing people, the Serkawa, who feel quite comfortable at the mission station, failed, for thy said it was a Dukawa school, and Dukawa had warned them to stay away from it.

To the Dukawa, there seems little reason in attending the school if some benefits do not accrue to the participants. Since Dukawa are unlikely to become Muslims, literact seems to be a necessary preliminary for becoming Christian, for a literate "pagan" seems to be a self-contradictory cognitive category in Yauri. No number of Muslims attending the Dry School would convince them otherwise.

THE VOCATIONAL SCHOOL

Begun about 1966, the Vocational School evolved from and incorporated a series of earlier projects that never were quite successful. It is a combination all- purpose repair and construction station and vocational school offering on the job training. In brief, everything including large trucks, ferry boats, flush toilets in the Emir's harem, electrical wiring in the Divisional Engineer's house, movie projectors, floors, ceilings, and other assorted odds and ends are repaired or built by the staff at the workshop. Crafts such as auto mechanics, masonry, and electrical skills are taught to the apprentices who work in the shop.

Because the lack of trained craftsmen in Northern Nigeria had impeded developmental projects, a school that prepared skilled workers at no cost to the state assures the missionaries at least provisional protection. To increase that protection the missionaries have actively and successfully recruited Hausa for the workshop. The recruitment has been aided by the obvious *girma prestige)* enjoyed by the lay brother who operated the shop.

Such prestige is complemented by the ease with which the graduates obtain good positions. This positive feedback, in turn, makes positions in the shop quite valuable. Thus, opening of his own automobile workshop by a lose relative of the Emir who had been the foreman of the missionaries' workshop was a positive aid to the Dominicans.

The Dominicans have had the greatest influence with those most hostile to the Islamic Hausa ruler and farthest removed from their economic and political influence. While there are differences in norms between Dukawa and the Dominicans, the Dukawa associate with them quite freely. Conversely, the Gungawa are drawing closer to the Hausa. Intermarriage is increasing, and the *mallamai* encourage it. Obviously, the Islamic missionaries enjoy government support, greater numbers and greater ability to mingle among the local peoples, including intermarriage. The Kamberi present an example of a group whose members are willing to convert to either religion, depending on the circumstances. Since they offer a clear test of my hypotheses, they are discussed carefully in the conclusion.

HYPOTHESES FROM YAURI

In cases where an established religion is associated with the government in a situation of ethnic pluralism and stratification, that government is likely to exert pressure to bring about the conversion of members of other ethnic groups. Conversion will be successful to the extent that the government is successful in controlling the ecological situation of a subordinate group and its interactions with other groups. The greater an ethnic groups' ability to be economically self sufficient, the more likely will it resist governmental pressure for conversion. If an outside agency, proselytizing or otherwise, demonstrates its ability to aid a group is resisting governmental pressures, it is likely to win converts to cause.

In the case of successful governmental pressure for conversion to the established religion, those groups will undergo a change in ethnic identity after changing their religious behavior (cf. BARTH 1969). Members of groups occupying lower strata will also convert to the established religion if they must in order to gain benefits. However, they will not change ethnic identity and are likely to use their membership in the established religion to promote ethnic nationalism. Their view of religion is an instrumental one. Such converts, if possible, will use other means to relieve the pressure that the government is able to exert on them.

In all cases, members of ethnic groups choose religions for benefits they perceive as accruing to them. All other things being equal, religion serves as an ethnic boundary marker in situations of ethnic composition, group members will adhere to that religion. In the last analysis, religious and ethnic identity are but sub –categories of *persona* (one's rights and duties), a means for structuring situations to gain perceived advantages.

TESTING THE YAURI HYPOTHESES IN OTHER NIGERIAN AREAS: THE KAMBERI : AGWARRA , BORGU DIVISION, KWARA STATE

There is an Irish Catholic mission station at Aqwarra in Borgu Emiriate, Kwara State, less than thirty miles from Yauri. Near it there is a United Mission Society station under the direction of a Dakarkari pastor. At the same time the government is committed to the furtherance of Islam. Therefore, superficially at least, the Yauri and Borgu situations appear the same. There are, however, a number of dissimilarities that suggests an in- depth study would be profitable. There are, for example, many more Christians in Kwara Statw than in the former North- Western State. The number of mission stations is greater than in the North- Western State. In short, Christians throughout Kwara State, while a minority, benefit from the presence of a large number of Christians in the State. Further, while Yauri is ethnically heterogeneous, it is an anomaly within the Sokoto State, for Hausa, and the Hausa—Fulani dominate the state. Kwara State, on the other hand , is an ethnically heterogeneous state comprised of Busawa, Hausawa, Kamberi, Gungawa, Lopawa, Nupe, Fulani, Yoruba and a number of other groups. The Nupe and Yoruba have significant numbers of Christians, and an all-out governmental campaign of conversion would add to the State's already great problems.

Therefore, although Agwarra is in the Muslim Emirate of Borgu, the missionaries are much freer from outside influence than are those at Yauri. New Bussa, the site of Kainji Dam and capitol of Borgu Emirate, attracted workers throughout Europe as well as West Africa and Nigeria. The vast majority of these workers were Christians and a pattern of tolerance and mutual respect grew up in the Emirate, aided by similar patterns throughout the state.

THE MAGUZAWA, ZARIA, NORTH-CENTRAL STATE

The Malumfashi area in Zaria Province provides another example of competitive conversion in Nigeria. The Maguzawa, a group of about 100,000 traditional Hausa , are a source of embarrassment to Islamic missionaries and the government , for the officials' position is that the North is Islamic , and to be a Hausa is to be a Muslim. The presence of these non-Muslim Hausa leads the government to announce significant conversions in the newspapers, for Zaria (Zazzau) area has traditionally no other ethnic groups present and therefore no outside ideological composition. Furthermore, since Maguzawa is a Qu'ranic term meaning infidel, it is not surprising that conversion to Islam and Christianity brings about a new change of name to Hausa.

THE IGBO

In general, the dominant Igbo value seems to be that of "getting ahead" or "rising up" (Uchendu 1965). A person must not only "get up" in society but must be seen rising up. Ekechi (1971: 103-115) argues that Igbo chose to convert to Catholicism because it best enables them to actualize their dominant values, that of bettering themselves. I have argued elsewhere (Salamone 1974 a) that there is a strong association in the Igbo ethos between chastity and success. Therefore, there tends to be a pre-adaptation in the Igbo value- system toward Catholicism. However, the dominant value is still success, and OTTENBURG (1971) presents an important example of a Muslim Igbo village. He is very clear in associating conversion to Islam with conspicuous signs of success.

THE YORUBA OF WESTERN NIGERIA

The Yoruba provide an example of a group that has large numbers of members in a number of religions: Islam, Catholicism, traditional religion, and various branches of Protestantism, ranging from Anglicanism to the nativistic Cherubim and Seraphim. Throughout Nigeria there has been a general falling away from traditional religion; for example, the Nigerian census of 1963 only lists 7.9% of the population as not being either Muslim or Christian (PARRATT 1969:113). Although the census data are open to question, they do not reflect rather accurately the fact of a drift away from traditional religion to Islam and Christianity. Significantly, the Yoruba, the most urban people in Nigeria and one of the more urbanized people in the world, seem to be explicit in Yorubaland.

TESTING SPECIFIC HYPOTHESIS

In this section I wish to use each of the four areas described above to examine a specific hypothesis derived from the Yauri case study.

THE KAMBERI, AGWARRA, BORGU DIVISION, KWARA STATE

Hypothesis: The greater an ethnic groups' ability to be economically self- sufficient, the more likely will it resist governmental pressure for conversion. If an outside agency, proselytizing or otherwise, demonstrates its ability to aid or group in resisting governmental pressure, it is likely to win converts to its cause.

Most Kamberi in Agwarra resist Islam and turn to those branches of Christianity can offer them some means of preserving their indigenous values and identity. The Kamberi who associate with the mission station assert their ethnic pride more openly than do most other Kamberi, an action encouraged by the missionaries.

The most noticeable difference between Dominican and Irish Catholic strategy is the different value each group places on plural marriage. The Dominicans delay Dukawa baptism until the danger of plural marriage is lessened. After baptism they carefully help screen prospective brides for their converts. The Irish missionaries believe that such a concern with marriage approaches a kind of monomania, hampering conversion efforts, and drawing attention from the essential message of Christianity. They also believe that changes in Catholic theological thinking make such an approach rather simplistic.

Irish Catholics are not the only Christian group having success in Agwarra. The United Mission Society (U.M.S.) also has a rather active following. Their congregation is mainly composed of members who live together in a communal village. These members came from Yauri and Borgu and have been bended together to strengthen and preserve their faith. They tend to be much more active in proselytizing than are U.M.S. members in Yauri or Shabanda. Consequently, one is conscious of the much more dynamic nature of the U.M.S. Members go out parading throughout Agwarra District in search of people to attend their services. The music and shouting serve their purpose, and people who had not planned on attending church services often do so.

Those who attend either U.M.S. or Catholic services in Agwarra tend to become more westernized than those who do not, even though the Irish, unlike the U.S.M. do not actively promote western behavior. U.S.M. members are easily distinguishable from other Kamberi because of their westernized behavior and possessions. Further, while retaining their traditional Kamberi politeness, they do not display any signs of the behavior local people label timidness that is a marked feature of traditional Kamberi.

At Agwarra Kamberi are choosing Christianity as a means of becoming modern while preserving their distinction from Hausa Muslims. The U.M.S. continues to flourish. However, since the coming of the Irish missionaries they have not been so successful as the Irish missionaries who have been careful to interfere as little as possible with traditional Kamberi religion and have begun to learn Kamberanci (the Kamberi language) while using earlier converts to translate prayers and the mass into their language. The Irish clearly see their role as one that will strengthen the Kamberi *vis- a-vis* outside authority. The Kamberi seem to be responding to the Irish strategy, one that the different political situation of Agwarra permits. Those few Kamberi Muslims in Agwarra are reminiscent of Kamberi Muslims in Ngaski District,

Yauri; i.e., they become Muslim to preserve their ethnicity while rising to positions of some power from which they might aid their people. Unlike the Gungawa, they do not identify with the Hausa , and conversion to Catholicism , Protestantism , or Islam is a means of preserving , not changing, their ethnic identity where there is societal agreement that the cultural meaning of religious conversion also embraces ethnic change (see PADEN 1973, especially 45-55).

The Maguzawa, Zaria, North-Central State

Hypothesis: Conversion will be successful to the extent that the government is successful in controlling the ecological situation of a subordinate group and its interactions with other groups.

Converts change their behavior and no longer call themselves Maguzawa. While the Maguzawa are not a separate ethnic group, they seem to be in the process of becoming one (BARKOW 1970). Certainly converts to Islam from the Maguzawa experience an identity change comparable to that of the Gungawa. In both cases, the change is culturally approved, and social patterns for the change have been in existence for hundreds of years. For both the Gungawa and Maguzawa, conversion to Islam has been a culturally approved means to increase prestige while undergoing a change in group affiliation.

On the other hand, both in Yauri and Malumfashi people convert to Catholicism in an effort to obtain benefits promised by their conversion. In some ways, these benefits are passive , i.e.; they keep away Islamic penetration and are intended to preserve one's ethnic identity. That identity can be a "real" one as in the case of the Gungawa, or it can be an "emergent" one. Following Barknow (1970) one can argue that conversion tends to increase the difference in the ethoses of the converts, and non- converts increase until these become so great that a new ethnic group emerges. Thus, he argues that the Maguzawa are an emergent ethnic group, and that those who convert to Catholicism may be doing so to emphasize their difference from the Islamic converts. The same argument holds true for the Gungawa in Yauri.

There are also "active" benefits obtainable from conversion, viz, material benefits from the mission. BARKNOW (1970) offers evidence for converts to Islam who are engaging in these types of changes. REUKE (1970) attest to the fact that converts to Catholicism change their interaction patterns, as do Islamic converts. In brief, people of the same religion are most likely to associate with one another. Catholic converts tend to spend increasingly amounts of time at the Dominican mission station while taking on the mannerisms and values of mission personnel. In Yauri religion is already an ethnic boundary marker, while at Malumfashi it is becoming one.

The Igbo of Southern Nigeria

Hypothesis: All other things being equal, if religion serves an ethnic boundary marker in situation of ethnic competition, group members will adhere
to that religion.

There are both Christian and Muslim Igbo and it seems clear that religion
tends to have an instrumental value of the Igbo (Ottenburg 1971), as it
does for the Gungawa of Yauri. Thus, in cases where Igbo must distinguish
themselves from Northerners they emphasize their allegiance to Christianity since Islam is inevitably associated with Hausa.

The Igbo case supports other data that suggest that the first generation
of converts choose the new religion for reasons that have little to do with
its beliefs and rituals (See Sahay 1968 and Salamone 1972: 224-225).
Certainly, the Igbo clearly present an example of a group that values the
maximization of opportunities to such an extent that there is no hierarchy
of occupations. Any occupation that provides wealth and the prestige symbols it commands count on enabling on e to better his status. Thus, it is
not surprising to find Igbo using religion instrumentally to maximize their
opportunities.

The Yoruba of Western Nigeria

Hypothesis: In the last analysis, religious and ethnic identities are but sub-
categories of *persona* (one's total rights and duties), a means for structuring
site of situations to gain perceived advantages.

In Ile-Ife, 70% of the people profess Christianity. As PARRATT (1969:114)
notes that sets Ile-Ife apart from many other areas in Yorubaland where
Islam tends to gain the majority of converts from traditional religion.
PARRATT (1969:119) argue that the major reason for the greater success
of Christianity in gaining converts in Ile-Ife is education. Mission schools
alienate people from the traditional religion while offering a ready substi-
tute for the newly educated elite. Significantly, both Islam and Christianity
offer higher status to the convert, thus viewing conversion as a means for
raising his status. PARRATT seems to imply that a convert chooses the religion of highest status at any given point in time.

Status alone, however, is not sufficient to account for the differential
rate of conversion in Ile-Ife. PARRATT (1969:117) found other variables
operating in the conversion process. As expected, however, is the tendency
of parents to convert to the religion of their educated children. PARRATT
continues beyond these "sociological" factors to discuss what he labels
"religions" factors in conversion. These tend to be those I would describe
as belonging to the categories of world views and ethos. Briefly, PARRATT
discusses the way Islam and Christianity impose order on a complex world
while enabling the convert to cope with problems of evil in ways he deems

more efficacious than were possible in traditional context. However, his data really suggest that status is the overriding reason for conversion among the Yoruba. In the Ile-Ife Christianity has the higher status because converts can "get ahead."

The Ibadan case that COHEN (1969) presents goes beyond Parratt's data, for COHEN discusses an example of the use of ethnicity and religion to maintain certain economic advantages. Both Yoruba and Hausa in Ibadan found its advantages to be Muslims. However, the Hausa had a strong economic need to differentiate themselves from other groups in order to maintain a monopoly of the Ibadan end of the trans- Sudanic cattle trade. The Hausa in Ibadan control the butchering trade because the Cattle Fulani will sell only to the Hausa. Significantly, man "Hausa" have Yoruba parents. In order to increase their members and strength, the Hausa community allowed non-Hausa to pass into Hausa society as long as these new members spoke Hausa, were Muslims and otherwise followed Hausa customs.

Interestingly, when Yoruba conversion to Islam threatened Hausa ethnic distinctiveness in Ibadan, the Hausa discovered other religious means to differentiate themselves from the Yoruba (Cohen 1969: 185).

The result of the Hausa's distinguishing themselves ritually from Yoruba's Muslims was to end the danger of failing to maintain a separate ethnic identity. The ritual separation of Hausa Muslims from Yoruba Muslims retarded the growth of informal social interaction that the increase of Yoruba conversion to Islam and the consequent sharing of places of worship had entailed. Cohen (1969:185) observes that as Yoruba –Hausa interaction decreased interaction among Hausa increased. The need to maintain their separate ethnic identity is rather clear, for ethnicity presented the most efficient way available for the Hausa to achieve desired economic and political goals (Cohen 1969: 186-190).

The major point I wish to draw from Cohen's study is the fact that while being a Muslim is essential in Northern Nigeria to being a Hausa, being a Muslim is not co-extensive with being Hausa. When it is not, there may be danger to the preservation of Hausa distinctiveness; the Hausa find new means of accentuating differences. Interestingly, the Hausa of Ibadan pursue a traditional pattern by stressing the purity of their version of Islam *vis-à-vis* the Islam of those who surround them. This differentiation does not prevent the recruitment of members from other ethnic groups. It merely prevents the loss of the ethnic category "Hausa" by preserving its distinctiveness from other ethnic categories.

Conclusion and Implications for a Theory of Competitive Conversion

The relationship of religious change to ethnicity in competitive conversion situations has been a major theoretical concern of this paper. The evidence

leads me to conclude that the closer in status position a subordinate group
is to a dominate group, the more likely is religious change to lead the ethnic
change. In addition, when the major ethnic boundary marker between the
two groups is a religious one, a change in religious behavior on the part
of the subordinate group is likely to lead to ethnic identity change, supporting the contention that the first change occurs in the behavioral realm
(religious change) and in turn that change facilitates a social- psychological
one (identity change). However, a consonance of values, for example, high
prestige accorded behavior associated with the religion of the politically
dominate group, eases religions change. Not every group that converts to
the established religion, then, is likely to undergo an ethnic identity change
as the Yauri and Agwarra cases indicate. Members of groups occupying relatively low status positions are likely to convert to the established religion
in order to increase their opportunities to obtain access to political and
economic offices which the government controls. However, these converts
are more likely to undergo the ethnic change. If an outside religious agency
effective in enabling a subordinate group to resist pressure for conversion
is present, then it is likely to enlist converts wishing to preserve their ethnic
independence. The new religion is apt to become a symbol of resistance
and, thus, an ethnic boundary marker. It is more likely to be an effective
means of ethnic preservation if the proselytizing agents present it in a manner that emphasizes the consonance of its belief and value system with
those of the indigenous religion.

The Agwarra example illustrates a major corollary of this theory: When
the government does not pursue a strong policy of change, groups are free
to choose alternate means for promoting their interests, and those means
which best help to resist forced change will be chosen. Those means that do
not threaten their basic values will be chosen most readily.

The evidence is strong that the most self- sufficient groups are those who
are able to resist ethnic and religious change. These groups have the least
interaction with other ethnic groups, and they also are least involved in the
wider economy. In other words, thy neither grow products for trade nor are
they traders, teachers or civil servants. They live in areas where the government finds it difficult to maintain pressure. It seems reasonable to state the
following as a general rule: In an ethnically plural society, the greater an
ethnic group's interaction with other ethnic groups, the more vulnerable it
is to external pressure for change. If a government wishes to promote behavioral change, it can most easily do so by controlling the options open to
the group it wishes to change. An important means for doing so is religion.
This study suggests that the relationship between religion and ethnicity is
but an aspect of the more general relationship between symbol systems and
the maintenance of distinctive identities, ranked or not, as the Maguzawa
case illustrates. As such, it adds to anthropological understanding of the

uses groups may make of cultural symbols in articulating social relationships and signifying changes in them.

It is clear that ethnicity is a concrete representative of a more general category. It is a means for articulating identity in particular situations. When these special conditions are not available for structuring given interactions, other means for establishing identity will be used, as the Ibadan, Yoruba, Hausa and Igbo cases demonstrates (Cohen 1969; Salamone 1975 a and b). As ethnic group is a type of political action group. Ethnic boundary markers, like religion, are symbolic means for demonstrating allegiance to particular groups (Barth: 1969). Since Christians in Yauri do not undergo ethnic identity change, it would be a mistake to conclude that the meaning of conversion is conceptually different for Muslim and Christian converts. Both seek to added access to power through conversion and therefore become members of what Max Weber termed parties. In one case, that of Gungawa's becoming Muslims the change is more obvious because of the accompanying change in ethnic identity. However, in all cases of conversion in Yauri what is happening is that people seek to change their social class, status (rights and duties), and party (power group). In short, they seek to gain greater access to power as the Igbo materials most clearly demonstrate. A string implication of the data is that an ethnic group is conceptually really a sub-group of class, status and party. It is a means for structuring interaction among certain kinds of people and this is part of identity theory.

Although religious conversion is the stated goal of Dominican missionaries, material changes are the immediate results of their actions. These material advantages, however, are in reality quite fragile. Even a larger and more powerful Christian community would probably not be sufficient to save the Dominican mission. The government has shown that when it feels qualified to take over missionary enterprises such as schools or hospitals it will hesitate to nationalize Euro-American Christian missionary property. In a test of power, the Dominicans must lose. Furthermore, while a few Christians may benefit through their identification of Christians convert in Yauri. In sum, in competitive conversion situations, the overall advantage belongs to the group that offers the largest number of people the most secure access to power and its consequent benefits. How it does so and what power and its benefits consist of are existential questions empirically verifiable for each case.

9

Religion as Play—
Bori, a Friendly "Witchdoctor"

On play we may move below the level of the serious, as the child does; but we can also move" above it—in the realm of the beautiful and the sacred.

—Huizinga

Huizinga found it surprising that anthropologists had paid little attention to the interrelationship between play and religion. With very few exceptions that neglect seems to have persisted into the present. Analysis of reasons for that neglect would require a separate paper. However, the existence of that neglect is a fact that has retarded the development of a more complete qualitative understanding of the religious experience.

By insisting on the serious nature of religion while treating "play" as synonymous with "frivolous," scholars have failed to focus on an important aspect of the sacred, namely, its playful nature. The sacred, as Huizinga, following Plato, states, is supremely playful. Indeed, Levi-Strauss' identification of anomalous categories with the sacred is a case in point. Play soars beyond ordinary boundaries and creates a world in which extraordinary things are possible, where the unthinkable is thought and the forbidden is performed as a commonplace. Perhaps the difficulty inherent in treating the sacred and play as compatible categories lies in a basic misunderstanding of the nature of play. According to Huizinga the major characteristics of play are "order, tension, movement, change, solemnity, rhythm, rapture." These are the very characteristics of ritual play and, I would add, of religious belief as well. In a very real sense, religion is a game with clearly defined rules, a goal or objective, a "playing field," and a means for procedure. It does indeed take people outside themselves. In short, it is play.

In the following passage Huizinga summed up the point for what he termed "primitive" or "archaic" ritual and then immediately broadened it to include all religious rituals.

> Primitive, or let us say, archaic ritual is thus sacred play, indispensable for the well-being of the community, fecund of cosmic insight and social develop-ment but always play in the sense Plato gave to it—an action accomplishing itself outside and above the necessities and seriousness of everyday life.

This chapter attempts to apply Huizinga's insights to one case, that of the Gungawa of Yauri and Borgu Divisions in Nigeria's North Western and Kwara States., and by applying them to suggest extensions fruitful for cross-cultural investigations. The goal of the proposed suggested extensions are to present a hypothesis explaining at least part of the connection between play and re-ligion: the sacred and the profane are really two aspects of the same reality. It is not merely that they alternate with each other: that game, for example, may be held on the sacred field after rituals are performed. Rather, it is the inextricable union of the two in the same event that emphasizes the insepa-rability of the concepts. 'Whatever is sacred is also profane, and conversely, whatever is profane is also sacred. More strongly, each is what it is because of the presence of the other, not in spite of it. It is this paradox that is at root the cause of the play element so profoundly present in religion. It is play that allows one to approach the sacred while at the same time signaling its sacredness—its apartness, for as Douglas points out, "Whenever in the social situation, dominance is liable to be subverted, the joke is the natural and necessary expression, since the structure of the joke parallels the structure of the situation." This play quality of the scared, exemplified in ritual, may also be used by religious practitioners to communicate their approachability. This may be especially necessary in the case of part-time specialists who also engage in secular occupations, as is the case among the Gungawa.

Elsewhere I have described the Gungawa at length. Suffice it here to provide a brief summary. Until the completion of Kainji Dam in the late 1960s forced their resettlement, the Gungawa (island-dwellers) were a riverine people who practiced exploitative alternation of resources, shift-ing from onions to millet, guinea com and rice as the season and occasion warranted. Fishing supplemented their income and complex and friendly arrangements with the Serkawa (professional fishermen) preserved fishing boundaries.

Today the Gungawa find themselves on extremely poor farm land, land especially ill-suited for onion and rice cultivation. In addition, their move-ment from riverine positions and the other ecological changes consequent on the building of Kainji Dam have abrogated their agreements with the Serkawa, and the Serkawa have taken over the dried fish export trade once dominated by the Gungawa.

Faced with no real alternatives, Gungawa increasingly used a long established pattern of ethnic identity change and became Hausa. The procedure for doing so is well-known in Yauri. They became Muslims, spoke
only Hausa in public, swore of f the consumption of indigenous alcoholic
beverages, dressed in a Hausa manner and called themselves Hausa. Such
behavior gain them tangible and immediate benefits and was in keeping
with a traditional function of Gungawa identity, an identity that has served
to incorporate new groups into Yauri and Borgu societies while supplying
members to the ruling Hausa group.

One of the major characteristics of the Gungawa has been their pragmatism. They have quite openly borrowed cultural practices from other groups
in order to maximize their opportunities. This has gained them a consistent
reputation of hard-working industrious people, an evaluation shared by the
British, Dukawa, Hausa, Kamberi and members of other groups who have
come into contact with them. This pragmatism has been quite adaptive
in the multi-ethnic setting of Yauri and 'Borgu. It has facilitated Gungawa
interaction with each of the other groups in the area. One of the major
mechanisms for facilitating ethnic interaction has been the transethnic
importance of Gungawa religious practitioners particularly that of the man
whose title is Bori.

THE GUNGAWA'S IDEAL RELIGIOUS LEADER

Among Gungawa, real power is cloaked in modesty, for the naked display
of power is culturally condemned. As Harris pointed out, the truly powerful
official in a Gungawa village, the retired Balkari, takes a "semi-humorous"
title such as "Had Enough," "Resting," "Can Feed Myself." It is this man's
contention that he has finished with the exercise of power and will only
occasionally stoop to use it when his people prove too foolish to handle
their own affairs. For example, during an especially severe riot between two
villages resulting from a wrestling match the former Balkari appeared and
asked why an old man ready to die had to be called from his rest to settle
the affairs of children. His presence was sufficient to quell the riot immediately, and he quickly returned to his rest.

Those who possess power among the Gungawa are those who least appear to and who most deny their own influence. They tend to make the
least display of their power, to dress more simply than others and to live
more modestly than those who may appear to exercise power. Furthermore,
there is a palpably benign quality to those with real as opposed to apparent
political power among the Gungawa. What is true of political leadership is
a fortiori applicable to religious leadership. Each village has a priest (Wahunu), described in the following passage.

An important personage in the village life is the Wahunu, who, for want of a better description, may be termed the village priest. To Wahunu is entrusted the making of prayers and supplications at the communal shrine or shrines of the village. He does not, however, interfere in any way with the individual shrines of each household which have been inherited and are in the care of individual families. To Wahunu is entrusted the care of all the property sacred to the village shrine, and he himself may be distinguished by his staff of office with its rings of iron... Wahunu, although an important person in the village life, is, as befits the village priest, a benign personage, and his main interest is centered in the good health and people of the village.

The village priest (Wahunu) is primarily concerned with the spiritual life of people of one village. Harris implies quite correctly that the *Ubwa* (doctor) may be concerned with the needs of people of more than one village. Furthermore, he is a doctor, a healer, who works through visible things to cure diseases which are frequently "spiritual" as well as physical and no clear-cut distinction is made between religious and secular practitioners. In fact, the Gungawa and others in the area generally regard the *Ubwa* as more powerful than any other practitioner because he deals with both spiritual and physical cures. Among these *Ubwa* is one who is not only more powerful and famous than any other *Ubwa* but is, as I shall argue later, the chief priest of all Gungawa. Harris' description of the position and status of the *Ubwa* in general is an important one.

Boka (Hausa) or Ubwa is the village doctor, skilled in the use of herbs, and sometimes killed as a fortuneteller, not all the islands have an Ubwa, and consequently those who are practiced in the art of herbs sometimes travel far afield and have a considerable income.

The Boka, at the Island of Hella (whose title is Bori) is far-famed throughout Nigeria, and it is no unusual sight to see, in the cosmopolitan crowd in the market at Yelwa, natives of Abeokuta, Warri and the Southern Provinces, all of whom have come up for treatment by this Boka and his famous speaking tree. This tree, which is a baobab, is sacred to the Bori spirit Doguwa (Inna), and is said to give answers to the questions put to it by Bori.

Further evidence of the repute of Gungawa doctors is given in Gunn and Conant. After summarizing their description, I will describe the role of the man who was the Bori in 1972 and try to amend their description and Harris' where appropriate, for they fail to present an adequate description of the role of the Bori. Nor have they set that role in its proper theoretical perspective.

Medicine and its practitioners are held in high repute among Gungawa. People come great distances to receive care from their doctors. In addition to being famous for medical skill, Gungawa *are* considered especially skillful *bori* practitioners. In fact, as, Harris suggests, the most famous of these practitioners are doctors. The fact that the most famous of these doctors occupies the inherited position named *Bori* underlines the relationship.

There is some confusion among non-Gungawa, especially Hausa and European ethnographers, of the religion *(maigiro)* and magic *(tsaffi)*. Both in religion and magic *bori* (spirits) are used which are often termed *aljani* to fit them into an Islamic framework. 18 In fact, the use of the term *bori* leads some people to confuse the work of the doctor *(Ubwa)* with that of Hausa spirit possession specialists. Gungawa doctors do not cause spirits to possess anyone. They do talk to the bori on behalf of their clients and convey their responses. It is also important ton ate that they are not possessed by spirits and that the spirits do not speak through them. The client can hear the spirits as well as the doctor, although perhaps more faintly. The spirits do tend to speak in an oracular fashion, demanding interpretation.

The spirit most associated with Hella is *Doguwa* (Inna). In addition, the Bori of Hella has hereditary ties with the keeper of a very famous and important shrine to *Ubangba* (the strong) in the neighboring village of Mnuh. That shrine is currently under the care of the Bori's patrilateral uncle. The Bori thus, draws on the importance of his association with what is essentially a fertility shrine and his famous talking familiar spirit. The significance of this alliance or union of magic and religion in one person will be discussed below.

THE BORI OF HELLA

Hella is part of Yabo village (a governmental administrative village unit) in Gungu District, Yauri Division; North-Western State. In 1966 it had 104 adult males of Yabo's 380 adult males (ca. 1,520 people) while the whole of Gungu District had 2,691 adult males (ca. 10,764 people). Niger Dams Resettlement figures in the NDR archives at Yauri differed slightly from those of the various District Heads.

For example, their figure for Gungu District was 2691 adult males as opposed to the 3 l09 counted by District Heads. However, both agreed on the figure of l04 adult males for Hella. The allied village of Mnuh, also within Yabo, had either 39 or 56 adult males, depending on whose figures are correct. In appearance, size and every other aspect, Hella is typically Gungawa. In short, it is neither the largest nor the smallest of Gungawa villages. Its uniqueness lies in the fact that its *Ubwa* (doctor) is the Bori, of chief priest of all Gungawa, a fact not really recognized by Harris or Gunn and Conant.

Physically, the current Bori is not impressive, and he does all in his power to emphasize those aspects of his physique that remind his fellow Gungawa of a benign trickster. He is about fifty years old, short and slightly overweight, a characteristic he does all in his power to exaggerate through the manner in which he wears his clothes. These he wears carelessly draped over his body, so that his gown opens at his stomach. Whenever Bori: notices that anyone is looking, he protrudes his belly to draw an inevitable and predictable laugh. In reality, Bori still possesses a fine athletic build, a legacy from his youth when he was the champion wrestler of the Gungawa. His wrestling scars, the result of a badly healed shoulder break, are displayed as badges of honor.

In sum, Bori's manner is benign, and he enjoys playing the buffoon. For example, at an intravillage wrestling match at Mnuh, he came shouting and laughing from: Hella to greet me. Failing to pull me away to his own village, he left and then returned with a calabash of guinea com beer *(giya)*. He then began a mock wrestling match with another elder which quickly became a contest to see who could pull enough of the other's gown to expose, the most rump. None of the wresters showed any pique at having their scene so easily stolen by Bon.

Among resettled Gungawa, Bori is one of the few who still follow old occupations. He still goes on the river to fish. In addition, he weaves fishing traps and sells these to the Serkawa. Bori is saddened by the Islamization of the Gungawa and of his own village. In his village, for example, only four people are not Muslim—he, two of his ten sons, and one brother. However, he bears the Muslims no malice, for they did what they had to do.

He demonstrates that lack of malice in a very direct manner. In times of trouble all men, he says, come to Bori and he refuses no one—Christian, traditionalist, or Muslim. As he quite accurately observes, his fame extends from Sokoto to Ibadan and people of all ethnic groups *(kabila)* and religions *(addini)* come to him. If they have no money, he still cares for their needs. If they have no shelter, he provides it. If they are hungry, he feeds them. In fact, Bori is willing to share his fee with other practitioners as he demonstrated when he sent chickens to the Catholic mission station with the message, "We are both in the same business. You cure men's outsides. I cure their insides."

Bori's tolerance extends to issues of faith as well as those of practice. On a visit to the Catholic mission station he was impressed with the sanctuary lamp and began to talk to it, believing that Jesus must live there since his own spirit, Inna, lived in a tree near his home on old Hella. Bori reasons that Christians pray to Jesus because he is nearer to them than God. As he says, "I believe in Allah. But I do not pray to him. He is too far away, too distant. My spirits are close to me. They understand my needs." If Jesus lives at the mission station, Bori is willing to consult him for advice as well.

As mentioned above, his favorite spirit, Inna or Doguwa, still lives in the sacred baobab tree at old Hella, on the flooded island. He is bitter that the tree was not replanted at new Hella. However, Doguwa still comes to see him. Interestingly, all the other spirits visit him only on Sundays, for they have abandoned the old tree and moved elsewhere. Bori can summon these spirits whenever he so desires, for unlike the otiose god they are near him. Even if they are in America, he said, "They will come at my call in the twinkling of an eye."

Bori can summon his spirits at any time. His preferred place of communion with them is a two room hut *(daki).* In the first room there is a miniature statue of a Kamberi spirit with a bow and arrow and two hoes. It is similar to a number of statues found in traditional Gungawa villages. The second room is divided from the first by a curtain and has the famous talking pats. A Fulani spirit occupies the second room and signifies his presence through rattling the pots in response to Bori's summoning shaking of rattles and verbal calls. Before calling the spirits Bori prepares himself by draping a sacred cloth over his shoulders and kneeling forward.

People who are present at the ceremony hear the spirits answer him. A good deal of playful banter takes place in which the spirit questions the motives of those who have come to Bori. Invariably Bori assures the spirit that the client is a good person who means him no harm. He begs the spirit not to harm the supplicant and to be kindly disposed toward him. Finally, the spirit renders his decision. There is an air of playfull1ness in the proceedings which demonstrate his closeness to the spirits.

As Bori is close to the spirits, so, too are the people close to him. There is no fear of him despite his clear possession of great powers, and even though he can curse as well as bless. For example, he has an altar on which he sacrifices chickens. These chickens can be sacrificed to kill Fulani cows that trample the farms of Gungawa farmers. Thus, the sacrifices that cure illness can also kill. Despite this tremendous power, there is no. fear evident that he will misuse it. His playfulness is used to communicate help fullness, approachability, and benignness in order to allay fears of misuse of power among Gungawa. It is behavior grammatically consistent with the transmission of his intended message, "I help them all. I am more powerful than them all." His gentleness, then, is not weakness any more than the humorous appearance of the *bori* (spirits) signifies their weakness. Their large heads on small bodies bring smiles to the faces of children, but they also signify the intelligence and wit of the *bon,* who are very much like many of the other trickster gods of Nigeria. Furthermore, they are reminders of the importance of "using one's head" in problem solving.

It is also important to add that the Bori's playfullness is not shallowness, for through his playfullness he is able to express basic Gungawa values, and he is fully aware of that fact. He is also aware that he is left alone to practice his religion because Christians, Muslims, and traditionalists from many ethnic groups throughout Nigeria come to seek his help.

As he says, "Those who prefer to talk with god (Allah) have become Muslims." Perceptively, he adds that what they really wish to do is to become like Hausa so that the government will leave them alone. The government of Yauri had been noted for its religious tolerance. However, under the late Northern Premier, Ahmadu Bello, conversion pressure became almost unbearable. It was then that waves of *Mallamai* (Islamic teachers) were sent from village to village to seek conversions. He has nothing to gain from becoming a Muslim and nothing to lose by refusing to convert. In fact, his conversion would cast him great lass of status (rights and duties) and would also be dysfunctional far Yauri society. In other words, it is to everyone's benefit to preserve the position of the Bari.

In order to understand the significance of this fact it is necessary to go beyond Gunn and Conant's and Harris' accounts and realize that the Bori is not just an important doctor. He is also a priest. In fact, he is the hereditary chief priest of the Gungawa who presides at their annual religious harvest festival, the only festival at which representatives from all Gungawa villages attend, signifying the ethnic unity of the group while reinforcing it. His position is further strengthened in that he is assisted at this festival, held at the end of the rainy season, by the keeper of the sacred shrine at Mnuh, the shrine of Ubangba (the powerful one, Gunganci) or *Mutamin bisa* (the man upstairs, Hausa).

CONCLUSION

This brief case study of the Gungawa Bori suggests, that cross-cultural investigation of the interrelatedness of the nature of play and that of the sacred will be rewarding. Both assert the existence of new possibilities, of a new order of things. They suggest the existence of a reality behind visible or existential reality. The arbitrariness of the world is also exemplified in sacred play. Furthermore, the playful aspects of the sacred while not detracting from its grandeur do make it more approachable.

There is deep significance in Bori's statement that he never talks to Allah because he is too far away. He says he believes in him, but he is too distant to care for the everyday problems of people. Therefore, belief in an otiose god is relatively emotionless, bloodless, and rather abstract. Certainly it is not original to note that even in highly monotheistic systems people create intermediaries who are more real to them than a distant god. Innumerable examples abound in the literature regarding these "minor spirits," ranging from turning their statues to the wall to warning Jesus that if he does not grant a favor the applicant will tell his mother on him.

Whatever else they are, these intermediaries are playful creatures who aid people to approach the sacred through providing them with a sense

of greater control over it. Thus, play removes enough of the fear of the unknown to make the sacred work for society. Bori is an example of one who
is highly skilled in the grammar of playfulness as befits a societal interme-
diary with the sacred. In fact, Bori is himself a sacred person he occupies
(or because of his occupation of) an anomalous category. His playfulness
brings the scared close to the Gungawa, something quite in keeping with
their pragmatic ways.

Bori has even greater significance. While the ruling Hausa have put
greater pressure on the Gungawa to convert to Islam, they need to preserve
the position of the Bori for their own uses. What this fact entails is that
some Gungawa must remain traditionalists, for the Bori's role requires that
he be a priest as well as a doctor. In order to be a priest, he must have a
congregation. It is no accident that Mnuh, where the sacred shrine is located
has remained traditionalist, for Bori draws some of his status from his relationship to that shrine.

Finally, both play and the sacred suggest the game-like quality of sociocultural life. It is this intimation of the reality behind reality, pointing to the
arbitrariness of any given social structure and its generative culture that reinforces the feeling that life itself is play, following rules in a set-apart arena
for action. This perception lends power to the lived-in reality of a given socio-cultural system. Play and sacred ritual suggest the possibility of change,
for this very reason, that is that all existing arrangements of socio-cultural
variables are arbitrary and not really eternal. New games can be played
with different rules. In addition, both lend themselves to reinterpretation,
for both are made-up and ambiguous. It is this constant perception of their
double meaning that gives them so powerful a role in life, for it provides an
opportunity for the possibility of change under the guise of persistence. In
this, games, and play are kin to the joke, for it is in the nature of the joke to
be ambiguous or, better, to see the dual nature of reality and to comment
on it. It is, in fact, the double meaning inherent in the combination of the
sacred/profane (this world/other world) dichotomy that gives the sacred its
power and the combination is itself play. It was this that Plato refers to in
the passage which most succinctly recapitulates, this paper's theme: "Life
must be lived as play, playing certain games, making sacrifices, singing and
dancing, and then a man will be able to propitiate the gods, and defend
himself against his enemies, and win in the contest."

Frank Salamone with children in market.

Market at Yelwa town.

Frank Salamone taking notes in a village.

Women thrashing grain in village.

Man preparing to pray in a village.

Sule, my Hausa Huck Finn. Sule was knowledgeable, the son of a village head but a scamp who was out of place in his culture

Young girl on the edge of her village near a bicycle.

Women carrying grain to market.

Yakubu Hanci, a wrestling champ, and his family.

10

Hausa Islamic Practices

In understanding the religion of the Hausa, it is important to focus on their Islamic practices, especially the syncretistic nature of those practices. Given the landscape in which the Hausa exist, the Islam of many Hausa groups is syncretic. Faulkingham (1975) notes that the Muslim and "pagan" Hausa in the southern Niger village he studied believed in the same spirits. Both believed in the same origin myth for these spirits as well. According to the myth, Allah called Adama ("the woman") and Adamu ("the man") to Him and bade them to bring all their children. They hid some of their children. Allah asked them where their children were. They said that they had brought all their children to Him. He then told them that the hidden children would belong to the spirit world. Faulkingham states that these spirits explain everything; the primary efficacy belongs to spirits.

The Hausa, therefore, share in the common Nigerian practice of maintaining systems of belief with ancient roots in the area alongside the universal religions of Islam or Christianity. These beliefs combine belief in family spirits with relationships to the primordial spirits of a particular site, providing supernatural sanction to the relationship between claims on resources. Indigenous theology links dead ancestors to the spirits of place in a union that protects claims and relationships to the land. Spirits of place include trees, rock outcroppings, a river, snakes, and other animals and objects. Rituals and prayers dedicated to the spirits of family and place reinforce loyalty to communal virtues and the authority of the elders in defending ancient beliefs and practices. In return for these prayers and rituals, the spirits offer their adherents protection from misfortune, adjudication, and divination through seers, or shamans. Evil is appropriately punished, for shamans or diviners work with the spirits to ensure good and counteract evil.

The continuation of traditional religious rituals and beliefs among the Hausa is not incompatible with counting oneself as a Muslim, for among the Hausa, individual participation in Islam varies according to a number of variables, including wealth and power. The more wealth and power one has, the greater the strict adherence to Islam. Furthermore, traditional Hausa religion, which the Maguzawa ("pagan" or "traditional Hausa," who are considered "people of magic") continue to practice, attracts a number of Muslim Hausa at one time or another.

This religion is spirit-centered. Following Islamic Hausa hierarchical principles, the spirits form hierarchies of good and evil. Sacrificial offerings and spirit possession are prominent characteristics of the worship. This family-centered religion has a number of diviners who serve as curers. Moreover, the majority of Muslim Hausa, who participate in the spirit possession cult, or Bori cult, are women and members of the lower classes.

Jacqueline Nicolas (1967), for example, states that most members of the spirit possession cult are women and prostitutes. In other words, they are socially marginal people. Michael Onwuejeogwu (1969) argues that Bori cults have homogeneity of organization and meaning throughout Hausaland. Moreover, they are, in his opinion, vestiges of Habe religion. Faulkingham (1975) disagrees with these findings, noting that there is more diversity in Hausaland than Nicolas and Onwuejeogwu grant. Muslims and *arna* (pagan) believe in the same spirits but Muslims claim that they do not need to perform rituals to these spirits. In fact, however, many do perform them; depending on the occasion and additionally they consult the *bori* doctor for aid.

One finds the 'yan daudu in these marginal areas of religion. In this system, men who are more or less exclusively homosexuals (not always, but often transvestite or at least effeminate males) have sexual relationships with men not culturally distinguished from other men. These "men who talk like women" form a link between the old non-Muslim Hausa and the Muslim Hausa, indicating where stress lines still exist between the old and new Hausa identities, for the coming of Islam to West African societies necessitated a rethinking of numerous cultural and social arrangements, not least of which were the relationship between men and women and the organization of family life.

As noted, Muslim Hausa social organization is highly stratified. Not only is stratification based on occupation, wealth, birth, and patron-client ties. It is also based on seniority and gender, even within the family. The system is one also marked by patronage. Wealth and power confer great prestige on men, who form patron-client ties. The stress on power and dominance permeates society, except in its marginal area. One's status is also determined by the status of one's family, and within the family males, at least theoretically, are dominant.

Both traditional and Muslim Hausa form patrilineal ties. The Muslim Hausa build their ties on a patrilocal extended family that occupies a compound. The head is a male who directs cooperative activities are under the direction of a male head, and compound members cooperate in agriculture and share in its products. Occupational specialties are pursued on a more individual basis. There is a great deal of formal respect and prescribed avoidance behavior among Hausa. The *mai gida* (compound head) expects great deference. Women generally are secluded whenever finances allow.

The participation of women in the bori cult among the Muslim Hausa, however, is not necessarily a sign of their lack of power. Kabir (N.D.) states that the status of women in early Hausa society was high. In his words, they were "not confined." They interacted freely with men, marrying at a later age than is now common among the Muslim Hausa. They were able to own their own farms. They were also important members of the Bori cult. Furthermore, they had a significant role in domestic and clan religious rituals. Interestingly, some Hausa groups had matrilineal inheritance and it was not uncommon for elite women to be queens or titleholders. The famous warrior queen Amina was but one of many famous Hausa queens. The Hausa even had a title for women in charge of the bori, Bori Magadjiya.

Diviners, or shamans, foretell the future and deal with personal problems. They fit into the scheme of religious specialists, a scheme that includes priests and magicians. The boundary among the categories is a shifting one at best. Diviners continue to play an important part in determining the causes of luck, both good and bad fortune. This includes the nature and cause of disease. Among the Hausa it is necessary to point that many of the Muslim holy men are themselves types of diviners who make amulets, which include decoctions of the ink in which pious texts have been written. They also manipulate sand patterns or use the stars to tell the future.

Significantly, there is some discussion of males who attend Bori rituals as being homosexuals. The Bori rituals among the Hausa appear to be rituals of inversion, and among the Hausa homosexuality is considered an inversion of appropriate male heterosexuality. The Bori cult is widely understood as being a refuge from the strongly patriarchal ideal of Hausa Islam. Thus both women and effeminate males find some respite there. Although ranked low in official Hausa hierarchies, Hausa males are not only strongly attached to their mothers and sisters, they also have a fear of the mysterious power of women, a fear found in many male dominated societies.

Although the Bori cult may be a "survival" from pre-Islamic Hausa religion, it differs among the Muslim Hausa from that practiced among related peoples, such as the Gungawa, or among non-Muslim Hausa, such as the Maguzawa. It has a different meaning for these Hausa. Thus, when Besmer (1983) states that the spirit rides the possessed and that this is somehow a symbol of homosexuality, it does not mean that it has the same meaning for the Maguzawa, Gungawa, or other non-Muslim groups who have the Bori cult. Among the Muslim Hausa homosexual transvestites, or 'Yan Daudu, play a prominent role. Daudu, a praise name for any Malidoma, or ranked title, here specifically refers to the Prince, a bori spirit who is a handsome young man.

These Yan Daudu sell various foods at ceremonies, mainly luxury foods such as fried chicken, and serve as pimps for prostitutes. Women who attend Hausa Bori rituals are deemed to be prostitutes. Rene Pittin (1983) lists three activities for Yan Daudu: procuring, cooking, and prostitution. She argues that there is a close tie between prostitutes and Yan Daudu. Moreover, the Yan Daudu in combining male and female roles mediate between men and women, occupying an ambiguous category. Living among the prostitutes further provides a disguise for men seeking homosexual activity. Protection and discretion are provided through this arrangement.

The Bori cult provides a niche for marginal people of all kinds, not simply women or homosexuals. Butchers, night-soil workers, musicians, and poor farmers are welcome there. Mentally disturbed people of all classes similarly seek refuge among the Bori devotees.

HAUSA CONCEPTS OF MASCULINITY AND THE 'YAN DAUDU'

There has long been an argument between advocates of nature and nurture regarding the function each has had in shaping human behavior. Recently, socio-biologists like Chagnon (1997, 1988), Wilson (1975), and Fox (1997) have had particular influence in shaping the argument regarding the inherent, or biological, nature of masculinity. The significance of the cultural construction of masculinity and femininity and of gender roles in general has been relatively neglected in the elevation of biological theories in the social sciences and their employment to explain cultural issues. I am not denying the importance of biology, simply stressing the manner in which culture gives meaning to it in its social landscape. (For relevant works on sociobiology see Barkow, et. al., 1992 and Boyd and Richerson 1976, 1980, 1986, and 1994.)

Specifically, this chapter examines the manner in which the Hausa people of Nigeria define ideal masculinity. That definition has a role to play within the complex ethnic sociocultural framework of West Africa in which the Hausa operate. Much of what it is to be a Hausa, and, therefore shape Hausa interaction with their neighbors is inextricably bound within the Hausa concept of masculinity. Challenges to that concept, and reinforcements of it, come from men and "men who talk like women," the *'yan daudu.'*

Ideal masculine behavior and challenges to that behavior flow from a cultural definition of masculinity shaped to permit the Hausa to gain success as rulers and traders within their cultural landscape. Maintenance of ethnic identity vis-à-vis other groups is essential in structuring daily interaction in the West African landscape. This ethnic identity maintenance is particularly crucial at the borders of the area, where groups can and do switch ethnic identities to gain favorable positions. Therefore, although the Hausa are concerned with guarding their concept of masculinity throughout their territory, they are exceptionally careful in safeguarding their concept of the ideal masculine role at the borders where new recruits to the Hausa identity are made.

HAUSA WITHIN THE CONTEXT OF
WEST AFRICAN HISTORY: ETHNICITY AND GENDER

Gender relationships and concepts of masculinity must be understood within the context of Hausa history and ethnic relationships. The Hausa have been in the process of expansion for many centuries. Much of that expansion has been a peaceful one, based on their skill at statecraft and commerce. In turn, a great deal of their statecraft and commerce is built upon family relationships and negotiations. Patrilineal family ties are the strands that tie the web of relationships together.

A good deal of business is conducted with handshakes and one's word. To repeat, the system of markets, traders, and families binds together the various parts of the state and subsequently the state itself is bound to outside units. For example, village markets in rural areas meet periodically, on three or four day cycles. These markets are tied to those in larger settlements that have daily markets. In turn, the larger markets are bound to a still larger central market in the regional capital. Officials tied similarly to the central authority govern each of these markets.

Similarly, all Muslim Hausa social organization is stratified. Occupation, wealth, and patron-client relationships play a part in the system but birth is at its root. Family is a key factor, perhaps the key factor in the hierarchical ladder. Sons are expected to follow their father's occupation and his wishes. Society, in theory and ideally, is held together by filial loyalty. The patron-client relationship is patterned on the father-son relationship and loyalty to the Sultan and emirs, indeed to all officials, is that of family members to one's father.

Although less complex in social organization than Muslim Hausa, the Maguzawa are also organized along patrilineal lines. Their villages are composed of exogamous patrilineal kin. Both Muslim and "pagan" Hausa form their organizations around male figures. The Maguzawa, however, retain greater privileges for women freer to go out in public, usually exposing their breasts with no reproach. The Maguzawa do not hold to wife-seclusion in any circumstance. For the Muslim Hausa wife-seclusion is an ideal and put into practice by those who can afford it. It helps distinguish them from their neighbours and serves as an ethnic boundary marker. Moreover, patrilateral kinship provides the fulcrum on which marriage alliances are formed, with men generally seeking marriage with their patrilateral parallel cousins, further emphasizing the male tie.

Men serve as household heads and are responsible for agriculture, collecting activities, marketing, sewing, laundry, building repairs, and transportation. Women are responsible for cooking, house cleaning, childcare, and also follow craft specialties and carry on trade, often through young daughters. Women are expected to be modest and to stay within the household unless accompanied by male family members or older post-menopausal women.

Historically, the Hausa and Hausa-Fulani ruled over local tribes, appointing village heads. These local communities were held as fiefs to feudal lords. Again, this system emphasized male rule and a particular image of masculinity in which calmness and male solidarity were essential. The subject tribes often were not Muslim and their women were allowed greater freedoms. Therefore, control of Hausa women was essential in structuring ethnic relations and maintaining ethnic boundaries. Hausa position within the social structure and the cultural landscape determined gender relationships and cultural definitions.

British colonial rule, beginning in the early twentieth century, made changes in the general system. In general, however, the British system of indirect rule simply strengthened the central authority while pretending to rule through local rulers. The British relied heavily on their Hausa-Fulani allies to maintain control of Northern Nigeria. In Niger, the French made no pretext of indirect rule and simply centralized the system openly. The result was a greater emphasis on male rule as personified in the dual mandate of colonial and native authorities.

Finally, the Hausa became more identified with Islam under colonial rule. The British found it necessary to strengthen Muslim leaders who were their allies vis-à-vis "pagans" who sought to resist the imposition of colonial rule or Hausa hegemony. The British perpetrated the fiction that Northern Nigeria was mainly Islamic. The truth was different in 1900. Allegiance to the West African Fulani Islamic ethos of male dominance helped unite Hausa and distinguish them from surrounding "pagan" peoples such as the Gungawa, Kamberi, and others. (See Greenberg 1947, Michael Smith 1955, Salamone 1998. 1993, 1985 for various accounts of material in this section.)

11

Hausa Culture and Personality

Discussions of culture and personality in various societies frequently make use of theories of personality development which have originated in our own culture. Such a theory of possible psychological development has been developed by Erik Erikson to account for kinds of psychopathology which he feels can develop not only in our own society, but which he and his followers have applied to humans in all cultures. While it can be argued that even Western cultures like our own are not all identical even if we .restrict attention to Europe or the United States, the application of such a theory as Erikson's to *any* and every non-Western society is certainly open to critical questions, of the anthropologist interested in cross-cultural differences.

A controversy has arisen concerning the application of Erikson's ideas to certain West African cultures. Essentially the controversy has raged between followers of Erikson, on the one hand, and followers of Marvin K. Opler, on the other. Those who follow Erikson believe that all men develop psychologically in the same manner regardless of cultural and societal differences. Some of Erikson's followers would neglect the alternate meanings attached to similar practices by different cultures.

The danger of attaching too much importance to a few child rearing practices, in fact, has been aptly illustrated by Marvin K. Opler (1969, pp. 9-11). Opler discusses Erikson's contention that the Sioux Indians' roaming of the Plains, hostility and bravado are functions of stored-up frustrations stemming from the restrictions of the cradleboard, long nursing interrupted by the eruption of milk teeth, and the consequent thwarting by duly irritated mothers. However, the Ute Indians have similar child rearing practices, but the Ute's culture is distinct from the Sioux's at every point. Similar practices had different meanings and purposes in the Ute and Sioux societies.

It is just the symbolic realm beyond the person that many neo-Freudians, accustomed to looking for intrapsychic phenomena and pathology, fail to see. In fact, it would probably be tempting for disciples of Erikson to interpret Hausa culture and personality in terms of mother g neglect and family rejection and see this as the basis for mistrust. The poor, twisted meek distrustful, "typical" Hausa to emerge from such a picture would bear little resemblance to the reality. If one focuses only on the nuclear family and neglects cultural societal and historical factors, one will never begin to comprehend the complexities of Hausa culture and personality.

Therefore, we contend along with Marvin K. Opler that child rearing while, important is not a *primum mobile*. Child rearing must be seen in the wider context of enculturation from which it derives its importance. The dominant influence proceeds from culture and society to the individual, rather than from, the family to the individual. The family, we believe, is shaped by the needs of the culture rather than the other way around. Following Marvin K. Opler (1969) and Abram Kardiner (1961) we believe that each culture has developed from a series of adaptive processes to meet physiological and psychological needs. A culture can exist only so long as it is felt to meet certain important needs by its members (Kardiner and Preble, 1963, p. 214). To say this is not to maintain that such a society is "better" or "more progressive" than others. It does mean that people feel that it is important, and, therefore, will try to keep it functioning. One way of preserving a culture is to establish institutions that will socialize individuals and encourage them to develop in ways favorable to the society.

It is the author's purpose to examine the above theories in relationship to one society, the Hausa of Northern Nigeria, an extremely complex people. In a chapter called "Pluralism in Pre-colonial African Societies", M. G. Smith (1969, p. 14) discusses the differences in historical development among the various emirates in Hausaland, essentially the Northern Region of Nigeria. Such divergent developments have resulted in vast differences in the life styles of the people of the emirates. So much is this true that facile generalizations about "the Hausa" are to be regarded with definite suspicion. Indeed, the very term "Hausa" has many possible meanings. In its most comprehensive application it refers to. anyone who speaks the Hausa language, a *lingua franca* in Northern Nigeria, Chad, Mali, Niger and parts of other West African states.

In its narrower applications it can mean only those speakers of Hausa who are Muslims. But even here one must be careful, for such a definition includes Fulani who conquered much of Northern Nigeria in the holy war (jihad) of Usman dan Fodio of 1804 and following, and other ethnically diverse people while it excludes the Maguzawa, pagan Hausa who ethnically are kin to the original Hausa rulers. The difficulties do not end there. For example, in Kano dissident Hausa helped the Fulani overthrow the established regime. There. Hausa were called "Hausawa" by the Fulani to distinguish them sharply from the "Habe", the Hausa who did not cooperate with the *jihad*. The term "Habe" means "slave" or "serf" and was applied to many Hausa even though these people were Muslims. In many Hausa emirates, Habe were not allowed any rights or any share in the government because the Fulani did not consider them true Muslims. However, at Zaria, Habe and Fulani have become increasingly assimilated and have worked together fairly smoothly.

The point of the above is that one must be careful in writing about the influence of culture on personality to be sure that one is describing the right culture and its proper setting. For example, one cannot describe a Fulani practice and attribute it to all Hausa. It is the author's-contention that Hausa culture is a very complex one, and, therefore, one must be extremely careful in discussing the interaction between Hausa culture and Hausas. It is our further contention that Hausa culture uses strong supportive measures throughout a person's life to aid him in meeting the expectations of Hausa society. In short, we are arguing against a too facile application of Erik Erikson's ideas to any non-Western culture. Unlike some of those who follow Erikson, we believe that a given practice does not have to lead necessarily to a given result in all societies. Each practice must be understood in its interpersonal societal setting. Therefore throughout this paper the author has limited his generalizations to particular Hausa and to point out differences between Hausa and Fulani. References are made to some Yoruba practices which are similar to Hausa practices in order to emphasize the fact that similar practices can be found in different societies utilized for various purposes.

Perhaps, a few words on Islam as practiced in Northern Nigeria will illustrate my point. Since M. G. Smith has called the coming of Islam one of the more important events in Hausa history and since the Fulani fought a *jihad* against the Habe in the early nineteenth century because of the supposed lack of purity in the Habe practice of Islam, it seems relevant to view Islam in Hausaland first (Smith. 1960. p. 3). As pointed out above many Hausa the Maguzawa, are not Muslim. In fact, the Maguzawa have resisted Islam since 1456. Further it is noteworthy that at the time of the Fulani jihad of 1804 most Hausa were not Muslim. It is true that the Habe rulers were Muslim but to be Muslim was highly profitable for these men especially after the fall of Timbuktu and the consequent rise in the commercial importance of the trans-Saharan routes from Egypt and Tripoli to the Hausa states (Greenberg 1946, p.3). In brief, the Habe were not especially sincere Muslims who felt a need to lose themselves in one of the higher religions in atonement for horrible sins.

As Greenberg (1946) has pointed out so well actual contact between the residents of Kano (Kanawa) and Muslims from North Africa was brief.

Literature rather than people was the main acculturative element. It was through playing a key role as mallams (Muslim teachers) that the Fulani gained a strong foothold in Hausa society. The Fulani reconciled Islamic and pagan beliefs by comfortably fitting Islamic beliefs into the ideational system of the Habe. For example the Muslim jinn {spirits) were identified, with the *iskoki* (spirits) of the Maguzawa. Nowhere else in the Muslim world are *jinn* so personalized as to be given names (Greenberg, 1946. p.10). The point is that the acceptance of Islam by the Habe was not done out of great religious conviction. Neither was it the result of a lack of confidence in the traditional religious system. The acceptance of Islam was a logical move on the part of a people trained from birth to accept opportunity and to feel free to move about in a society wider than the nuclear family of father mother and children.

It is in this light that one must view practices surrounding birth and parent-child relationships. No Hausa adult is regarded as an adult until he becomes a parent. Therefore, parenthood is an important stage in the development of a person's life marking the passage youth to adulthood. As such, it is marked by important ceremonies. It is in this light that the ritual purification of Hausa mothers is to be viewed. To conclude from such practices, common in Hebraic and Islamic societies, that motherhood is not desired or that sex is regarded as vile would be to misinterpret grossly the significance of the purification rituals. The cleansing is ritual and not really hygienic. This should be illustrated rather clearly by the substitution of cold water or herbs for the prescribed boiling hot water. Furthermore a woman's status is determined not by her husband's status but by the number of children she has. Therefore, each childbirth is a *rite de passage* for her and as such each is marked by a special ritual. It is not surprising that the first childbirth is most ritualized while consequent ones are less so (Smith. 1954 p.20).

Indeed far from being the rather puritanical occasion it might seem, Hausa childbirth in contradistinction to Fulani childbirth is rather comfortable for the mother. She stays in her husband's compound and is surrounded by her female relatives and. if possible her female childhood companions (*Kawaye*). She and her child are cared for by them. Therefore, her days of recovery are ones of complete rest. The child has the complete attention of his grandparents' for the first few days of his life (Smith. 1954, pp. 26, 126, 144). Far from suffering from a lack of affection, the baby is surrounded with love from his birth. The point is that he receives this love from a number of sources other than his parents, for in later life he must come to regard his family as being composed of more than the nuclear family.

Too much can be made of the mother's not feeding the child for the first' three days of his life. As Opler (1969) has pointed out what matters in child

I rearing is that a child be given affection in a societally approved way not necessarily that it be given by his parents. Further, the mother refuses to breast feed the child for only three days, the period when modern science recognizes her milk to be of poor quality. The Hausa child is fed, is loved, and is cared for by people. He is fed a watered-down version of guinea corn (dawa) porridge, and he is given water to drink. Modern science has discovered that nursing mothers: often must supplement their child's diet for the first few days because of the poor quality of their milk. Keeping the child from the mother not only emphasizes their different statuses, an important function in the highly stratified Hausa society, but it allows the mother to recuperate from childbirth. Indeed, to believe that a child must crave immediately for one particular breast, his mother's, is to be guilty of the most romantic of fallacies regarding inherent mother instincts. A child does need love and care, and the Hausa child receives an abundance of both. His grandparents shower him with extreme tenderness soon after birth. In fact, he often, to his chagrin receives his life-long nickname at this time from his grandparents (Smith, 1954. p.l44).

It is true that there is a lifelong avoidance relationship between parents and children. This relationship is more rigid among Fulani than among Hausa, but it does exist among Hausa. However, the Hausa tend to limit the avoidance to first born children and lessen the avoidance among succeeding children till the last born are not publicly avoided at all. The *dan faxi* (avoidance) relationship must be viewed in the wider context of Hausa society. If one does this, one sees that the "shame avoidance" relationship tends to reduce tension in a society. This tension-reducing quality is extremely necessary in a highly stratified society such as that of the Hausa (Smith, 1955, p.4S). A Hausa, in theory, must give; obedience to his superiors, but no superior of intelligence will demand too much of any Hausa. Indeed, one reason Habe despises Fulani is the Fulani refusal to understand this (Smith, 1954, p.272). One reason for the Hausa's attitude toward authority is that avoidance relations help him increase his circle of friends and regard his people as consisting of more than the members of his mother's compound. One result of this attitude is that the Hausa can always leave the scene whenever the pressure gets too great or authority demands too much. Dry, who wrongly argues that the Hausa contract few strong emotional attachments, contradicts himself when he writes correctly, "With this widespread security it is easy for any member of the society faced with a difficult situation to solve his problems simply by going away from them. This running away from any situation of strain is the normal pattern, and the consequent easing of tensions before they become internalized results in an extremely low incidence of neurosis" (1956, p.170).

However, one note of caution must be inserted. To infer from the above data that Hausa society is peaceful and that Hausa will unite against outside enemies is false. Historically, the traditional Hausa states have warred against each other, and one reason for the success of the Fulani *jihad* was what Keith Otterbein has labeled internal warfare, warfare among groups sharing the same culture. As mentioned above, some Hausa cooperated with the Fulani against their own people. It must also be noted that the Hausa, often depicted as groveling traders, were in the process of driving out the Fulani when the British intervened (Smith, 1960 and 1969).

Having said the above and having issued some warnings, we want to return to parent-child relations briefly. While it is true that avoidance relations have generally accomplished their purpose, teaching Hausa to rely on a wide range of support, it does not follow that parent-child relations are cold. In public there may be avoidance between mother and child, but in private no one has to urge her to fondle and caress her baby (Smith, 1954, p.l44). Although the child is chided publicly and told that he is a disgrace to the family, such scolding is ritually sanctioned and tends to act as a liberating element for youth by giving them common grievances against their parents and forcing them to be on their own, or at least to feel that they are on their own.

Similarly, what is erroneously called in the literature "adoption" serves the purpose of extending the boundaries of a Hausa's relationships. A child is "adopted" by people, usually his grandparents, who have a deep emotional attachment for him. The "adoption" is by no means necessarily permanent or even mandatory. It is an act of filial piety, and it is usually pleasant for all concerned. Granted that such a relationship usually takes place at the age of two or three when a child is weaned, in fact it is often part of the weaning process. Granted also is that at such a time sexual relations are legitimately resumed between parents. What we will not grant is that this separation causes great sexual guilt in the Hausa. To rid oneself of that illusion one simply has to read about *Tsaranci* practices in Hassan and Shaibu (1952, pp. 58, 68) or elsewhere. *Tsaranci* is similar to petting except that it is socially sanctioned and traditionally did not lead to sexual intercourse. Each adolescent had a *Tsaranci* partner often chosen by one's parents. One never married his *Tsaranci* partner. The purpose of the *Tsaranci* institution was to familiarize one with anatomy and sexually stimulating Procedures before marriage so the marital awkwardness would not 'occur. Further, *Tsaranci* served to work off sexual drives in a fear-free, guilt-free atmosphere that fostered healthy sexual attitudes. Consequently, the Hausa have very few sexual problems or inhibitions. To explain the high 'rate of divorce among Hausa one does not have to go 'back to child rearing practices such as child avoidance or sudden weaning. The Yoruba do not have child avoidance relationships, but they do have sudden weaning. But in both societies the easiest explanation for traditionally high divorce rates is the easy access women have to the market and in their ability to compete freely with men (Dry, 1956, p.160).

   Such a fact has greater relevance in explaining the high divorce rates than does the patrilineality of the Yoruba or the bilaterality of the Hausa. If men are distrustful of their women in either society, there is a real economic reason to be so. It is impossible in a chapter to discuss many aspects of Hausa culture and personality which are greatly intriguing; for example, the Hausa theory of mental illness which holds that all mental illness is the result of spirit possession (Greenberg 1946, pp. 30 ff). Further, the role of bori (spirit) possession and the various types of deviancy tolerated and not have had to be largely ignored. What has been discussed has been done in order to illustrate the relationship between culture and personality among the Hausa in the light of Marvin K. Opler's ideas. It has been agreed that culture has influenced child rearing patterns and not *vice versa*. Two relationships, ritual cleansing after childbirth and parent-child "shame avoidance" were discussed in the larger context of Hausa culture. The brief discussion of Hausa Islamic practice was intended to distinguish it from the more rigid Fulani version. It has been argued that the Hausa child undergoes a socialization process that relies heavily on supportive measures to mold the child for his role in a highly stratified society. That society provides many outlets for the release of tension, including flight and, homosexuality. In a future paper, the author hopes to discuss the epidemiology of Hausa mental illness.

   The Hausa child is a child of his society more than of his nuclear family. To apply Erikson's methods uncritically to Hausa society would be to miss that rather obvious fact. Rather than seeing "shame avoidance" relations as functional within a society an Eriksonian anthropologist might be tempted to see them as intrapsychically damaging. Using Opler's insights one can see the Hausa child as material from which an adult can be fashioned. The society provides supportive measures all along the way in order to facilitate that fashioning. As we have tried to show in the paper, one must regard not only a child rearing practice as important but the function of that practice and its meaning within the wider framework of the society.

   "While not a *primum mobile*, then, child rearing may be viewed as social, as self, and as sexual identification-dependent upon the cultural conditions of existence that weigh so heavily on the adults, and hence children of the world" (Opler 1969, p.36).

12

Erikson in Nigeria: Exploring the Universality of the Theory of Psychosocial Development

with Virginia Salamone

Biology is destiny (Sigmund Freud)

Personality, too, is destiny (Erik H. Erikson)

I (F. Salamone 1969-70) have taken issue with the universality of the psychosocial crisis "trust versus mistrust" that Erikson (1950) posits for infancy, his first stage of development. In so doing, he indicated that separation from parents at an early age among the Hausa of Nigeria was a common practice that did not lead to a mistrust of the social environment but rather led to a generalized trust of an environment broader than the immediate nuclear family. This attitude of generalized trust is encapsulated within a Hausa value that enfolds developmentally as a theme within Hausa culture. Examination of this value, named *kirki*, through a developmental perspective enables those interested in, the study of a culture's ethos to include a dynamic element to its study. Simultaneously, a developmental perspective grounded in Hausa sociocultural reality bares the relational and situational nature of cultural values as they become nodal points in the elaboration of cultural themes. Additionally, Gilligan's (1977, 1982) legitimate concerns regarding gender bias in much developmental work are addressed through an approach which traces a core cultural value, *kirki*, through an emically derived life cycle for males and females. Simply, at each stage of their life cycles males and females express *kirki* in an age and gender appropriate manner.

One of the authors (V. Salamone) began significant preliminary explorations of this theme in an earlier publication. In that publication she traced emically derived meanings for *kirki* from a developmental perspective over the Hausa lifespan. As she notes:

> *Kirki* defies literal translation into English. Jerome Barkow (1974) identifies "gentleness" as a likely synonym. Description and interpretation of *kirki* in the ethnographic literature focuses upon its contribution in structuring male interaction. That *kirki* appears to be a characteristic solely operating in male interaction is more likely a consequence of men conducting the research using male informants than the absence of *kirki* in the lives of Hausa women. With few exceptions, Mary Smith's "Baba of Karo," ethnographic data on *kirki* have been collected by men who explore this predominantly Muslim culture through the actions and perceptions of its male members.

Kirki provides the Hausa with an. essential element for their social mask. It is essential to their economic activity which benefits from the ability to move among and identify with a vast number of potential customers. *Kirki* woven into the individual's social mask does not have one ideal manifestation but rather presents itself in a range of acceptable forms. Ultimately, the purpose is to smooth the way for 'friction free, open-door relations (1991: 116).

Since "Baba of Karo" there have been other studies of Hausa women, notably the papers in Coles and Mack (1991), Barkow (1971, 1972), Coles (1990, *1983a, 1983b*), Mack (1990), Pellow (1977, 1985, 1987, 1988), Pittin (1979, 1983, *1984a, 1984b*, 1987), F. Salamone *(1986b)*, and Schildkrout (1978, 1982, 1983, 1986, 1988) among others. In spite of the ethnographic and theoretical richness of these works, nonetheless, it is perplexing to note that no development or application of the Hausa value of *kirki* to women's life is made in any of these works, in spite of Gilligan's (1977, 1982) clarion call to revise androcentric "global" theoretical constructs, specifically those relating to moral cognitive development.

This study, accordingly, seeks to return to an earlier theoretical concern with the applicability of Erikson's developmental schema. That concern has been augmented and refined to include gender issues, the role of a specific value (the Hausa *kirki)* in fostering moral and identity development, and the applicability of Kohlberg's theory of moral development in a Hausa case including males and females. In the conclusion, the authors address specific concerns of Gilligan regarding androcentric bias in developmental theories and assess what value in general developmental theories may retain in aiding comprehension of cross-cultural development.

KIRKI AND EGO DEVELOPMENT

Each culture provides a concept around which people can shape and judge their identities, for the Hausa *kirki* is that concept, providing what Morris

Opler (1946) labeled a "theme." Black (1973: 519) views these themes "as underlying forces affecting cultural phenomena, on a diffuse macro level." These themes do not impose uniformity on behavior but allow for variations around a theme. They establish guides for behavior. The actual behavior, nevertheless, occurs in real situations. Therefore, the values are relational and identity emerges from the fit between a general cultural theme, such as *kirki, and* existential reality.

Specifically, the Hausa inquire whether a person's behavior, accounting for age, gender, socioeconomic status, family position, time, place, the sociocultural factors of others engaged in the behavior, and audience is behavior worthy of a person displaying *kirki*. If so, they will further calibrate and determine to what extent it possesses *kirki* and in what manner it falls short of it. Clearly, *kirki* is not an absolute value. Rather its expression is relational, depending on a number of emically evaluated factors in Hausa life. Among those factors are many pertaining to the Hausa concept of the lifespan (V. Salamone 1991).

The Hausa have four stages in contrast with the eight Erikson delineated. Moreover, they distinguish each stage according to gender, explicitly recognizing a dichotomy between male and female development. Moreover, as we demonstrate further in the article, the Hausa acknowledge the cultural complementarity of these differences. Men and women inhabit different worlds but these worlds depend on each other and cannot exist in isolation.

In addition, without *kirki* the Hausa cannot continue to exist, for *kirki* is an ethnic boundary marker setting them apart from neighboring peoples. This fact emerges clearly from Abdullahi, an educated Hausa trader who shared his reflections during his long trading stopover within Ibadan, a predominantly Yoruba city. Re interprets *kirki* as a behavior crucial to Hausa identity, a behavior that Hausa believe is distinctive to themselves and would not be evident in other groups. For example, Abdullahi states emphatically that "Yoruba do not have *kirki.*"

Kirki, therefore, appears to serve a dual identity function within Hausa culture; namely, it distinguishes 'Hausa from "others" and it defines for Hausa members just what it is to be and behave as Hausa should. More specifically, it communicates Hausa identity to out-group members while thematically defining age, gender, and sociocultural status appropriate Hausaness to the in-group. Thus, although it meets Morris Opler's general criteria for a "theme"—it is an underlying force that contributes diffusely to the development of macro level cultural phenomena—it is not an "unconscious" or even out of awareness phenomenon. There is nothing repressed about it nor is it operating at a hidden or unexamined level. Hausa, as is evident in many interviews including that with Abdullahi, recognize the word and are able to discuss it articulately.

There is, as we have said, an appropriate *kirki* for each stage and station in life. Abdullahi explains that *yaran kirki* (*kirki* for young children), those who are *karamin yaro* (a little boy) or *jariri* (little girls), consists of the following:

The child who possesses *kirki* is quiet and does not cry. It just looks at things and doesn't touch them. Parents judge who has the best *kirki*. The child with *kirki* does not abuse elders and other kids. We call such a child *yaran kirki* (Abdullahi 1990).

It does not appear that at this stage there is much difference between males and females. Although girls are supposed to be a bit quieter and even at such a young age should begin to defer to their brothers. There is a converse to *kirki* which the Hausa term *banza*. The *banza* (worthless) child cries for no reason. This is a sign that he'll be *mutamin banza* (a worthless man). He will be beating other kids, causing trouble (Abdullahi 1990).

A young girl who is *banza* will refuse to help in the home, not defer publicly to men and "act like a young boy." Starkly, then, *banza* is the diametrical opposite of *kirki*, and the fear exists that a movement away from *kirki* is a movement to its opposite, non-Hausaness. The message is obvious. To be a non-Hausa, clearly, is to be worthless.

The manner in which Hausa attempt to correct children who do not possess *kirki* demonstrates their belief that *kirki* results from some sort of nature-nurture interaction. Note that Hausa parents examine their children's behavior in order to evaluate their portion of *kirki*. Regard further that there is a perception on their part that at least some portion of *kirki* is innate. "Parents judge," Abdullahi states, "who has the best *kirki*." However, if a child displays little or even no *kirki*, parents seek to instill some measure of it, thereby demonstrating their belief that at least a child can learn behavior appropriate to *kirki*.

Hausa parents first attempt to correct *banza* behavior and instill *kirki* behavior through guidance and attention. Since one meaning of *kirki* is "gentleness" or, perhaps better, "consideration," it is logical that the Hausa do not approve of violence in child raising. It is also logical that this guidance and attention stretches beyond the nuclear or even extended family to the most relevant wider community concerned with the child's behavior. As one of the author's wrote regarding Hausa childrearing patterns some time ago he has seen as still applicable after seven field trips, "The Hausa child is a child of his [or her] society more than of his nuclear family . . . one must regard not only a child rearing practice as important but the function of that practice and its meaning with the wider framework of the society" (F. Salamone 1969-70: 44).

Along with guidance and attention, themselves two basic elements of *kirki*, parents employ other means to move a child closer to *kirki*. They employ proverbs as being gentler than direct confrontation, something itself contradictory *tokirki*. The Hausa prefer the indirect method and the go-between. In grandparents they have the perfect intermediaries. Hausa children enjoy a joking relationship with their grandparents, affording them the greatest latitude of speech and behavior (Salamone *1985a*). They know that they can count on their grandparents for guidance and love no matter what others may feel toward them. Consequently, when their grandparents chastise them the message is doubly clear; namely, that their behavior is inappropriate and requires correction.

Family meetings regarding youngsters who continue to prove difficult follow other measures. These meetings seek to bring the weight of the relatives to bear, appealing to the youngster to "have sense" and consider the shame he or she is bringing on the family. Since Hausa value freely-given deference in contrast with coerced obedience, they are loath to resort to force to command obedience from their children (see Salamone 1969-70: 42, and M. F. Smith 1954). In addition, although they have not yet matched the Fulani in their ability to mask their innermost emotions, they do provide a generally self-composed, dignified, and genial mask to the world. Therefore, to employ violence to force what should be given freely is to lose face and increase personal shame.

At that point even the patient Hausa may admit that the child is simply incorrigible—a "bad seed." As Abdullahi insists, "Some people are just born bad. They have no sense and will not listen. What can *you* do? Even God won't *force* them!" He states it in a manner that clearly indicates both his bewilderment that some people are incapable of understanding something so obvious and his disgust at that failure. It was a gesture I had noted many times in Northern Nigeria and had watched closely. An elderly man who cooked *for* me, coming out of retirement in his pity at my incompetence, took two young boys in hand and often corrected them in the same fashion, shaking his head and murmuring *"banza"* at them. When their behavior especially aroused him, he would mutter *"shega"* (bastard) at them. Never did he hit them nor raise his voice. The scene was touching, amusing—and effective.

A young man *(saurayi)* is expected to be gentle and courteous. To learn how to be unfailingly so, he accompanies his father and assists him with whatever he does. The Hausa, in common with many other African groups, apply an imitation theory of learning in which a child learns through watching and imitating a skilled adult. (See Fortes 1938 *for* a detailed example of imitation at work among the Talensi of Ghana, and Gearing 1973: 1229-1232 for a lucid discussion of the implications and importance of his study. In this example, he also identifies identification and cooperation as key elements in learning recognized by the Talle.)

A young man follows his father to town. They work together. He cuts wood for fire and food. He brings it home from the farm. He puts it on the donkey. If your father has money, you'll be educated or sent for training in some craft. If not, your father will train you in his handiwork—shoes, clothes. Whatever we're making it in our own culture (Abdullahi 1990).

Abdullahi, himself, is a product of that system. He followed his father into the long-distance trading business, shuttling between Kano and Ibadan. There are strands of relatives along the route and into side areas, controlling each aspect of the movement and transaction of goods that seemingly appear so mysteriously. In common with other *saurayi*, he was expected to be gentle, courteous, and hardworking. Once a *saurayi* learns his trade, he is to work for ten or fifteen years in order to save enough money for marriage. Not surprisingly, rich men marry at a younger age than poor men and the kinds of marriage available to them are greater.

The literature agrees that women marry soon after menstruation. Menarche is a sign that they are ready for marriage since they can bear children. What Echard (1991: 210) reports for Adar in Niger is reasonably comparable with Hausa elsewhere. She states: "Accordingly, women first married between ten and twelve years of age and in any case, before the age of fifteen—subsequently change husbands, and therefore houses and association with patrilineage, several times before reaching menopause." In contrast, a man's first marriage, according to Echard (1991: 210), takes place no earlier than twenty and, more likely, closer to twenty-five. Even young men, therefore, are appreciably older than their first wives.

Those men whose first marriage is nearer age twenty than twenty-five are almost invariably wealthy. The wealthy can afford to dispense with his bride's dowry, even giving her family money for her dowry *(kayan daki)* if necessary to retain their pride and her financial independence. Although even a poor man may "want" a particular woman enough to waive her dowry overlooking its absence, people mention such an act as terribly romantic and, therefore, rare. For typical Hausa, dowry is part of marriage. A dowry *must* consist of items in' units of six: six bags of rice, six bags of millet, six different fabrics in a gown, and so on in a similar fashion. In an important sense, then, a *saurayi's kirki* is to prepare himself for marriage and the full assumption of adult responsibilities. No less important is a *budurawa's* preparation for marriage. Her *kirki* parallels that of a man's. Specifically, she also "follows" her mother and learns from her how a proper Hausa woman is to act. She learns to select material, make cloth, cook, clean dishes, and the thousand tiny details that a woman must master to be an *uwar gida* (mother, literally "mother, of the house").

One of the *budurawa's* major tasks is to fetch water. In an arid land, water encapsulates a nexus of meanings and relationships. It is the *budurawa's* responsibility to master these meanings and maneuver easily through the intricate paths of social relationships. Neighbors play a major role in these relationships, symbolized through the regular borrowing of water from each other. Women rely on each other for aid in coping with the inescapable vicissitudes of their lives. Echard (1991: 210) provides a strong indication of the nature of these vicissitudes: They are transients who; deprived of all access to a status based on a relationship to production and all rights to their descendants, are clearly limited to tasks of biological and social reproduction. Recent changes whether of a cultural or economic nature (such as the spectacular growth of Islam or the development of the market economy) have only accentuated male domination through the suppression of certain practices and the development of others which, until recently, remained marginal (most notably, marriage with seclusion)."

A young girl, beginning at age five or six during the period termed *jariri* and continuing through the period labeled *budurawa* may aid her mother through selling kola nuts, oranges, cakes of various kinds, lunches or otherwise engage in "penny capitalism" (Schildkrout 1980 and 1981). Such work, of course, not only serves to provide economic security for her mother but also to enable her to expand her cognitive map of sociocultural reality. Truly, she has an opportunity to observe, imitate, and identify with a wide range of social life, moving more freely at this period, before her first marriage, than she most likely ever will in her life again.

Interestingly, although Hausa state that both males and females reach the age of reason at the same time—about five or six—they mention corporal punishment as a viable option for correcting misbehavior only when mentioning correcting females. Guidance, of course, is still an option and it is not to be assumed that young girls are physically abused. Indeed, it is safe to declare that mothers rather than fathers would routinely "spank" their daughters. However, wife abuse unfortunately is not rare and the evidence is that it is growing (F. Salamone 1974, 1976; Echard 1991).

Since divorce has traditionally been common in Hausa society and marriage for life rare, relations between husband and wife tend to be formal and their lives complementary but somewhat separate. Men are expected to provide a house, work diligently, and care for the children materially and spiritually through providing counsel. .A man is expected to be quiet and hardworking. His children come to him for advice. He does what he sets out to do. He is kind to his wife and provides for her as he should (Abdullahi 1990).

Somewhat resignedly, Abdullahi asserts that first marriages tend to end in divorce. Nonetheless, the husband is expected to seek help in preserving the marriage. If there is trouble, and the expectation is that there will be, he will approach her family. The wife's family will take her back and talk to her. After three or four days, she will return. If she still "disobeys," her husband will divorce her. Often, that may be exactly what the woman desires, for women are not totally helpless dupes. Women, at the least, have the power to embarrass their husbands and to manipulate reality to do so (F.

Salamone *1986a, 1986b*, 1976; Sanday 1981; Rogers 1975; Gilmore 1990).
Aware of that fact, husbands generally find it easier to grant wives a divorce
rather than live with a woman who wishes to depart.

The entire adult period of life is termed *ango* for men and *amarya* for
women. It is the period in which people are at the peak of their powers,
dealing with everyday problems, continuing and preserving the culture
while preparing for its future. In actuality, however, Hausa allow for many
differences in the way in which people live through these periods. Women,
for example, enter and leave the married state through divorce and widowhood. Divorced and not yet remarried women are not expected to express'
kirki in the same manner as married women. There is, recall, an appropriate
mode for expressing *kirki* for each contingency of life. Moreover, women
who opt for prostitution between marriages have their *kirki*, and being a
prostitute or courtesan is a viable option for Hausa women and not necessarily an impediment to a respectable marriage. (See Pittin 1983, 1979, and
Barkow 1971 for cogent discussions of the distinction between prostitution and courtesanship, the meaning of courtesanship, and its significance
and role in Hausa culture and society.) Baba of Karo's story (M. F. Smith
1954) illustrates this alternation of life styles and their complementarity in
women's lives. Each mode offers a woman something the other does not.
In turn, each demands something unpleasant in return.

Men, too, go through alterations in their life paths. These changes, granted,
tend to present a more direct and unified image. The young father, for example, is quite different from the aging *pater familias*. However, the link between one and the other is a rather coherent and direct one. Even the varied
occupations a Hausa male follows do not form an in coherent pattern. After
all, a farmer who has another craft or two and who travels occasionally in the
pursuit of trade is not an unusual character, nor is his activity at odds with
being a husband, father, or community leader. It is important to recall, furthermore, that Hausa while stressing obedience to authority do not wish authority to weigh heavily upon themselves. They tend to solve their problems
through flight. A diversified *curriculum vitae* provides a legitimate opportunity
to travel while earning a living. When things cool down, the Hausa man can
return without having lost face or being compelled to face unpleasantness.

For the Hausa the last stage of life is old age. The Hausa call men in this
stage *tsoho*; women, *tsohuwa*. Their *kirki* is to deal with children. They correct bad children. They make everyone happy. They give advice. That is the
most important of their work. People come from other towns to get advice.
They will tell you whatever happened, including the whole history of the
area (Abdullahi 1990).

Hausa willingly talk about their grandparents and the joy they have
brought to their lives. There is a joking relationship with grandparents, and
grandparents and their grandchildren routinely address each other familiarly,

calling one another *"abokina"* (my friend). Young boys delight in "threaten-ing" their grandfathers with stealing their wives from them or in "stealing" food from their grandmothers. This joking relationship with grandparents extends to grandparents on both sides—even to step grandparents—and is the same for males and females. It continues into adult life.

The fact that Hausa address all grandparents by the same term *kaka* in-dicates their cultural equivalence. Simply put, grandparents "exist" to pro-vide secure havens for their grandchildren. They are a source of social and cultural wisdom, providing a standard for *kirki*—judging, with the heart as well as head, right from wrong.

The grandparental elders are the protectors of the knowledge of right and wrong—all problems go to them for solution. They might go to some-one powerful to seek assistance on behalf of an erring grandchild. One of the authors recalls a *saurayi's* step-grandfather approaching him to aid his grandson who was in the hospital as a result of an illness resulting from drug abuse (F. Salamone 1974).

There had been a disagreement resulting from the young man's habit and he had been dismissed from his position in the author's employ. Notwith-standing the argument, his grandfather came to the author for help, admit-ting his step-grandson's "lack of sense" but excusing it as part of the folly of youth and a fault of the times. He argued persuasively that established people had to have compassion and show in our actions an example for youth to follow. Of course, he persuaded the author to do what he could for his grandson.

The whole meaning of *kirki*, nonetheless, was in that old man's gesture. *Kirki* reveals itself in selfless actions meant to demonstrate to other's appro-priate behavior. It is a moral concept expressed through appropriate behav-ior. It is not, however, simply an emotional concept. The Hausa are clear on this point. It is in Kohlberg's terms "a cognitive-developmental... theory... translated into a rational and viable. . . educational ideology" (Kohlberg and Mayer 1972: 450). *Kirki* is something good to think about. Indeed, it clearly requires a lifetime of thought to understand. It is, therefore, a devel-opmental concept, unfolding over the course of the lifespan. Each stage of life possessing its own proper measure and variation of kirki contributes to a holistic understanding of its meaning to Hausa ethos.

DISCUSSION

Kirki is a theme deep within Hausa culture. Abdullahi claims it is not taught through Islam, "only through the elders and in our culture." Without *kirki*, it is safe to state, there is no Hausa identity. Proverbs relating to *kirki* urge the point. .Three examples suffice.

Alheri dankone baya paduwa kasa banza. This proverb—"Happy the small area before dust made it a useless land"—is used to prod people to do some good as they pass through life. Abdullahi first translated it as, "When you pass through life you must do some good. Even a little evil turns the land useless while a little good makes it blossom." The power of *kirki* to promote harmony in life flows logically from the belief that the good of all people are interconnected.

Another proverb states, *Barewa tayi gududanta vayi rarrape.* Literally, it says the antelope runs and the child cries. Aside from its obvious meanings that each creature has its appropriate action and should not be forced to do what it is not yet capable of doing, a good developmental principle, it has other meanings. It is used to remind people to provide models of behavior for youngsters. How else can a child know what is appropriate for an adult to do unless the adult model that behavior? Otherwise the child will never grow past the crying stage.

Finally, *Sai bango yar tsage kadangare kan sami mushi ga.* Precisely, unless the road is straight you cannot enter the hut. The .Hausa employ this proverb to warn mothers-in-law not to meddle in family affairs unless invited to do so. Through extension, they warn all those who would meddle without knowledge or invitation not to do so. *Kirki* refers to knowing how and when to act appropriately. Rushing in to interfere in other people's affairs is not appropriate behavior. In all things, caution and decorum must prevail. Precipitate behavior is not seemly. In all things, the Hausa must appear unrushed, collected, and in control of emotions.

Individual behavior in social relationships is strongly tied to the Hausa ethos. The Hausa ideal is to be in emotional control and to avoid displays of what would be considered unseemly emotion. Imposing emotions from the far ends of the spectrum, for example, ecstasy, profound grief, and rage upon social encounters, is seen in Hausa culture to cause an imbalance throughout the social universe. Moreover, maintaining one's place in the Hausa hierarchy is closely tied to appropriate displays of *kirki*. Breaches and missed opportunities require an active group response. Whenever the group must mobilize to restore balance to the social universe, rank in the hierarchy is jeopardized (Barkow 1974).

Social situations appropriate for the display of *kirki* are frequently satisfied through displays of generosity. Using Dell Hymes's (1962) distinction between competence and performance, *kirki* can be viewed as a component of personality, the sincerity of which can only be assumed through overt actions performed at the appropriate times. Using generosity as one measure, the wealthy Hausa would seem to have the edge over the poor Hausa in the performance of *kirki* (Barkow 1974). Yet linking the performance of generous acts to *kirki* can be misleading.

Hausa regard the poor man who gives his mite to beggars in good cheer to fulfill the obligations of *kirki* with no less respect than they view the wealthy man who gives from his greater wealth. The child who, with cheerful carriage, assists his juniors displays *kirki* no less than the adult patron who aids his client. At every age and at every level in the social hierarchy, Hausa are offered opportunities to display sincere *kirki*. Every aspect of Hausa society is charged with the energy of *kirki*.

The Hausa maintain that God gives riches to people in trust. The more important a person is the more he or she must display *kirki*. Everyone in life must take care of everyone else, with God taking care of the entire community. Great riches bring great responsibility, for they offer a person greater opportunity to display *kirki*. If a person meets his or her obligations in a manner satisfactory to the community, then the Hausa adult possessing a blend of competence and performance in *kirki* is rewarded with sanction to move through the geographic and social space of diverse groups.

Michael G. Smith (1959) characterized Hausa culture as one of patron-client relationships.

> Factors including birth-order, family, prestige, and individual personality assist the Hausa in determining the patron-client nature of all relationships in their highly stratified society. Socialization practices active throughout life assist the Hausa in determining whether (s) he should view self as the patron responsible to a client or a client responsible to a patron in a particular relationship. The patron-client nature of Hausa culture is maintained in part by the practice of *dan faxi* and *tallafi*.

Tallafi, or child adoption, is a method used to extend the social ties of a Hausa child. Commonly, it occurs between the ages of two and three when a child undergoes weaning. At that time a new child typically appears in the family. The older child's leaving coincides with the younger child's appearance and serves to emphasis a distinction between them as well as to teach the older child the limits of a nuclear family's ability to satisfy all his or her emotional needs. At the same time, it also demonstrates the role of the extended family network in meeting the needs of its members, for those who adopt the child tend to be its maternal grandparents, aunts, uncles, or other or fictive kin. Thus, the child, who rarely resides far from the parents, is provided communal support and nurture while learning about the extent and boundaries of his or her social world.

Although *tallafi* is the general term for Hausa adoption, Hausa distinguish two specific types of adoption according to duration. *Dan ruko* indicates long-term adoption. This form is most similar to Western life time adoption. *Dan yaye* indicates short-term adoption, as short as three or four months. It is similar a Western practice of sending older children to their grandparents while the new child settles in. There .are a number of factors that are decisive in choosing one form of *tallafi* or another: economic conditions, number of children, desire to cement alliances, lack of children in a relative's or patron's family, and other social and cultural considerations.

The *dan faxi* relationship is a lifelong one in which a woman and her eldest son engage in mutual avoidance behavior. The purpose of this behavior is to mark her change of status from that of wife without a male child to one who has produced an heir. The continuance of avoidance behavior—the taboo on saying her son's name and his on mentioning hers, for example—is a constant reminder of her social position and the prestige it accords her. Members of the community, for example, will refer to her teknonymously as "the mother of Sule" *(uwar Sule)*, for example. They will express their approval of her status through the increased politeness of their greetings and in other displays of courtesy.

A father and son also exhibit mutual avoidance if the son is his mother's first male child. The father never addresses his son directly, but speaks through intermediaries, often the son's paternal uncles. He sends him supplies, money, and watches over him carefully but distantly. Again the relationship marks status. It also forces the child to search outside the nuclear family for emotional support and to realize that the wider Hausa community can supply what the more immediate nuclear family lacks (M. G. Smith 1959). The literature, surprisingly, does not mention that the *dan faxi* or *dan fari* relationship also may extend to women. However, a father's eldest daughter must avoid direct conversation with him and deal with him through intermediaries, carefully avoiding firsthand contact (Abdullahi 1990). The reasons parallel those for avoidance with male children. Significantly, a mother does *not* avoid direct contact with her female children.

Internalization of the demands of *kirki* begins in childhood. A Hausa child whose family members have themselves internalized *kirki* and view it as part of their generative responsibility is rewarded when *kirki* is displayed in childlike- fashion in age-appropriate situations. This childhood activity lays the foundation for adult displays of *kirki*, and integral and essential value in adult Hausa relationships. Its timely display serves to reduce the stress associated with social interaction, thus diminishing the possibility of conflict. Hausa marketing economy relies upon the individual's ability to develop numerous social ties and to sustain those ties as you move through a wide network of suppliers and customers. *Kirki* is a social commodity culturally constructed which enables the Hausa to fulfill their roles as prime entrepreneurs throughout Nigeria and the rest of West Africa (Mahdi 1979).

CONCLUSION

We began this chapter by expressing concern with the universality of Erickson's scheme of development. Additionally, we noted Gilligan's concern with sex bias in development schemes, notably with Kohlberg's levels and stages of moral development. In order to address these issues, we chose a thematic concept in Hausa ethos; namely, that of *kirki*. Our purpose was to examine the meaning and application of that concept across the lifespan and by males and females. One further objective was to examine Erickson's assertion that true development requires an increasing emergence of the ego—or the loss of self-identity.

It is clear that *kirki* functions multivocally within Hausa culture. It is clear, indeed, an identity marker between' Hausa and others. Moreover, it is a measure of "Hausaness" within Hausa society. Simply, those who exhibit more *kirki* are somehow more Hausa. Although a Hausa exhibits *kirki* through behavior, they see no dichotomy between thinking about morality and actual behavior as the proverbs above demonstrate. Behavior springs from the presence or absence of *kirki*. Those who have *kirki* will behave in a responsible and gentle manner. Those who do not will be *banza*, and their behavior will approach that of groups least like Hausa. Over the course of the lifespan, a Hausa learns more about the meaning of *kirki*. There is an appropriate *kirki* for each stage of life and for each position on the social scale. Moreover, there is an appropriate *kirki* for each gender and each status within that gender—parents, grandparents, widows, divorced women, prostitutes, businessmen or women, *ad infinitum*. *Kirki* has many manifestations that stem from one source.

The Hausa in discussion come enticingly close to confounding *kirki* with the Hausa soul, life force, or "genius." In a manner close to Kohlberg's conceptualization (Kohlberg 1966; Kohlberg and Gilligan 1971; Kohlberg, Levine, and Hewer 1983), Hausa see a progressive development of moral thinking. Unlike Kohlberg, they see that thinking as intrinsically applied to moral behavior. Behavior flows from a state of being and thinking *(Barewa tayi gudu danta yayi rarrape)*. Moral thinking revolves around the guiding theme of *kirki*. It is an organizing and referential theme. It mobilizes appropriate behavior and all behavior is referred to it for evaluation. Thus, when thinking about themselves Hausa assess their identity in terms of its fit with the demands of *kirki*.

We conclude that Erikson is radically correct in his contention that all development is ego development or it is nothing. Nevertheless, we also maintain that ego development must be empirically understood or it is a meaningless generality. Certainly, for Hausa ego development, their sense of identity, involves increasing ties of relationship, multiplying bonds rather than moving toward independence. Moreover, Erikson's eight stages do not fit the realities of Hausa society, either today or in the past. The only way in which they could fit them would be to make a Procrustean bed of them. However, the fact that there is an emically derived view of progressive development strengthens the overall position of developmentalists. Certainly, the fact that Hausa also posit separate development stages for males and females also lends support to Gilligan and others (Belenky et al. 1986) who view many development theories as and androcentric. The Hausa data suggest that their own global theories are not universally applicable as stated but the fundamental issue of separate development emically defined is the crucial one in our view.

In sum, examination of the Hausa theme *kirki* suggests that the concept of developmental stage is more than a Western construct indiscriminately applied to indigenous cultures. These cultures have their own views of development that perceive it as a progressive series of stages. Certainly, Erickson's and Kohlberg's global theories require significant modification before application to indigenous cases is possible or profitable. However, the Hausa do see development as leading to greater self-knowledge; that is, identity. They define identity more communally than he does. Moreover, they do appreciate moral cognitive development as an unfolding of understanding and thinking about moral issues. These issues tend to concern *kirki*. Nonetheless, they do not distinguish between thinking about *kirki* and exhibiting its influence in behavior. *Kirki* speaks to a person's essence, in a rather Platonic fashion, and a person (male or female) behaves according to his or her essence and cannot help doing so.

The Hausa data also suggest that female cognitive moral development parallels but is different from male development. Again, it is necessary to reiterate that specific Western theories of Gilligan and Belenky among others are not directly applicable to indigenous cases. However, the indigenous Hausa categories are univocal in supporting those who contend in the need to attend to separate but related development schemes for male and female.

Finally, the Hausa data are clear in asserting the need to heed relational elements in development. Erikson terms his theory a psychosocial theory of development. Yet he argues that ego development requires disentanglement from relationships. Granted that it can be argued that an individual must disentangle from unthought about relationships so that (s) he can enter relationships in a conscious manner. But the emphasis is nonetheless on the individual. Attention to indigenous systems sensitizes us to the value of culturally defined relationships and the manner in which these enter into day-to-day relationships. The next phase of this research will examine the salience of *kirki* in the "modem" world and the specific manner in which it helps structure interaction with other Nigerian groups with diametrically opposed thematic concepts of appropriate behavior.

13

Muslim African Women and Kinship

It is important to discuss the role and status of women and Islam to understand the Hausa more completely. Islam brought about a number of changes in the lives of sub-Saharan African women, including changes in patterns of kinship. It is also important to note some distinctions regarding formal and popular Islam. In sub-Saharan Africa, as elsewhere, these two forms of Islam may differ significantly from each other.

In common with other universal religions, Islam caused a shift in allegiance from the tribal or lineage unit to the broader community. Inheritance provides a clear example of this shift. Before the coming of Islam, matrilineal societies generally provided for inheritance to males. Islam was concerned with reforming this practice.

The providing for inheritance for women served to shore up the family's strength. The Qu'ran provides for inheritance by determining that fixed amounts of shares are distributed according to categories of heirs. First among the women are the closest female kin. The next to share are the closest male relatives. These changes helped provide for women along the categories of kinship.

WOMEN AND MARRIAGE

The Qu'ran does not specifically allow a woman any voice in choosing, accepting, or rejecting a husband. Although divorce is possible for a woman, it is more difficult for a wife to sue for divorce than for a husband. Additionally, a man is allowed four wives in a specific circumstance and as many concubines as he can afford.

In Africa some Muslim women do get additional sexual rights under local practices. If a man is unable, for some reason, to impregnate one of his
wives, he may turn a blind eye to adultery in hopes that someone may get
her pregnant. A variation on this practice is for a man to bring in a mend
to impregnate a wife. The husband will continue to be the social father of
the child and add it to his family. There is also the practice of the levirate;
sometimes called "ghost marriage" in one of its variations.

In this practice, a man's younger brother inherits his older brother's
widow. Any children they have are counted as those of his older brother.
The younger brother is bound to raise these children as his brother's. The
group continues and kinship categories remain filled.

THE INTERACTION OF LOCAL CUSTOMS AND
ISLAM AND THE IMPACT ON WOMEN'S LIVES

The manner in which Islam has influenced the lives of women demonstrates the power of local culture in interacting with Islam. The Hausa of
Nigeria, for example, provide a clear illustration of the manner in which Islam, as a total way of life, has reinforced the patriarchal power of the Hausa
of Nigeria's northern areas. Hausa women are put into *purdah* (seclusion)
directly upon marriage if their husbands can afford to do so. They are cut
off from contact from all males but kinsmen. There are strict regulations
regarding their public movements. For women, marriage is the only path
to virtue. Consequently, marriage is common for young girls between the
ages of ten and twelve.

In Senegal, to consider another example in sub-Saharan Africa, women
are subordinated to men, although they are not veiled or secluded. Nevertheless, polygyny is allowed and the inheritance laws favor men. Within
kinships groups, however, women do exert power. This power increases
with the maturity of age and the networks women build up over time. Thus,
Among the Wolof, the largest of Senegal's ethnic groups, women exert a
good deal of power. Islam further strengthened the patriarchal power of the
Tukulor kingdom in Senegal, coming to them earlier than to the Woloff
any trace of women holding leadership roles was obliterated among the
Tukulor by the eleventh century. The Wolof resisted Islam until the end of
the nineteenth century.

Among the Wolof, Islam decreased the status of women. Traditionally,
Wolof and Serer women had some degree of status and prestige because
they retained elements of matrilineality in their kinship system. Currently,
however, in Senegal inheritance operates to the detriment of a woman's
interests. Muslim women are given only half of what their brothers receive
in inheritance. Wives receive almost nothing on the death of their spouses.

These inequities are found systematically through every degree of kinship, favoring men over women.

CELEBRATIONS AND KINSHIP

Kinship and friendship overlap, and friendship itself is a kind of fictive kinship. Celebrations among the Muslim Hausa underscore and illustrate this point. Men and women are separated for most of the events. For example, the naming ceremony has two parts. In the early morning, the ceremony occurs at the mosque. It is for men only. The baby received its name. There is then a later celebration that begins late in the morning.

This ceremony is for women. It generally gets loud and takes up most of the remainder of the day. There is ceremonial drumming, performed by males. These Hausa drummers begin with Hausa style music but move to a more generic Muslim style as the day continues. Then music fills the air and women dance with one another. They find time to eat, dance and talk.

There is generally a separation of functions at weddings by gender. However, there is some overlap. For example, on the wedding day in front of her female friends are hidden in the doorway and relatives of both sexes, the bride must recite the last of the Qur'an. This recitation, mainly for the benefit of the men, takes place either at her father's house or that of the groom. Some ethnic groups, such as the Hausa of North Nigeria generally separate the sexes at tile parties that follow The Muslim Yoruba do not.

WOMEN'S RIGHTS AND KIN

As with so much else in Africa, a woman's position and rights are tied to her own kin and their power to protect her. If a woman lives near her kin, she is likely to be looked after by her family of birth. Among the Hausa, for example, there is a close tie of friendship between a man and his sister as well as between him and his mother's sister. Thus, male members living near their female kin tend to protect them.

There is also the opportunity for financial support should anything happen to a woman's husband or should she be divorced. Family members can intervene in the case of marital problems or help support women who are dismissed by their husbands. There is also a better opportunity for visits between family members should they live close together.

There is a close relationship, of course, between a patriarchal system, such as found in Islamic Africa, and the manner in which kinship separates the sexes and subordinates women. Local custom may moderate this subordination somewhat but it does not erase it. Scholars have frequently seen sex/gender systems generating the kinship system in a society.

In Muslim Africa, women carry on a great deal of the work of production and reproduction through their kinship ties. That system reaffirms male rights to women work. One strategy that women use to get around some of the difficulties of the system is to avoid males who have power over them as much as possible and to form alliances with other women and men, such as sons or brothers, who can aid them. In sum, women employ strategies that make the system work for them.

ISLAMIC FEMALE FRIENDSHIP IN AFRICA

Islamic women in Africa, or elsewhere, are bound by the prescriptions of the Qu'ran to have only friends in their households and to be attractive only in their homes. Their husbands will blame them if any other man finds them attractive. To decrease odds that this will happen, women can only visit their friends after nightfall. Close friends do keep in touch with these night visits.

Men generally stay out of women's quarters in other homes and only rarely enter these quarters in their own homes. They feel freer in visiting older sisters and other female relatives than do in visiting younger sisters and other relatives. In these female quarters, then, women have a great degree of freedom.

Although women in Nigeria, for example, know little about their husbands' ages, occupations, or income, they do have their own networks and keep up on the state of their extended families. Rituals also provide other opportunities for Islamic African women to marriages, naming ceremonies, and other rituals are constant. Women meet, develop connections, and exchange information without any male presence. Through these networks they influence developments throughout their families.

MARRIAGE AND FRIENDSHIP

The bride is never present at a traditional Hausa wedding, while the groom is typically present if the wedding is his bride's first marriage. The woman receives her guests and gifts at her father's home. Her female relatives and friends take care of the preparations for the celebration. The women announce the marriage through taking cakes and other treats home with them, thus spreading the news of the marriage.

Married women generally are not close to their husbands. They share their intimate secrets with their friends and female relatives. African Muslim women provide security for each other in these tight primary groups. Women's primary groups, for example, are quite important in places like the barracks of Kano, Nigeria. The barracks area of Kano is part of the new section of town and the layout of houses is quite different from that in the Old City of Kano. In the Old City there is a clear division of public and private space and women's spaces are safely placed in the back areas where they are away from the public gaze. Men not of the household cannot enter the female quarters and wives have their privacy secured.

The barracks houses, however, do not afford this privacy. The old entrance hall is gone and there is no public space to replace it. The outer area is not shaded as in traditional houses. Therefore, men spend their days near mosques or in other areas away from the barracks. Women, thus, have almost sole occupation of the barracks area and can develop their friendships. The barracks area also differs from the Old City and even other new neighborhoods in Kano in the almost virtual absence of women's kinship networks, for many women there have come from other areas of Nigeria. They have, however, replaced their kin in a sense through extending their non-kin female networks throughout Kano through visiting female friends all over the city.

TYPES OF WOMEN'S INTIMATE RELATIONSHIP IN AFRICA

Women in Africa find that intimate associations with other women may supersede the ties of kinship and marriage. Friendships tend to be distinguished by age groups first. Then they talk about friends of fortune and neighbors. These friends of fortune are people with whom they greet and whom they invite to various feasts. The next level of friend is the "bond-friend," those who have mutual obligations of support and gift-exchange. Above these friends are the "most-trusted friends," those with whom people share their most intimate secrets. This relationship generally lasts longer than most marriages. It transcends living near one another.

In general, women form a mutual aid society of friends. They watch each other's homes, children, and send food to each other. Friends aid a woman who gives birth far from her female relatives. They take over all household duties for the first week. When the baby's naming day arrives, at the end of that week, a woman is generally able to resume her household tasks.

When spouses quarrel it is a female friend who generally intervenes to heal the breach and who seeks to keep the dispute from escalating out of bounds. She counsels patience and restraint to both parties. Moreover, in Africa relationships are rarely if ever between just two people. The entire community is involved. Therefore, when people are involved in conflict, the community in the form of an audience who act as intermediaries is present.

FRIENDSHIP AND CLIENTSHIP

In many Muslim African societies clientship is an integral bond of social life. Clientship relations tie together people with differences in their relationships, such as, differentials in status, wealth, or generation. Superiority and inferiority become the basis of the obligations owed to the partners. Clientship provides an additional means of support for women. The inferior in the relationship receives the aid of her patron whenever needed. Thus, in the case of ritual celebrations, feasts, or other religious occasions she has the help and guidance of a patron. In return, clients owe deference and aid in turn. They help raise the prestige of their patrons in the community. Generally, a kind of friendly loyalty prevails and marks the relationship.

CO-WIVES AND FRIENDSHIP

Although most people expect the co-wife relationship to be marked by jealousy, and jealousy is often a part of that relationship, there is another aspect of Muslim co-wife relationships in Africa—one of friendship. There is the dimension of cooperation and the sharing of secrets to counterbalance that of competition. Polygyny often fosters collaboration among women. Cultural conditions and attitudes within specific contexts help shape the manner in which relationships develop. For example, if the co-wife situation is one of sororal polygyny, in which sister or cousins marry the same man, then the possibility for cooperation and friendship increases. Age is significant in the forming of friendships among co-wives. The closer in age, the more likely are friendships to be formed. When a man brings a younger wife into the group of co-wives, then there is liable to be trouble, especially when he favors her in many ways. However, when women are about the same age, "woman-talk" is more likely to take place and foster friendship.

In the course of performing daily tasks, women talk to one another. They also must share their leisure together in the compound. They talk about the things of their daily life. Thus, the harvest, illness, food shortages, and gossip fill their conversations. Friends discuss pregnancies, sexual relations, and contraception. These are sensitive issues and require co-wives to be close friends.

MUSLIM HAUSA CONCEPTS OF
MASCULINITY AND GENDER RELATIONS

Islamic missionaries, originally merchants and wandering teachers (*Malla-mai*) and later government sponsored and trained teachers; believe that Islam is the proper religion for men. Islam, they teach, is compatible with the nature of man. It does not ask the impossible of converts. Human nature needs guidance but it is not depraved. Man by nature is concupiscent. Instead of condemning this concupiscence, Islamic teachers among the Hausa have stressed the wisdom of allowing four wives and as many concubines as one can afford. In Nigeria, wife seclusion is an Islamic ideal but one not found except among the wealthy Hausa. Its idealization, however, as a goal is an indication of the sex role specificity that Hausa Muslims cherish.

There is a cultural ideal of masculine superiority in which the *maigida* (household head) is the complete master of his home. Reinforcing this ideal is the cultural emphasis on wife seclusion. Any type of seclusion, even the milder forms practices among most Muslim Hausa, conflict with pre-Islamic custom and practice. Therefore, Barkow (1971: 60) argues that Hausa Muslim women frequently turn to courtesanship to escape the confines of married life, seeking to return to the more carefree period of their adolescence.

Hausa Muslim men look with disdain on the practice of other ethnic groups, which permits the relatively free mixing of men and women in public. They do not like to have women near men even when women have withdrawn to a nearby area to carry on their own activities. There is a great fear of being polluted by the too close presence of women. Moreover, there is a fear that women will betray their husbands, given the opportunity. Since Hausa men expect to betray their wives it is not difficult to see the origin of their concerns.

Hausa Muslim men have a strong double standard regarding non-marital sexual intercourse. It is legally impossible for a married man to commit adultery with unmarried women. If his wife catches him, he expects her to condemn and attack him, but she cannot divorce him for his actions. Indeed, she cannot divorce him if he has sexual relations with a married woman. On the other hand, a woman may have sexual relations only with her husband, but if she is still nursing a baby, she may not even have sexual relations with him.

A married man has the obligation to treat each of his wives equally. That restriction requires that he have sex with each of his wives in turn and in providing them with children. Only when a woman has a child is she fully an adult, and only when she has a grown son is she fully secure and protected. Thus, the pressure on men to perform sexually is great. It becomes even greater when one realizes that only wealthy men can have four wives and that wealth generally comes to a select few who tend to be advanced in years. These men tend to fear that their wives are liable to commit adultery if they do not satisfy them sexually and also provide a child, preferably a son, to them.

Thus, there is tremendous pressure on Hausa males to play a difficult masculine role, one that puts a great deal of pressure on them to provide quiet, calm, leadership while proving their sexual prowess daily. Their failures are "taken to the public" by their wives who harangue them in the loudest possible manner, throwing their sexual shortcoming in their faces for public amusement. Similarly, failure to provide a wife with a child can lead to further insults and public humiliation. It is a pressure from which many Hausa males seek escape in various ways.

CONCLUSION

Imam has written that there is no single Islamic view of sexuality. He offers a cross-cultural view of Muslim practices over place and time. He writes that the "honor-shame" complex is rare in sub-Saharan Africa. For instance, in Hausaland 'honor' killings are unknown, even as a bad joke. Men marry prostitutes eagerly and women may be known to be prostitutes by their families. It is not a favored profession but women are not killed for it either—much less for suspicions of non- or extra-marital affairs (Imam 1994).

He also notes that cliterodectomy is not found in all Islamic countries. It varies according to the customs of the area and the interpretation of Islam given in the region. Thus, although found in a number of areas, female genital mutilation in other countries with Muslim communities it is wholly unknown (e.g. Algeria, Tunisia, Pakistan, Singapore) or (as in northern Nigeria) not common among Muslims and considered to be a pagan practice (Dorkenoo and Ellsworthy 1992, Mandara 1995). In fact, by contrast, in northern Nigeria a baby girl may be made to undergo hymenectomy (8) to ensure she can be easily penetrated, although this is apparently a disappearing practice (Mandara 1995).

Muslim discourses of sexuality vary not only by community, but also over time. For example, northern Nigeria has been dominantly Muslim at least since the 18th century, some argue the fourteenth century. But, even in the last sixty or seventy years there have been changes in the discourse of sexuality such that *tsarance* (Hausa—institutionalized pre-marital lovemaking or sexual play that stops short of actual penetration) which used to be a common and unremarkable practice up to the 1940s and 1950s (Smith 1981) is now considered to be unislamic and 'rural.' To the other extreme, girls are frequently now not being allowed even to dance at the *kalangu* (Hausa—drumming and dancing held each market day—Imam 1994).

There is thus some justifiable dispute about what constitutes legitimate Islamic practice as opposed to local Muslim interpretation. Even in Nigeria among the Hausa Muslims there is a continual change in response to colonialism, outside fundamentalist pressure, and modernization. The pressures of Muslim Hausa masculinity, therefore, are increased by the confusion that changes generate. There is a marginal area of doubt and old traditions. The 'yan daudu occupy that marginal zone between old and new definitions of Hausa and male and female relations. They form a liminal category that subverts general views of Hausa masculinity and gender relationships. As Gaudio notes (*Africa Today* 46: 3/4) study of the 'yan daudu sheds light on the manner in which masculine and feminine identity are constructed in Hausa society, and the ways people use language both to reproduce and to challenge those constructions." Susan O' Brien's "Pilgrimage, Power, and Identity: The Role of the Hajj in the Lives of Nigerian Hausa Bori Adepts" suggests the position the 'yan daudu inhabit, a category betwixt and between and therefore sacred. She notes "host populations have consistently attributed to them otherworldly powers that have marked them as different from the local Muslim populace." Bori practitioners, including the 'yan daudu, have played a great part in promoting these other worldly powers, emphasizing their sacred and dangerous position on the margins of Hausa society.

Given the Hausa position as a category on the margins as it is since it unites so many disparate peoples and ideologies, it is to be expected that those in power seek to control its meaning. New recruits to the Hausa must prove their adherence to the identity. Within the landscape of West Africa in which the Hausa operate the Hausa occupy a unique niche. Males must be able to predict what other males will do. Family determines position and men provide the means for identifying with family. Gender behavior is rigidly defined for the Hausa Muslim. Women and men who act like women, the 'yan daudu threaten the operation of the system and provide a source for instability.

Presence of the 'yan daudu category, neither men nor women, offers glimpses into possibilities of alternate realities, as anomalous categories are meant to do. Moreover, the 'yan daudu have sexual relations not only with homosexuals but also with otherwise heterosexual men, offering a possibility for at least a temporary escape from the rigid demands of Hausa Muslim masculinity. Their presence, protected by traditional religion, offers a comment on the arbitrary nature of cultural definitions and the mutability of even rigid definitions.

14

Hausa Wrestling and Ethnic Boundaries

Some years ago (Salamone 1973-74) I wrote an article about the use of wrestling as an ethnic boundary marker in a Hausa Emirate named Yauri. The Gungawa, a minority group in a multiethnic emirate, used their style of wrestling to mark them off from other groups in the area, especially the dominant Hausa. In 1990 I witnessed the Hausa in Ibadan using their wrestling to distinguish themselves from the dominant Yoruba in the area and to forge closer ethnic ties among their members; especially their youth and other ethnic groups who live in the Hausa dominated area of Sabon Gari (new town) within Ibadan. I offer a study of this Hausa boundary maintenance in light of my earlier work on the Gungawa in Yauri Emirate.

The fact that the Hausa are famous for their markets and trading and need to maintain a separate ethnic identification in Ibadan and to incorporate new members through recruitment is significant in understanding the Hausa. Their vast trading network is held together through ties of clientship and kinship. Many if not most transactions are sealed with a handshake, not with written contracts. Thus, ethnic ties are essential to the maintenance and perpetuation of the system. In sum, Muslim Hausa social organization is characterized by a complex system of stratification, based on occupation, wealth, birth, and patron-client ties. The Hausa prize wealth and use it to form patronage links. However, wealth also brings with it the burden of great responsibility. The patron-client relationship binds all Hausa men to some extent.

THE YORUBA AND WRESTLING

The importance of ritual for the Yoruba, including wrestling as ritual and as a component of ritual, has been noted in many places (Aster 1998, Bar-

142

ber 1989, and Asiwaju 1975, for example). In my earlier article I suggested that ethnic boundary markers should be analyzed as possible socializing mechanism for ethnic group members. In this article I have attempted to demonstrate how this process occurs among the Hausa of Sabon Gari, Nigeria. Moreover, I have returned to them to note the dynamic nature of establishing boundary markers. These are not simply accidental or ascribed characteristics. They are actively created distinct indicators of identity located among other similar markers.

Earlier I stressed the event-processes that go into the cultural construction of identity boundary markers. The case of the Hausa in Ibadan reinforces the notion of how flexible these markers are and how creative the process of cultural construction is. Additionally, these processes are not simply a matter of "once and for all." They are ongoing processes, ritually repeated in order to fortify the socialization and enculturation they entail Indeed, as I argued earlier (Salamone 1972) so strong are these ethnic identity changes they directly or indirectly resemble conversion processes.

The complexity of these characteristics is clear when one reflects on the fact that in Ibadan the Hausa are distinguishing themselves from other Muslims while in Yauri the Gungawa (Reshe) were making themselves distinctive as "pagans" from Hausa Muslims. The process in Ibadan is more subtle as Abner Cohen (1969) wisely noted many years ago. Cohen also indicated something too often forgotten; namely, that there are identity differences among Muslims inhabiting the same area and, therefore, one cannot assume an absolute agreement between them on all issues, especially issues impinging on vital interests. We in the West generally understand this distinction for Christians but too easily forget it for those of other religions.

Part of the complexity was shown in the brief examination of how the leaders of Sabo protect their community through maintaining good relations with those in power in Ibadan.(Salamone 1998). Not only is this process an example of restorative justice it is a clear lesson to residents of Sabo of the worth of membership in the Hausa community, not to mention the complexity of Hausa identity itself. Clearly, the Hausa Waziri is protecting the power and prestige of the Hausa elite. However, in return he only can function effectively through delivering the goods; specifically, in protecting those for whom he is responsible. The interconnectedness of the process is a testament to Marcel Mauss's classic treatment of exchange in *The Gift* (2001, original 1923). Mauss observed that gift-giving establishes networks of obligations and relationships in society, strengthening social solidarity.

Such strengthening is necessary because ethnic groups are not homogeneous. Their boundaries are permeable and are frequently crossed. After all, ethnic groups are, as both Abner and Ronald Cohen noted, political action groups (Abner Cohen 1969, Ronald Cohen 1978). They exist to aid their members to achieve various goals. This goal-oriented function of ethnic groups helps account for their dynamic nature as well as their concern for power. The power of the Waziri and those whom he represents rests clearly on the support of the community just as much as the community's protection in the midst of those in other communities who wield potentially hostile power rests on the effectiveness of the Waziri and other Hausa elite. There is patently interdependence, thus, all efforts that strengthen community creation and solidarity must be carefully articulated to achieve these goals. Wrestling is an important part of this multifaceted process.

It was true in the 1973 case that boundary markers served to define some of the major themes of their community's culture as well as promoting social solidarity. It is still the case among the Hausa of Ibadan. Wrestling recruits community members while reminding them of the need for membership in the community and of the benefits that membership will ensure. There are explicit and implicit messages at the wrestling events held each Friday afternoon after Mosque attendance. Essentially, these messages affirm the unity and the necessity of that unity of the Hausa people in the face of Yoruba power in Ibadan. Wrestling is simply a metaphor for Hausa identity.

15

The Waziri and the Thief: Hausa Islamic Law in a Yoruba City, a Case Study from Ibadan, Nigeria

Nancy Munn (1973, 579) defines rituals from the "inside out" "as a symbolic intercom between the level of cultural thought and complex cultural meanings, on the one hand, and that of social action and immediate event, on the other."

It is from that perspective that I wish to examine a case study of Hausa law in the Yoruba city of Ibadan, Oyo State, Nigeria. I argue that the Sarkin Sabo and his representatives, including the Waziri, in dispensing justice and governing Sabo provide just such a ritual manifestation of a "symbolic interaction between the level of cultural thought and complex cultural meanings, on the one hand, and that of social action and immediate event, on the other" to which Munn refers. Following Kiernan (1981, 6), moreover, without slighting either one. In an article that aids in that task, Lubeck (1981, 70) reminds us that:

> Colonial rule did not interfere with Islamic practices in the Sokoto Caliphate. In fact, indirect rule created an alliance between a faction of the Muslim aristocracy and the colonial state in which foreign trading firms, acting through layers of agents, linked the pre-existing peasant household and market sectors to the capitalist world economy.

In his classic study of the Hausa Sabon Gari (new town) in Ibadan, Abner Cohen (1969 1974) described a logical consequence of the amalgam of sacred and secular in African society, the Hausa, as well as the manner in which the Sabo was linked through the Hausa – British alliance with the capitalist world economy. Moreover, this study seeks to extend Cohen's work to the post-colonial state served to establish an affiliation with the post-colonial state in Nigeria. It does so by focusing on a court case involving the Waziri of Sabo. A brief presentation of the history of Sabo further clarifies the case and enables contextual examination of the relevant social and cultural factors involved. Sabo, after all, must be understood as a consequence of the extension of British colonial power in Nigeria. The extension of that power enabled the Hausa to found dispersed trading centers throughout Nigeria and, indeed, British West Africa. Their power, however, rested on their ability to control those in their constituency. Appropriate analysis of the nexus of historical, political, social and cultural factors in this process will further the understanding of that unifying concept for interpenetration of the sacred and secular which Kiernan seeks.

HISTORY OF SABO

Hausa migration in West Africa is a long term phenomenon (Adamu 1978). The Hausa began to enter the Yoruba areas of what is today Nigeria in the 18th century. Although the *jihads* of the Fulani Islamic leader Usman dan Fodio and his supporters were unable to penetrate the Yoruba interior. Their adventures did alert the Hausa to the various possibilities of the area, especially trade.

By the early 19th century Hausa merchants and Fulani cattle herders had begun settling in tandem in Yoruba lands, including Ibadan. Ibadan became a kind of camping ground and center of Hausa activities in what is now western Nigeria. Among their joint ventures was the trafficking of slaves in the trans-Atlantic slave trade, mediation in the cattle trade between north and south, and control of the middle portion of the caravan between the Hausa States and Yoruba sections.

In common with other Hausa settlements, that in Ibadan developed into an important trading center with Hausa controlling and regulating the flow of trade. In turn, the Hausa became responsible for maintaining law and order within the settlement and representing the settlement to the ruler of the region. Moreover, "the settlement" includes more than just the Hausa area within the city of Ibadan. It encompasses all the Hausa, and indeed even non- Hausa "strangers" in the region. As Miangu (1990) records:

> Note also that not all the people from the North speak Hausa or Fulani. There are the Nupe from Kwara and Niger; Zuru from Sokoto: Gwari from Kaduna and Niger, and Kamberi from Sokoto. Even most of the people from the Jos area don't know the Hausa or Fulani language but they are still regarded as Hausa or Fulani. Even the people from Benue State such as the Tiv, Idoma, Igala and the rest are addressed as Hausa by the Yoruba, Igbo, and the Kalabari.

In addition, there were differences among the Hausa themselves. Some were frees or escaped slaves who settled on farms. Other Hausa had left home in disputes with their father, seeking a new start in life. Some entered the transportation network, carrying goods from the north to the south in "burden transport," aiding in the complete Hausa control of the North-South trade network through forming the transportation link in that connection.

In time, the majority of Hausa and Fulani settlers in Ibadan came from the Northwest and Northeastern regions of Nigeria. The Northwest section includes, Sokoto, Niger and parts of Kaduna, Kwara and Katsina States. The Northeastern area includes the rest of Katsina State as well as Kano and Bornu States. The settlers from this region comprise most of the cattle dealers while those from the Northwest supply most of the farm food and fish found in the market.

The original Hausa settlement in the Ibadan was at a site named Omiadeyegun, along the Abeokuta Road. Because the Hausa considered this settlement too distant form the town, they moved to a new location named Oji Oba in Yoruba. In Hausa it was called Kasuwar Sarki (emir's Market). The move was successful in increasing Hausa trade and population. Unfortunately, it also increased Hausa crime or what the Yoruba perceived as Hausa crime since they lumped all "strangers" together as Hausa.

After World War I, in order to control crime, the Yoruba rulers decided to move the Hausa and other strangers to an unoccupied area in the Mokola and Race Course section of Ibadan near the army barracks. At the same time the area was underdeveloped bush and a dumping ground. Nonetheless the Hausa accepted the area and the responsibility to rule it and bring about law and order. As a symbol of their hope and dedication, they named it New Town, Sabon Gari and every other Hausa settlement in the south, east and west of Nigeria has carried that name. Not only in Sabo in Ibadan the oldest Hausa settlement in the southern part of Nigeria, its rulers have been the ultimate chiefs of all other Hausa settlements. In order to control crime in Sabo, the Hausa realized that they needed a formally recognized leader. There had been no overall ruler of the Hausa in the Yoruba areas. As Miangu (1990) states:

> There had never been a ruler or leader among the Hausa and this was one of the main things that contributed to the different crimes there. When the Hausa settled in their new area, Sabo, they also decided to have a head. Now that that had come to stay together, practice their religion, they also needed a ruler, a ruler who is honest and outspoken, who would represent them and protect their well being, a responsible person with manners.

Since the British colonial government had recently installed a paramount chief in Ibadan, the Olubadan, the Hausa felt the time was ripe for petitioning the new chief to recognize their own leader. The Olubadan saw the wisdom and advantage of doing so and installed Mallam Audu Maikandiri as the first Sarkin Hausawa in Ibadan. Although there is general agreement among the Hausa that Audu was an intelligent and moral person, he was not a Nigerian citizen. The Hausa in Ibadan, therefore, asked him to resign his position, feeling that their interests would be better served in any disputes by a Nigerian citizen.

After a court case, which Audu lost, the Hausa elected a new Sarkin Hausawa, Alhaji Bature dan Makama. In typical Hausa fashion, a friend of Audu's had been allowed to serve as interim ruler pending dan Makama's election. Dan Makama chose Alhaji Audu Dunguru as his Waziri. Together they worked to develop Sabo and increase the number of Hausa resident there. They worked to coordinate their efforts with the other stranger groups in Ibadan, ensuring Hausa hegemony over these groups. Unfortunately, dan Makama died within a few years of taking office. His son, Alhaji Amadu Bature , found the burdens of office to be greater than he could bear and so he went to Oyo, the district capital, and the British Divisional Officer (DO) to accept his resignation. The DO did so but could not decide on a successor. Therefore, he sought a qualified Hausa volunteer who would willingly assume the burden of office.

Dan Bature's Waziri, Alhaji Audu Dunguru, stepped forward and was accepted to all concerned. During Dunguru's reign, relations with the Yoruba rulers of Ibadan as well with those other ethnic groups resident in Sabo were solidified on cordial terms. It was Dunguru who worked out the broad outlines of Hausa – Yoruba political cooperation in Ibadan in which the Sarji would guarantee peace in the area and be allowed to settle Sabo's problems unmolested by the Yoruba. In turn, he supported the OluIbadan's political interests and represented those interests to the Hausa in the North when need be. Over the years , the Hausa have even tactfully differed with their Fulani allies when they were forced to take sides in matters they Yoruba rulers of Ibadan deemed essential to their interests- such as the *jangali* (cattle tax).

Cohen (1965) made clear the value of the Hausa – Fulani alliance to the very existence Hausa rule in Sabo. The prevalence of the tsetse fly in the Ibadan area makes it imperative to import cattle from the North in large quantities. Since all sales are on credit, it is essential that there be exquisite coordination between all elements of the Hausa community involved. Ethnicity becomes a ritual symbol in the transaction. It is vital that Hausa stand out clearly from Yoruba in Ibadan and that Sarkin Sabo and Waziri demonstrates their ability to rule the area clearly.

Cohen is correct in asserting that this highly developed sense of ethnicity is not found in the Northern Hausa homeland. In enclaves, however, such as Sabo, differences among individual Hausa which are freely expressed in the Hausa homeland would tend to fragment a community which demands a high degree of unity to survive. Therefore, Hausa practices found in Northern Nigeria are given additional importance in Ibadan. Cohen, for example, eloquently develops this argument in reference to the Hausa practice of clientage in Ibadan.

The landlord is a pivotal figure in the life if the Hausa settlement of Sabo. He must know the dealers who trade there intimately. Additionally, he controls lodgings in Sabo. There were in 1990 still only thirty landlords in Sabo, the same number that Cohen noted in 1965. Meantime, the population of Sabo grew from Cohen's estimated 5400 to about 10,000. Sabo's remarkable unity is to a very large degree the result of the united front these landlords present in the face of Yoruba buyers. They have employed the traditional clientage relationship to bind other Hausa to themselves. As Cohen (1965, 15) notes:

> The Hausa throughout the region, indeed throughout northern Nigeria, monopolize the sale of cattle and control all cattle markets. (They form) a widespread network of highly interrelated communities.

In order to maintain this network it is sometimes necessary to ally themselves with local authorities against even their Hausa or Fulani allies from other areas. Thus, siding with the Fulani on the matter of the *jangali* (cattle tax) was not isolated instance of Sabo's Hausa going against their allies. Cohen (1965, 16) discusses the reasons for the Hausa Sabo joining the Yoruba dominated Action Group after independence rather than the Hausa Northern Peoples Party. By joining the Action Party, the Sabo Hausa insured a pressure group within the party to protect Sabo's interests. It also showed an allegiance to the implicit deal with the Yoruba that ensured Hausa rule in Sabo in return for loyalty to local Yoruba rulers of Ibadan.

The current composition of Sabo offers some insight into the complexity of ruling Sabo. While Sabo is reputedly a Hausa area, it is actually composed of people from a number of different ethnic groups, religions, and occupations, each of whom looks to him to maintain law and order and settles disputes. In a sample of residents of Sabo conducted in 1990, 51 respondents gave a Hausa place of origin, 57a Yoruba and nine gave "others". While all who identified themselves as Hausa also stated they were Muslims, the Yoruba were split exactly evenly between Christians and Muslims. There were no Hausa "traditionalists" but there was one Yoruba traditionalist who was an herbalist. The overwhelming majority of Hausa were traders with a scattering of mechanics, herbalists, students, tailors, and professional people.

The Yoruba were more diversified, including traders, farmers, mechanics and various professional men and women. The Hausa population came from all the various areas of Hausaland with the largest number coming from Zaria. Moreover, it was obvious that many had stayed in Sabo for most of their lives, with some being there almost from its founding days after World War I. Some Yoruba as well, had stayed in Sabo for over 40 years.

It is essential to note that I addition to Sabo there are other Hausa settlements in Ibadan. These were not developed at the time of Cohen's study and those that were just coming into existence at the time of his study were, understandably, overlooked. The Sarkin Sabo's rule, however, does extend beyond just Sabo as both he and the Waziri made clear to me. Others in Ibadan agreed with their assertions. Quite simply, space in Sabo proper is at a premium and controlled by the powerful landlords and their descendants who established themselves during the original settlement of the area. The system the Dunguru dynasty developed for ruling Sabo, however, has adapted itself to these new settlements. Primary among these more recent settlements is Bodija. On July 4 1976, a group of Hausa established an animal park market, in Hausa, *kara*. It soon became, with the help of the Fulani, the largest animal market in Ibadan.

In February 1990, the Sarkin Sabo dedicated a wrestling and boxing field in the market at Bodija. This arena allows the Hausa to continue their traditional activities and distinguish themselves from others in the area. Bodija is also the center of prostitution, gambling and traditional medicine. Shasha, founded in 1979, is another prominent Hausa area. It is noted for trade in food spices, tomatoes, onions, sweet and hot peppers, chickens and other agricultural products. It is close to a Hausa motor park from which long distance trucks continue trade with the northern Hausa regions of Nigeria.

It was Dunguru who began the landlord system which Cohen (1969) described and analyzed so well. Wealthy Hausa built homes in Sabo and rented space to others, going surety for their conduct while residing in Sabo. By having corps affluent Hausa merchants with vital interests in Sabo, Dunguru both reassured the Yoruba and had allies in maintaining order and advancing Hausa interests in Ibadan. Moreover, the presence of these wealthy Hausa led to the building of a school, shops, and a mosque. Dunguru's achievements seem even more remarkable when one notes that he began his career as a handicapped street beggar.

His son Alhaji Mamman Audu Dunguru succeeded him in office and built on his foundation. His son, Alhaji Shuaibu Mamman Audu, succeeded him and began to expand the Sarki's power through initiating a system employing *Shugabas*, or heads, over other Hausa settlements in the Ibadan region. These *Shugabas* served to settle disputes between Hausa ad other ethnic groups in the region.

The Shugabas or leaders are responsible for hearing matters and discharging mattes. The Shugaba must be a learned person, who can act as judge whenever [necessary]. Cases among the Hausa should not be taken to Court. First they should see the Shugaba or Wakili [the Islamic judge, also in Sabo the Waziri]. If the Shugaba is not able to settle the matter, then the case is forwarded to the Wakili, from the Wakili then to Sarki. If the Sarki cannot settle the matter then it is taken to the Court (Miangu 1990)

It should be added that the Waziri travels among these Shugabas, representing that Sarki's interests, and takes a significant part in cases. The Sarki, understandably, seeks to keep cases from reaching courts outside his control. His ability to control the area requires him to be able to settle disputes in manner seen to be just. His reputation is the best guarantee that he can do so. Accordingly, he and his Waziri must be approachable and be involved in day-to-day affairs of the area. They cannot simply descend upon them on judgment day and render decisions. Therefore, they must cultivate the virtue the Hausa term *kirki*, a virtue marked by courtesy and composure at all times (Salamone and Salamone, 1993 and V. Salamone, 1991).

Kirki defies literal translation into English. Jerome Barkow (1974) identifies 'gentleness' element to their social mask. It is essential to their economic activity which benefits from the ability to move among and identify with a vast number of potential customers. *Kiriki* woven into the individual's social mask does not have one ideal manifestation but rather presents itself in range of acceptable forms. Ultimately, the purpose is to smooth the way for friction – free, open- door relations.

Kirki provides a theme around which the Hausa organize their lives, establishing a guide for appropriate behavior. Specifically, the Hausa inquire whether a person's behavior is worthy of a person displaying *kirki*. Hausa take into account situational variables such as age, gender, socioeconomic status, family position, time, place, the socio-cultural factors of other engaged in the behavior and audience. Clearly, *kirki* is a relational value, depending on a number of factors.

The current Waziri, Alhaji A. Dahiru Dunguru, personifies the virtue of *kirki*. He is reputed to be a person who is approachable and generous, quick to aid and to settle disputes. Since the Waziri plays a prominent role in the case that I will present and analyze, I will provide some background information on the position, the current Waziri and his family. The position of Waziri is an important one at Sabo. The Waziri acts for Sarki. It is his responsibility to find accommodations for strangers. In turn, he can refuse admittance to undesirable strangers, Hausa or otherwise, whom he deems potential problems. In addition, the Waziri collects taxes and pays Sabo's taxes to various government, traditional Yoruba governments, the municipal government and the federal government.

The present Waziri, Alhaji A, Dahiru Dunguru, lives in the same house his grandfather bought from the original Sarkin Hausawa, Mallam Audu Maikandiri. In common with many of Sabo's elite, however, he was educated in the northern part of Nigeria at Kaduna. Eventually, he was educated in Chicago and speaks fluent English as well as Hausa and Yoruba. Although he was educated in Kaduna, his family traces itself to Malumfashi in Katsina State. The current Waziri is the younger brother of the Sarkin Sabo. Their grandfather left Malumfashi for Zungeru when he lost his bid for the chieftaincy of Galadima. Since he was of the royal family, he felt he had lost face when the king makers passed over him for the position. In time, he established himself in trade in Zungeru and finally made his way to Ibadan where his family predominates in Sabo.

THE THIEF, THE YORUBA
MARKET WOMAN AND THE CONSTABLE

On 21 March 1990, at the Waziri's invitation, I accompanied him on his rounds. We began at Sabo about 9:30 am. The Waziri was somewhat embarrassed because he had lent his car to one of his brothers and had to hire a smaller car to take me around. Our first stop was Shasha where the Waziri had some business, including a trail involving a young Hausa accused of stealing from a Yoruba market woman and assaulting a Yoruba constable. The trial, which began about 10:15 am, took place in a large open courtyard outside the Shugaba's house. It was conducted mainly in Hausa, with translations into Yoruba and English for the benefit of the constable. The Yoruba market women spoke Hausa. The constable, not a Yoruba, understood and spoke the language. English summaries were provided for those whose Hausa or Yoruba might not be sufficient. There were about 20 elders gathered in judgment. They were arranged in a horseshoe shaped semicircle, under a large shade tree. Some were seated on chairs while others arranged themselves with their backs to a wall, under the shade of the wall's overhang. There were elaborate rugs placed on the ground for the use of participants. Completing the circle were the complainants, the defendant and some spectators.

Each of the elders felt free to interrupt and question the participants, seeking more information or commenting on that given. Eyes turned to the Waziri for guidance. With his big robes, large gold ring on his middle finger and stately presence, he was clearly the most important person present. Generally, he was content to let matters proceed without interfering. Occasionally, he would interject a comment or two to frame the case in a larger context or to focus attention on what he deemed most relevant.

The constable was dressed in his blue Nigerian police uniform, complete with tidy beret. He sat calmly on a chair at the head of the circle, facing into the horseshoe. When his turn came to give testimony, he did so in English since he spoke neither Yoruba nor Hausa well, coming from another area of Nigeria. The market woman and youth gave their testimony while kneeling. The youth, however, demonstrated a clear breech of decorum through appearing shirtless at a solemn gathering. From the beginning, he demonstrated his disrespect through his tone of voice, posture and dress. Even while kneeling, for example, he did so in a manner that demonstrated his contempt, failing to remain straight and managing to present himself in a lazy contemptuous fashion.

The basic facts of the case seemed fairly simple and straightforward. The young man, about 18 years old, had come to Ibadan a few months before. He had been a source of concern to the Hausa community, being rather rebellious and not appropriately respectful of authority. His open show of temper especially concerned the Hausa who dislike and fear open displays of unseemly emotion. He had worked for the Yoruba market woman for one day, lifting and moving her fabric goods and potters as well as running errands. When his daily work was completed he came to collect his pay. He claimed that he did not receive the amount agreed upon. The market woman argued that he had broken some of her pottery through sheer carelessness and that she deducted the replacement costs from his pay. The young man countered that he did not break the goods through carelessness and that he had only learned of the woman's intent to deduct the costs when he received his pay.

To recoup his losses, he argued, he took the money equal to what his employer owed him. In rather typical fashion, chaos ensued. The market woman chased him across the market aided by fellow- workers and patrons. Since Nigerians who catch thieves in the act routinely beat and even kill them, the young man was fortunate that a Nigerian constable halted his progress.

Unfortunately for his cause, he did not deem it so, for he chose to attack the constable before being subdued. This attack, of course, further compounded the youth's troubles. Again, he was laying himself open to serious personal injury and, yet once more, was fortunate in having the constable bring him before a Hausa court rather than before the municipal court. Even worse, he could have been "lost" within the system and learned how seriously the police deem an attack on a police constable.

The high reputation of the Sarki and Waziri entered strongly in the constable's decision to advise the Yoruba market woman to use a Hausa court. They believed justice would prevail, to their profit. Moreover, the Waziri would go surety for the young man, guaranteeing his good conduct and punishing severely any further recurrence. In fact, the Waziri did advise the youth that he had brought shame on the Hausa community through his actions. He instructed him as to what his seemly course of action should have been; namely to come immediately to the Waziri or Shugaba to complain of being cheated in his wages. The Waziri or Shugaba would have investigated the charges quietly and fairly to everyone's benefit. By his actions, the young man had limited the Waziri's options.

Moreover, through attacking a constable he had brought further un-
necessary trouble on himself. The Waziri reminded the youth that the
constable did not have to bring to the Hausa court. That he did so should
remind him that he was fortunate to belong to a people who care for
their members and try and take care of them. They implicit warning
inherent in this speech was made explicit when the youth continued his
defiance. Unable or unwilling to pick up the cultural cues the Waziri
patiently fed him, the youth continued to protest that he did not need
the Hausa to take care of him. He was perfectly capable of caring for his
own interests. After pointing out that recent events demonstrated that
he was not capable of caring for himself, the Waziri warned him that
his continued defiance jeopardized not only himself, but the Hausa. He
was willing to take some risk to aid a fellow Hausa but not when that
rascal was ungrateful and continued heedlessly to imperil the interests of
other Hausa in Ibadan. The Waziri warned the youth that if he continued in this manner, the Waziri and the elders would send him back to
his hometown in the North and have him placed in confinement there,
never to return to Ibadan. Additionally, the youth's relatives in Sabo had
agreed to this course of action and were shamed by the youth's defiance
of his elders. Having said that, the Waziri allowed the trial to continue.
The three major figures had their say. The elders and Waziri had theirs.
No other witnesses were called. The constable presented a summary of
witness reports and these reports were allowed uncontested by all save
the youth.

After an hour or so, the court decided that the youth, had acted rashly
in taking money from the market woman. If he had a dispute, he should
have brought it to the appropriate authorities who would have known how
to settle it. Moreover, he was given no leeway in the matter of assaulting a
constable and resisting arrest. The court commended the constable on his
restraint and his goodness in bringing the matter to them rather than to a
municipal court. They censored the youth for his actions in resisting arrest
and assaulting a constable who had saved him from the fury of the market
crowd.

They furthered fined the youth a large sum of money, my understanding was several thousand naira, and lent him the money to pay his fine to
the market woman and constable. The fine was paid immediately to the
complainants. The elders made it clear to the youth that the money was
a bond for his good behavior. As the Waziri had warned him, any further
trouble would lead to his exile and confinement in the North. Or, in a
matter of great seriousness, abandonment by the community in which
case he would face the wrath of the accusers unprotected in a court they
controlled.

ANALYSIS

Raybeck (1991) argues cogently that small- scale communities differ in their assessment and treatment of deviance and the deviant. In small- scale groups including, I contend, enclaves, primarily relationships prevail. The group coheres in the face of opposition, and its leaders primarily serve to present and protect the community's interests in an often dangerous and always intricate environment.

The "deviant" or miscreant in small communities generally has multiple ties to the community through family, friendship, and commercial networks. He is not simply s "thief", or "hothead" or worse "someone who disregards appropriate authority". He is potentially a contributing member of Hausa society. It is in the community's best interests to teach him how to behave. The trial, among other things, serves to educate him and to show him that without his community he is at the mercy of unpredictable and hostile elements. The very fact that outsiders demonstrates respect and trust to the Sarki, Waziri, Shugaba and the Hausa community is meant to instill in the youth a sense of ethnic pride and security. The array of elders along three sides of the circle demonstrates community solidarity in the face of the youth and his Yoruba accusers. He is, in a sense, outside the center of the circle, figuratively and literally.

Interestingly, the Waziri sits slightly behind the tip of the horseshoe, close to the accusers and accused. He sums up the arguments, asks leading questions and comments on the proceedings, clearly setting forth dominate Hausa virtues: respect for elders, community solidarity, the need to avoid shamming the community, seemly demeanor- in sum, all that the concept of *kirki* subsumes. His remarks, moreover, seek to persuade the youth to follow the true Hausa path and reject his individual road, a road that can only lead to his ultimate destruction. There is a clear connection between right behavior, legality, and morality. A person who has *kirki* will be a law- abiding, just, upright person- one who's every action accords with the good of the community. As Raybeck (1991) notes, in small – scale communities the good of the citizenry requires that it be slow to label the rule- breaker as deviant and, thus, beyond the pale.

Moreover, the power of the Sabo's leaders centers on their ability to control the Hausa population while representing and protecting their interests. That, in turn, requires them to persuade the residents of Sabo that they are legitimate leaders who understand the interests of its residents and how best to protect them. They must earn the consent of the governed and not force it. The recalcitrance of the youth is a direct challenge to the Waziri's authority and he deals with it patiently and even gently. He simply and incessantly lays out the consequences of the youth's behavior, using its occasion to strengthen community norms but also to help the youth conform to them.

The decision itself was a foregone conclusion at the start of the trial. The youth had acted in a very un- Hausa manner. He continued to do so during the trial, violating every tenet of *kirki*. Remember that it is in Hausa interests to keep cases from reaching courts outside their control. Moreover, the Sarki and Waziri control the area through settling disputes in a manner seen to be just. Their reputation is the best guarantee that they will be able to do so. Accordingly, they must be approachable by members of all ethnic groups in Ibadan. Above all, we have seen, they must cultivate the virtue of *kirki*, a virtue marked by courtesy and composure at all times (Salamone and Salamone 1993, and V. Salamone, 1991).

The Yoruba market woman and the federal constable knew that the Hausa elders would work to mend the potential breech in relations with two powerful segments of outside society: the market and the police. Women have great power in the market and the Hausa require access to markets to sustain their community. Moreover, Hausa control of their own community is strongly dependent on the willingness of police to bring cases to them before they enter municipal courts.

The fact that the elders did, in fact, substantially reward the constable and market woman through considerable financial remuneration simply showed their good judgment in using a Hausa court. The Hausa were not disconcerted by the necessity to "spray" some money to ensure continued good relations. The capability of keeping control of Sabo's affairs is worth a few nairas to them. After all, the ability and willingness to compromise is an integral part pf being a man of *kirki*.

CONCLUSION

British colonial power enabled the Hausa to spread their more traditional locations. Their migration, it is true, preceded British presence and control if Nigeria. British control, however, under the Pax Britannica ensured that peaceful migration and trade would come under their protection. With the migration, however, came the need for the working out of accommodations for the newly settled Hausa.

The system that evolved at Sabo became a model for other similar systems. Basically, an emir and vizier along with commercial elite undertook the responsibility for maintaining law and order in return for basic commercial privileges. The system, fairly well in place by the end of World War I, has served the needs of Hausa and other settlers while providing Yoruba rulers of Ibadan with their own benefits. They are able to govern a large foreign group within their system of indirect rule. Moreover, in crucial issues the Hausa will attempt to present the Yoruba view to their northern kinsmen. Although they do not relish doing so, they will openly side with the Yoruba on matters of vital interests to them is they see no other option open to them.

In turn, the Hausa must demonstrate their ability to control their constituency, including newly arrived settlers. Therefore, the case study is significant in illustrating a typical manner in which the Hausa solidify their ties to the outside community while reinforcing core values, encapsulated in the virtue of *kirki*. They pacify the constable and the market woman while seeking to reincorporate their errant youth. Their lecture to him is also meant for a wider audience. The elders clearly state their position and warn the youth that while patient, they are not infinitely so.

Kiernan's (1981, 6) argument, therefore, that a concept is needed to tie the sacred and secular together without slighting either one is a sound one. The Hausa concept of *kirki* certainly does so in an effective manner. The demeanor of the Waziri, quiet and calm, is the mark of a man of *kirki*. His certainty in the face of confusion calms the people and reassures them of the sanctity and surety of the law. The law is not a thing, moreover, it is a process that seeks to protect the community in the face of outside dangers. That lesson is driven home to the recalcitrant young men in numerous ways. The circle, for example, symbolizes the force of the Hausa community that will protect him and teach him, always being ready, furthermore, to embrace him once again.

The tree itself is a scared symbol being old and enduring and providing welcome cool shade on a hot day. Indeed, the value of coolness in Hausa society is well- known (V. Salamone 1991). The Hausa value people who can listen calmly in the face of adversity and who can seek to reconcile seemingly irreconcilable differences. Again, there are a series of symbols, ritually encapsulated in the trial that reinforce this value. For example, each person gets an opportunity to present the case calmly. Respect is accorded each presentation. People in the circle are free to ask questions and the Waziri generally waits until all other have spoken, not wishing to inhibit their advice and opinions.

The entire trial is presented in a ritualistic order. The young man must kneel. The constable sits on a comfortable chair, underscoring both his dignity and his outsider status. Three languages are used—Hausa, Yoruba and English—but deliberation is done in Hausa, a kind of canonical language. Translations are made in summary fashion as a courtesy to outsiders. Indeed, courtesy itself is the order of the day as befits a Hausa ritual. The healing aspects of the trial, internally and externally, are significant. The trial sought, as good rituals, to bring the group together and reinforce its values. At the same time, in conformity with the Hausa's special position in Ibadan, the Waziri was careful to heal the breach with those whom a fellow—Hausa had offered; namely, the constable and the market woman.

Ethnic groups, including the Hausa, have frequently used religion to safe guard those values mot tied up in preserving ethnic identity in complex interactions. Those values tend to assume sacred characteristics and therefore, to be protected through sacred sanctions. Symbols closely associated with a group's identity tend to be sacralised. After all, Durkheim taught us, religion us only society writ large. Using sacred symbols as identity markers assures that insiders and outsiders will take them seriously and structure ethnic transactions accordingly. Religion in Nigeria is master status, requiring that each of a group's other statuses are grammatical with them. I suggest that social groups will always employ religion, or its symbolic equivalents, to sanctify key identity symbols they use to distinguish themselves and define themselves and other social groups who are in constant social encounters with each other.

The sociodram's key symbols on 21 March 1990, illustrated a number of points about ritual, key symbols and the manner in which key symbols are used in rituals to reinforce core values in Hausa society. Cohen's earlier work on the Sabo Hausa noted that the survival and continuation of their community depended on their ability to maintain their economic position in the savanna-to-forest- trade. To do so they had to preserve their unique Hausa identity in the face of Yoruba challenges. Preserving control over their Sabo community, including dispute settlement involving community members and outsiders, was an integral part of their task. Moreover, from Munn's perspective, they demonstrate the manner in which ritual leads to action and the relationship between tropes, identities and social organization.

16

Student Teachers and Change

with Virginia Salamone

Student teachers in Northern Nigeria view education as a primary vehicle for change and themselves as major drivers of that vehicle, an attitude that aids research concerned with the involvement of student teachers in social development. To understand their involvement, we must examine the realities of Nigerian society that permit student teachers to act as cultural brokers, the characteristics of student teachers that allow them to become change agents within the Northern Nigeria context, and the manner and way in which they refashion open elements in Northern Nigerian cultural systems to effect an ultimate, elaborate bridging of Western and Nigerian cultural elements as well as intra-Nigerian ones.

Student teachers are ideally suited to move among the various categories of people involved in student teaching: supervisory personnel, faculty members, and secondary school students. They have something to offer each, and each has something to offer them. They are best able to manipulate the impressions that each group has of the others, for they are intermediaries between groups and the only people that have immediate dealings with members of all other groups. They also have the most at stake in the student teaching process: their own success or failure.

Thus student teachers in Nigeria appear to fit classic models of culture and power brokers; that is, they attempt to make themselves indispensable through their control of the symbols of power (Cohen and Comaroff 1976:87ff). They control those symbols by making themselves middlepersons in triadic relationships; in effect, they become key links in a series of dyads that replace the former three-way relationships. Fundamental to their control of power symbols, which they obtain by filling key positions, is their reinterpretation of cultural symbols to the members of the various groups, which they link.

We will concentrate on how student teachers in one area of Northern Nigeria, Plateau State, actually act as cultural brokers. This will shed light on a number of empirical and theoretical areas: the cultural and structural aspects of change in Northern Nigeria and Nigeria as a whole; the likely characteristics and functions of cultural brokers in similar postcolonial pluralistic societies; and the underlying structural and processual similarities among all situations in which brokers are found. An understanding of these areas should aid our comprehension of how brokers manipulate symbols to bridge the gaps between cultures and social development.

THE SETTING

Plateau State, in Nigeria's geographic heartland, is one of eleven new states carved out of the old Northern Provinces of Nigeria. Its rulers perceive education as an integral ingredient in development. Essential to educational integrity, particularly since the implementation of Universal Primary Education (UPE) in the late 1970s, are both the improvement and expansion of teacher education. Consequently, Nigeria's educators have made serious efforts to rectify past inadequacies, many of which were unavoidable.

To appreciate their efforts and to comprehend one source of power of well-trained student teachers, it is helpful to note some of those inadequacies, especially as they have affected the North. Largely because of the North's unique colonial situation within Nigeria, which the colonial administration dubbed "indirect rule," the North lagged far behind other sections of Nigeria in the modernization process, of which education is an integral part. Consequently, many of the teachers in northern schools are poorly trained. Large numbers, in fact, are not trained at all.

Typically, teachers at one level of education are those who have failed at the next higher level. For instance, students who fail to gain entrance into senior primary school may end up teaching the junior primary level. Universal Primary Education has added one more dimension to the problem, for it was introduced so rapidly that inadequate preparation was inevitable. Virtual illiterates are teaching in the UPE schools as Nigeria attempts to eliminate illiteracy in the North.

Efforts to amend the system include tighter enforcement of existing standards and promulgation of new, stricter standards. The former has compelled poorly prepared teachers to return to school for further education, no matter how long they may have been teaching. These teachers are often responsible for supervising their own student teachers. Stricter standards have encouraged prospective young teachers to go straight to the university, so they are often better trained than most of the teachers in the schools where they student teach. In the case of both returning teachers who have their own student teachers and of bright young teachers, it is important to note that we are dealing with role models who understand their power, know how to use it, and are in positions where they can combine knowledge and power to effect change. The typical Northern Nigerian school facilitates their exercise of power. It is poorly built, staffed, and equipped. The representative Northern Nigerian school has unscreened windows and no electricity or, at best, uncertain power, and is both hot and dirty. Furnishings and supplies, when available, are insufficient, of poor quality, or in need of repair. Textbooks are in short supply, old, and often inaccurate.

But there are exceptions. They tend to be private missionary schools, such as Hillcrest in Jos, and model schools, either newly built or old elite ones such as Government College in Keffi. Such schools exist for a number of reasons. Missionaries, for instance, never subscribed to indirect rule and its implications; to do so would have been to agree to keep Muslim areas as such and to allow Muslims to proselytize "pagans," such as those in Plateau State. Furthermore, Hillcrest was originally built for the education of expatriate children by American missionaries. Expatriate children included those of missionaries, political officers, and such. A few promising children of prominent Nigerians were always allowed to attend. Expectedly, their number has substantially increased in recent years. Hillcrest, however, has retained its Midwestern American flavor.

Government College in Keffi was built as a colonial showpiece to train, promising Northern Nigerian students for clerical and other positions in the colonial bureaucracy. An additional reason was to counteract what was obvious by the 1930s to even the staunchest defenders of indirect rule: southern Nigerians were monopolizing all the modern positions in the "native" services, even in the North.

Current model schools have a more truly Nigerian focus, which is to serve as models for improvement of Northern schools. In many ways, they are experimental and resource centers for other schools in their areas. Teachers in less well equipped schools can look to those schools for aid, advice, and equipment. Additionally, such schools often provide teacher training in holiday periods.

Student teachers who attend the University of Jos, the state's only university, are the only Nigerian teachers in the North prepared by training to make full use of the opportunities available in the model schools. Their familiarity, moreover, with videotapes, films, audiotapes, and other technologically advanced teaching aids that are nonexistent in the overwhelming majority of the Northern schools, increases their prestige in schools where they practice-teach; for constant propaganda has equated modernization, technology, and superiority in the Nigerian as well as Western mind.

Moreover, the constant media attacks on teachers, coupled with the popular consensus regarding their overall poor quality, have further undermined their self-esteem. Consequently, a process is established whereby superior teachers are lured into government and private positions, which are far more lucrative and prestigious than teaching. Teachers who remain in teaching, furthermore, tend to grow into their popular stereotypes; specifically, they fail to report to classes, read newspapers, conduct personal business at work, and commit other acts of misfeasance and malfeasance.

Largely as a result of the general low esteem in which they are held, teachers face real physical danger. School teachers, after all, have no real parallel in traditional culture. Religious teachers, *Mallamai* for Muslims and various other priests and doctors for others, still function in their traditional social roles. These more powerful modern actors are accorded due respect. In scorning their teachers, students simply follow adult example. So serious, in fact, has their disrespect grown that discipline, or its lack, has become a real problem. And the government has sometimes placed soldiers in schools to ensure law and order and to end the beating of teachers and destruction of school property.

An additional structural factor that enhances the power of student teachers and aids in understanding the setting in which they operate is Nigeria's ethnic heterogeneity and the consequent interethnic rivalry and hostility. The general issue has been treated extensively in numerous sources.6 Specific consequences for education, however, have scarcely been mentioned (see Salamone 1976 b and Foley 1977). British colonial policy exacerbated ethnic differences and rivalries (Dorward 1974; Salamone 1978). That policy had significant effects for education. A paramount result of the backward British administrative mentality in the North was the lack of a Northern educational infrastructure. Consequently, there are too few Northern Nigerian teachers at the secondary and university level, as well as too few Northern Nigerian student teachers at the university level.

Members of southern groups, predominantly Ibo and Yoruba, have stepped into the gap. They have been willing to do so for a number of reasons: ease of opportunity for higher education because of the pressing need for more teachers, the presence of role models from their ethnic groups and families in higher education, and transferability of educational skills and experience to more profitable endeavors, including education in the United States or United Kingdom. Their presence, however, creates a serious educational problem, for Northerners, even Christians, are not fond of Yoruba and Ibo. During Nigeria's Civil War, too often wrongly portrayed as a Muslim-Christian conflict, the predominantly Christian middle belt, of which Plateau State is an integral part, was violently anti-Ibo. It remains so today.

Students, therefore, receive Western education in schools from the hands of traditional enemies and strangers (Europeans, Indians, Americans, and others). Strangers, in fact, often appear to run the universities and teachers' colleges, for Europeans and East and West Indians head departments, direct student teaching, and seem to have entrenched themselves no less than in colonial days. Foreign experts from mid western American universities, with no previous knowledge of or interest in Nigeria, make quick trips through the area and offer detailed suggestions for changing the educational system before returning to their schools.

It is not puzzling, therefore, that student teachers are rather free to operate at their own pace within such a heterogeneous system. The ethnic hostility they face forces them to act as a cohesive group, promoting common goals. In spite of student hostility to their positions, student teachers represent to those students the access to power that successful completion of schooling affords. Students are used to being treated somewhat contemptuously. Indeed, inferiors, such as students, would not respect a superior who treated them democratically. As long as the hated southern student teachers demonstrate their connection with power, their presence will be tolerated.

Additionally, it must be remembered that the overwhelming majority of teachers in Northern secondary schools are non-Northerners. Student teachers, who generally are not Northerners, can use their outsider status to forge ties with other faculty members. Members of their own ethnic groups, predictably, afford them special protection in a hostile situation.

The setting in which student teachers in Northern Nigeria operate on the importance of education to development and its perceived need for educational reform, the current low regard for teachers, the high quality of teacher training at the University of Jos, the lack of discipline in secondary schools, and ethnic heterogeneity and hostility all function to place student teachers in a position of power in any conflict. Continuing Western influence in the schools, especially in the university, constitutes an ideal setting within which power brokers easily operate.

BROKERING CHANGE

Student teachers in Northern Nigeria have fewer constraints and more opportunities to exercise their influence than their American counterparts. 8 Their presence, quite simply, is necessary to the continued operation of Nigeria's secondary schools. Their absence would mean elimination of vital courses. Full-time teachers would face impossible course loads. In general, Nigerian student teachers do not teach a class or two for a master teacher. Rather they assume a full course load and function as regular staff members during their tenure.

In conjunction with teaching duties, they perform other essential duties. They construct and grade examinations. They supervise clubs and in many cases conceive and organize them. Their duties may include monitoring, assignments, field trips, tutoring, counseling, demonstrations and experiments, and a number of other tasks. Included is the informal updating of the faculty's education. It is little wonder, then, that schools vie for their services, for student teachers are seen as essential resources. Competition for their services certainly enhances university power. It also serves, however, to strengthen the student teacher's role as a broker, for they are clearly aware of their power.

The manner in which student teachers are assigned to schools further enhances their prestige. Secondary school officials make it known that they are seriously short of teaching staff and require student teachers in order to function. Usually, these officials contact university officials through mutual friends, who make it clear that such a favor will not be forgotten. No suggestion of monetary reward is made. The favor will, however, confer prestige on its donor. The donor will be "talked about" and recognized as powerful, a very serious cultural reward. Thus, instead of student teachers being assigned to schools as close as possible to either their hometowns or they are sent to schools where their assignment increases the prestige of university officials, a prestige that enhances their own value via reflected glory.

In general, the student teachers are better educated than a majority of the teachers in their host schools. There are two structural reasons for their superiority. First, one large category of student teachers tends to be "passing through" the system. Such students take student teaching either as a means of fulfilling their degree requirements to get a job in a government ministry or the private sector or as a step to further education in the Western world. Another large category of students consists of those in the Post Graduate Degree in Education (PGDE) program. By definition, these students have been teaching for a number of years, usually in superior schools in southern or western Nigeria, and are working toward obtaining appropriate credentials.

In common with many "strangers," these latter teachers use resources developed by earlier migrants from their group. Ethnic associations, already in place in Jos, ease their entrance in Plateau State's social life. Fellow ethnics in the university and secondary schools further strengthen their position. Thus, student teachers who are "outsiders" do not come as complete strangers to the city. There is already a means for entry into the city and state and its interethnic political and power relationships.

Power in a developing country eager for change is often found in being youthful and having close contact with Western mentors. Student teachers typically meet both criteria: they are young and Western personnel supervise them, Moreover, they have usually taken steps to familiarize themselves with the entire Nigerian scene, often including mastery of northern languages. Such credentials enable Nigerian student teachers to manipulate existing ties between structures, that is, to become brokers between schools and Western personnel.

There is a classic opportunity for such brokerage because of the inability of Western personnel to perform their jobs or reach their own goals without the help of student teachers, who in fact perform fundamental work for them. Student teachers are often used for research. They distribute questionnaires to staff and pupils, try new methods, make observations, and perform other research-oriented tasks. The supervisor is enabled, furthermore, to enter the school to carry out research tasks directly. Finally, student teachers interpret local reality, to their own advantage, to Western personnel. They immerse themselves in the day-to-day operation of the school, and they shape their supervisors' impression of those operations. To function as supervisors and to validate their role, it is essential to Western personnel that they know how to behave in the local setting; that is, they must understand the local school culture.

In addition, student teachers interpret the supervisory chain of command to their Western supervisors. Briefly, the University of Jos oversees the training of student teachers who are preparing to teach in secondary schools. The specific responsibility is given to the Department of Education. Within the department, responsibility is delegated to various area specialists. Outside the university, the federal and state ministries of education set teaching policy. Similarly, local education boards, principals, and master teachers exercise control over the student teaching process.-In reality, however, the student teacher is usually the only person in the chain in contact with every other person. Moreover, the only relevant relationship is that between the student teacher and supervisor.

A number of factors enable student teachers to assume such prominent roles in the student teaching process. Student teacher supervisors, particularly Western personnel, are typically too busy for the day-to-day contact necessary to forge ties with members of federal, state, and local education ministries, master teachers, and principals. Furthermore, outsiders rarely remain long enough to master the intricacies of the Nigerian educational system, a system that is seemingly second nature to Nigerian student teachers. Moreover, most of the student teachers are in education because close relatives have preceded them there. They know many key members of the educational establishment, and those whom they do not know of them through their relatives' intercessions. The personal (particularistic) nature of traditional Nigerian culture is thereby applied in what Westerners expect to be an area of universalistic endeavor, the educational bureaucracy.

University-trained student teachers, moreover, tend to be outstanding individuals who have already mastered many systems and cleared numerous hurdles. Most are probably preparing themselves for ministerial positions and regard themselves as already superior in teaching ability to many professional teachers, an accurate assessment buoyed by the lack of secondary teachers. Because of that lack, Nigerian student teachers, unlike their American counterparts, are full-fledged faculty members. They relieve professional teachers of burdens, help train them, and offer classes that would not otherwise be available to students. Such experiences tend to support their self-images and strengthen their resolve to pass through the system to more prestigious positions, a goal in which their ministerial supporters concur.

Given their strategic situation, it is not surprising that the 47 postgraduate and undergraduate students whom the senior author supervised were able to exert a great deal of power. In turn, because she controlled or influenced their attainment of desired goals, they were careful to structure the situation in order to present themselves in the best possible light, that is, to interpret reality for her. Because they, as well as their evaluator, judged their success in Western terms, their control was even greater, for they were all, to a greater or lesser extent, bicultural.

It is important to note that the culture-bound Western criteria used for judging successful teaching, in themselves rather schizophrenically divided between British and American standards, were often at odds with indigenous culture. Classroom organization, presentation, materials, and quality of presentation-all are patterned after Western models. Desks are arranged in neat rows. Quiet prevails. Lecture and demonstration techniques predominate. Innovation, which is prized, usually takes the form of finding a way to keep water frozen for an experiment without the benefit of electricity or using audiovisual aids in difficult circumstances. In sum, no formal notice is taken of the fit between Western concepts, materials, and techniques and indigenous needs.

The following examples will illustrate a number of the points under discussion: Western influence, student teachers' strategic positions, cultural conflict, and structural elements of education. The examples will help to clarify the role of student teachers in effecting changes.

He took conscious care to pattern his syllabus on American models. Specifically, he analyzed American secondary school syllabi, obtained from his own American-trained professors. He discovered what common units were covered in those syllabi and in what sequence. In contrast with the usual practice in Northern Nigerian schools, he developed behavioral objectives, continual evaluation techniques in contrast to one year-end evaluation, and direct student involvement in learning.

Two other students were assigned to Government College in Keffj, a school in decline from its former high standards. These young men spent a great deal of time developing interaction habits with students and among students themselves. They felt that northern students had *not* mastered the etiquette appropriate and necessary for successful classroom performance.

They, therefore, spent an inordinate amount of time teaching students to raise hands, not to call out, and, especially, to wait until the bell to be dismissed, a rather amusing, but significant, fact in light of their propensity to begin leaving their university classes when the clock signaled completion. They were seeking to instill the behavior in their students on which their Western supervisors seemed to place great importance. Their attitude regarding the class bell must be viewed in the same light. Significantly, the administration viewed these students as more mature than full-time staff. Even when their ideas were not accepted, they were still praised for their desire to innovate. In fact, the administration rejected their innovations because, as in the case of a proposed geography laboratory, there were no full-time teachers who could or would continue the project.

In general, however, there was no dispute with student teachers' attitudes that exposure to the new is a positive experience. Through their use of maps, both of these southern teachers sought to convey the concept of One Nigeria, of the Western nation-state. This, of course, is not simply a Western idea. It is also a part of the South's strategy for survival, a concept that it adopted after the Civil War (1967 to 1970).

The concepts of Western science and empiricism are not neglected. One of the student teachers somehow managed to preserve some ice for a classroom demonstration in an area with limited electricity and unlimited heat and humidity. This was the first lesson in the unit. The student teacher obtained the class excitement for which he had hoped. Students who had never seen ice before rushed from their seats to mob him, eagerly begging to know, "What is it? What does it do? How do you use it? How does it feel?" The class became a dramatic performance, which the student teacher took command of. He channeled student curiosity into scientific inquiry by following up on the next lessons. Carefully, he mapped out the next lessons in the unit on water and molecules, explaining that scientific principles, not magic, accounted for the miracle they had seen, touched, and tasted that morning.

A final example concerns a student who taught at Gindiri Girls School, a school controlled and administered by American missionary personnel. This southern student was the only one to have a white supervising teacher as well as a white supervisor from Unijos. He was provided with an outline and additional books to augment his lessons. Furthermore, he was the only student required to observe and imitate the style of his supervisor. The point is that his experience was similar to that of the average American student teacher, closer efforts to adapt his teaching style and materials to the type of student with whom he was dealing was far more pronounced than that of any other student teacher.

Interestingly, he displayed a great deal more interest and respect for local ways than any other southerner. Although the theme of One Nigeria was stressed, he did so in a far more pluralistic fashion than others. His teaching benefited because of his search for parallels in northern cultures with modern ideas, such as taxation. Significantly, his sensitivity and empathy with local culture enabled him to introduce changes more easily than any of the other teachers. Thus, he used pre- and post-testing and wrote important words on the board. He made specific mention to the students that what he was doing was done by successful American teachers.1! Furthermore, there was an emphasis on follow-through, bringing in other students. Periodically, there was a rewriting of lessons and an attempt to plan ahead. Scheduling was important to him, and extra assignments were given to keep up.

Example 1 shows that student teachers are responsible for curriculum development that seeks lasting changes. The emphasis is on having students perceive themselves as Nigerians, citizens of a united country. Example 2 demonstrates the importance of student teachers in reducing the load of regular teachers and innovating change in courses offered. When those students left their school, their classes ended. Their students were "doubled up" in other classes. Their concentration was on teaching survival skills: grin and bear it, good manners, and sportsmanship. They introduced new materials, and, perhaps more importantly, ideas for new methods of teaching.

The third example provides a case of a student teacher consciously seeking change through brokering between American concepts and ideas and local ones. His supervisors from Unijos and Gindiri were American white women. Both encouraged him to know and make use of his students' cultural and social backgrounds and to relate style and content to them. His teaching style demonstrated clearly the manner in which he perceived both his supervisory and student audiences.

Expressly, he took care to investigate the manner in which Northern Nigerian farming is carried out and the role of women in that occupation. Carefully, he elicited information from students concerning what they did. For example, upon their return to school at the end of the growing season, they stated that they had burned off guinea corn stalks and cleared the brush.

Seizing the opportunity to give names to the unknown he taught them to call what they did "slash and burn" agriculture, leading into a discussion its characteristic qualities. Similarly, he used other aspects of their cultural and social backgrounds-their status as converts in a missionary school, their role as women in a developing nation-as centerpieces for class discussions

CONCLUSIONS

Action theory framework (Vincent 1978) predicts that student teachers would be prime cultural brokers. They must know both the rules that structure their society and the ways in which those rules and their operation can be manipulated. Their own students are exposed to their reinterpretation of Western values and behavior as they strive to impress their Western supervisors.

Glick's (1975) article appears to deny that student teachers could be change agents. On closer examination, however, it is obvious that Nigerian teachers do not suffer from the obstacles to change that he outlines: lack of maturity, expertise, and experience, as well as suffering from other cultural factors such as fear of adult acceptance. Even American student teachers, moreover, can effect change in certain situations. The example that Glick (1975:4) offers is the situation in which "teaching teams which view as part of their mission a cooperative, collegial preparatory role" exist. In Nigeria, conditions hindering student teachers from bringing about change do not exist, whereas all three conditions that Glick notes as promoting a change agent role do.

Student teachers, therefore, find it easy to effect change. We have produced examples illustrating ways in which they do, in fact, bring it about. Those with whom student teachers come into contact must be pleased with their work or they will impede the attainment of student teachers' goals. "Success" is the general concept under which a host of goals have been subsumed. Further analysis would reveal interesting individual goals: a recommendation and aid for study abroad, joint publications help in securing a job, and, of course, good grades.

It is obvious that culture is not monolithic, and the student teacher is able to achieve goals because of its very diversity, as well as his own diverse role models. In transmitting his version of "culture," the student teacher gains an advantage in dealing with other groups, or even categories, of people. Moreover, the examples we cited suggest that in developing countries attempts to adhere to Western models lead to change as well as reinterpretation (Dorward 1974; Salamone 1978). As our third example suggests, greater cultural understanding is not proof against change but, in fact, facilitates it. "Understanding" without sympathetic insight and conformity to the cultural needs of the people may lead to changes that are non developmental and disruptive.

17

Children's Games in Nigeria Redux: A Consideration of the "Uses" of Play

with Virginia Salamone

Observations of three game played in Ibadan, Oyo State, Nigeria are used to demonstrate that play is more than self- contained activity with no purpose outside itself. These examples show that even "pure" play has social, cultural, and psychological functions.

Sutton-Smith has consistently argues that play that has an object outside itself is not play. For example, "this type of behavior is engaged in 'for fun's sake', 'for the pleasure of the action without thought to the consequences,' or because 'it is non-utilitarian'" (Avedon & Sutton-Smith, 1971, p.7). In another place he writes in similar vein:

> For me play is what a person does when he can choose the arbitrariness of the constraints within which he will act or imagine. In its most primordial form, an attempt to control the circumstances of habitual action by reversing the direction of the control. It may be, therefore, the ultimate source of all voluntary behavior on all the levels of action and thought. The player substitutes his own conventions and his own urgencies for those of society and nature. (Sutton-Smith, 1972, p. XIII)

Play is, therefore, self-contained with no purpose outside of itself, insulating that player in his or her own world into which no one uninvited may intrude. Play creates its own culture and is solipsistic, narcissistic, and self- reinforcing. Its only function is to encourage the autonomy of the individual.

Conversely, numerous scholars maintain that all play has an object outside itself; that is, it is purposive. These scholars include those who view play as therapeutic and consequently prescribe m play as therapy to cure social maladjustment and retardation.

In 1978, F. Salamone published an article following theoretical suggestions of Bateson (1972) and Goffman (1979) regarding the interpretative
value of tending to social frames and front and back stage areas of social
interaction. Specifically, he analyzed the manner in which children's games
in an ethically heterogeneous area in Nigeria served as mechanisms for
socialization and provide insight into the cultural imprinting of patterns.
He concluded:

> Children's games are a primary means for socialization. Through them, care-
> fully chosen and structured bits of reality are presented to participants. The
> games clearly reflect patterns present in adult life. These patterns are both
> cognitive and behavioral. In other words, the games teach patterns of thought
> (conceptions of reality) and the, or consequences, interactional results of
> those patterns. The rules of the games are, on examination, rules of life. The
> incidence and occasions of interethnic interaction or its lack are reflected in
> children's games. The lesson of the games is indeed preparation for life, or
> more aptly, life itself. (Salamone 1978, p. 212)

He did not intend to imply that children consciously sought to solve the
problems inherent in their environment through games. Nor did he ever
state that either games were not fun or all consuming. Indeed, the opposite
is true. The Nigerian children whom we have seen playing are absorbed in
the flow of their activity. That does not, however, negate that fact that the
games did serve to prepare children for the multiethnic social environment
in which they found themselves. Some games served as boundary markers;
others, as bridges; and still others, as a means for reproducing the ethnic
stratification system. Play, then, can be simultaneously an end in itself and
a means to an end. This double-edge feature is what makes play so inher-
ently powerful.

In studying play, therefore, it is crucial to attend to the different perspectives that flow from various levels of abstractions. Certainly, a methodology
concerned with the psychological dimensions of play, what play means
to a participant, has a different perspective on play from one concerned
with play's social or cultural aspects. The approaches are complementary,
not contradictory. Too often, scholars lose sight of that fact. Let us outline
some of the perspectives that scholars have employed in studying play.
Some have focused on the conscious aspects of play; others have examined its unconscious elements. Some have looked at play from an emic or
insider's viewpoint telling us what it feels like to play basketball with a particular group, for example. Other scholars have concentrated on an etic, or
outsider's, perspective, looking at how play reproduces social relationships
within a hierarchical structure, for example. There are those who have par-
ticipated more than they observed and others who have done the opposite.
Of course, many have crisscrossed the axes of the dichotomies. None of the

approaches is mutually exclusive of any other, and the permutations of the possible combinations are dizzying to comprehend.

However, in spite of the commonsensical notion of the compatibility of apparent opposites, when it come to presenting the data, researchers tend to lock in on one end of the opposition or the other and argue for its primacy ferociously. We suggest that perspective has a great deal to do with the conclusions. In our version of trying to combine the answers of the blind men to what the elephant looks like, we will examine some play and games in Nigeria in light of the earlier paper (Salamone, 1978) and the views of Sutton-Smith.

CHILDREN AT PLAY

F. Salamone's (1978) study of children's games confined itself to games in the multiethnic northern Nigerian emirate of Yauri. The games we examine in this paper take place in Ibadan, Oyo Sate, Nigeria. Ibadan is plausibly the largest city in sub- Africa with an estimated population of over 4 million. It is more accurate, however, to describe it as the world's largest village or, more accurately, as a series of quasi-independent villages (Olu Moloye, personal communication). A thorough study of the matrix of play roles in Ibadan would have to take that fact into account. Here, we wish to make a start in that direction as the International Institute of Tropical Agriculture, play at the now- misnamed International School of the University of Ibadan, and play at a private primary school in the Bodija section of Ibadan. Each area is in itself an almost separate world within the Yoruba-dominated world of Ibadan. Each world, however, has multiple ties with the other quasi-self-sufficient worlds within Ibadan and across the complex ethnic entanglements that constitute Nigeria.

The International Institute of Tropical Agriculture (IITA), for example, is an international enclave whose members come from many different countries in order to conduct experiments on the improvement of tropical crops. American philanthropic money financed its construction, and some of American's idea of a Hollywood Africa set on a Florida or California back lot went into its design. The Ibadan name for IITA is Little America, an apt description. There are, however, relatively few Americans working at IITA. During the period in which we are familiar with IITA, May 1989–April 1990, we could estimate that less than 10% of its expatriate contingent was American, including short- term consultants who passed through to perform special training tasks. African, Canadian, British and other technicians, agronomists, scientists, and daily workers were in the vast majority. Students from all over Africa formed part of the community, one that changed frequently as training courses rotated.

In spite of its American flavor, apparent in the hamburgers and french fries at its snack bar and the cleanliness of its swimming pool, IITA formed an integrated international community that included a large proportion of Ibadan indigenes. Play around the pool, then, offered an interesting perspective on international life in Ibadan, an opportunity to observe without being conspicuous as we were, briefly members of the community and our children were themselves engaged in play. We realize that we are conflating the concepts of play and games here but believe it is a justifies conflation, especially in light of Barnett's (1990) recent argument that if the lay person has no difficulty in discerning play then the scientist has had problems only because the scientist has concentrated on a behavior rather than on the playful child. What we saw at IITA were playful children playing at games. In the conclusion, we argue, moreover, that these games had more than mere psychological meaning; they expressed cultural and social meanings as well.

One game that we viewed each day at IITA when at least three children were in the pool was Marco Polo. It is a common game, played in many areas of the world. Like most popular games, it is simple and admits endless variations and combinations to its simple structure. The basic game consists of at least three kids in a swimming pool. Although there is nothing in its format that would appear to prohibit its being played on land, we never saw it being played out of the pool, a point that we feel is significant in understanding its message.

One child is "it" in this case, "Marco Polo". That child must give the other kids at least 10 seconds to scatter away to all corners of the pool. Of course, the child's eyes are closed during this and subsequent parts of its turn. After 10 seconds, Marco Polo calls out, "Marco". Each of the other players must respond immediately, "Polo". Using these responses to his or her calls, Marco Polo must locate someone else to be "it". When located, the other child must be tagged, more likely lunged at blindly and grabbed. The game resumes again, and cries of "Marco" with its response, "Polo," respond on lazy, hot afternoons, merging with gin and tonic, Star beer, and ice cold Coca-Cola.

If someone cheats by speaking, then the game starts again, and the inscrutable East, does not respond, "Polo" on cue, there may be anger but no set penalty. There is so much noise in the pool that the culprit can plausibly state that his or her response was lost in the din of the poolside. Even if caught red handed, no one can really do more that warn the offender not to do it again. Efforts to eject offenders never succeeded in our knowledge or our son's experience. The East can use silence to escape being captured, even though it is not, in our sons' term, fair for a player to do so.

Marco Polo is game that many can play. The more participants, the shorter the quest and, therefore, the turn. Many kids like to be "it" for prolonged periods. They like wandering around a cool pool with their eyes closed to the glare, relaying on the senses of sound and touch and using the movement of the pool's water to sense where someone might be. They also love controlling large areas of the pool for their game, displacing adults, bumping into them without risking reproach, and causing tolerated disruptions wherever they go.

Variations to this simple game are virtually endless. Some players, for example, try to blind fold those whom they seek to capture by splashing them furiously while approaching, putting each side on more or less equal footing. In turn, some who flee often confuse their symbolically blind pursuer through counter-splashes that may add to the perceptual disorientation of Marco Polo. Others flee underwater, providing a ready excuse for not responding to the call and making it more difficult for anyone to locate them. After a time, however, players do return from underwater excursions in order to be part of the game. There is no fun in taunting a pursuer if he or she cannot hear your silent taunts and react to them. There is little fun in being so far from risk that there is no danger of being caught.

The fun of the game consists of being able to skirt danger, taunt Marco Polo, and escape at the least second from furious rushes. Close attention to the manner in which different kids play the game does reveal individual and cultural differences among the participants. This game is open to all people from differing cultural backgrounds, members of both sexes, and all sexes, and all ages Adults can play (children urge them to do so), but must adults play briefly with their children not their own. Significantly, as personal experience taught us, it is not a game with much intrinsic merriment for those past their mid teens.

It is a game that children in an intercultural setting love. Thus, although a more traditional psychological analysis of idiosyncratic differences among the players would yield more important data, we prefer to examine more cultural psychological areas; that is, we prefer to look at the groups to which participants belong and to note whether these groups yield differences in style of play. Further, we consider the overall structure and meaning of the game, including in context, to hold an important cultural psychological message regarding the "use" of play in intercultural settings.

Before moving to an analysis, however, there are two other examples of play to be presented. According to Sutton-Smith (1972), play that occurs in adult controlled situations is not play. However, if we shift our attention to the playful child from an arbitrary focus on the structure of the situation alone, as Barnett (1990) suggested, then it is clear that on at least some occasions when adults control the playtime children can really play. Such an occasion, surely common to situations beyond those in Ibadan, is the physical education class.

In the Staff School of The University of Ibadan it was clear that the children, cooped up for much of the day, desired to get out of their classrooms into the relatively fresh air and play. Even in the dog days that hang heavy and linger just before the first rains, the outdoors has advantages for children over hot classrooms close to poorly serviced latrines. The eagerness while which the children begged to have physical education and engaged in supervised play activity attests to their individual playfulness. The obvious spirit with which they played games, included their glee and enjoyment, makes it clear that, adult supervision or not, these kids were playing on every level.

We must admit that one reason for the obvious abandon with which the children engaged in play was the presence of an American anthropologist with a video recorder. The recording, however, confirms my ethnographic impression that these were indeed playful children who were immersed in their games, rather than people who had read the latest play theorists and were attempting to act out the implications of those theories. Their playfulness is obvious; therefore, even though these children were playing under adult supervision, they indeed were playing.

One game the children played with gusto in this predominantly. Yoruba school was a traditional Yoruba girls' game called *Sin San* (ten ten). This game is found, in various forms, throughout Nigeria and other countries of western Africa. The Igbo, for example, call it *oga* (chief). The Akan of Ghana call it *ampe* and employ hand as well as foot variations. In *sin sin*, now played between any two girls at the school regardless of ethnic group, the girls break off into pairs of equals. The girls are roughly equal in size, age, strength, and ability. Each girl faces her chosen partner with hands on her hips. One girl is a leader, and the other must match her foot movements exactly with but a split second to react. The leader does intricate dance steps, attempting to confuse her follower. On the second, fourth, sixth, or eighth beat, the leader does a variation that the follower must catch. The follower seeks to match those steps and then responds with her own variations, much in the manner of a tap dancer's cutting contest or a battle of two jazz saxophonists. As they dance, the girls sing rhythmically. If there are spectators, these people clap and sing along. As the game progresses, the rhythm becomes more heated, and the participants more excited. The firs girl to win six passes wins the round. Then the girls switch sides. In brief, then, the game consists of self- elected pairs of girls playing in sequence. They use numbers, varying them rhythmically on off beats, dancing in a limited space, taking turns, and forcing themselves to pay attention to subtle cues in their partner's behavior.

In the midst of this type of play, the girls learn to imitate about each other useful for daily interaction. They discover how carefully they can communicate with each other through gestures and how well they can read each other's minds and anticipate actions. Obviously, some girls are more compatible than others. Grace under pressure, tested in some occasions among males through a version of what we in America term The Dozens, become obvious. Rhythms, movement, skill in versifying, and improvisation- all essential Yoruba talents- are fostered through this game. Although individual children may not realize that fact (many, however, do), the societal goals to get achieved.

Just as there can be play within games, there can be games without play. Similarly, there can be adult-directed games with or without play. Certainly, it is clear to any observer that nursery instruction almost anywhere in the world offers examples of both types of games. Here, we wish to present one final example of children's games that will enable us to address more thoroughly Sutton-Smith's (1992) speculations on play: adult-directed preschool games that clearly are not play for the children involved.

The example we use can be seen on any school day at a private school in the Bodija area of Ibadan. Its counterparts can be seen in virtually any preschool setting in the world. The owner and headmistress of this particular school is a retired primary school principal who has built a school along the side of a back road near a Catholic mission station. Her friendship with the Catholic prior has provided protection for her school, built illegally on land on which she has squatted. The prior counts among his parishioners that state government's permanent secretary. As friends of the prior, we were allowed free access to the school.

Each day that we visited the school we spent time observing its preschool children at "play". In the early morning, this play consisted of having the preschool teacher sit outside with them and have them repeat English various lessons. One lesson was the phrase we are *jumping, jumping, jumping* accompanied by kids jumping. That phrase could be varied by substituting *running, or walking,* or any other appropriate verb and its action. Sometimes the kids would repeat the alphabet or names of colors while jumping or running. The underlying theory was that if learning is fun then children will learn. In this school, clearly, the adults decided both what fun was and what was to be learned.

The video tape makes it clear that, although the children were not being mistreated, they did not appear to be either learning much or having a great deal of fun. At best, they did manage to get some exercise and fresh air. They were not having fun for many reasons. They did not understand English. Thus, the actions and words appeared meaningless. Moreover, they did not choose the game. It was not something, even, that they play on their own so that an adult's choice could appear to bestow a favor on them. They rhythm and pace of the game did not emerge from the play if children. Rather, an adult imposed it on the children "for their own good". The lesson appears rather obvious. Adults cannot impose plat on students.

When they do, children may get exercise and games may proceed. But no one will be "playing" those games.

ANALYSIS AND CONCLUSION

Sutton-Smith (1972) maintained that adult- supervised play is a contradiction in terms. Play is something that a person must freely choose. Moreover, play is not an end in itself. It is never for something else. Again, if it is not for something else, it is not play. He did not distinguish between play and games. His concern is essentially on the individual who plays.

It is in fact, that distinction, as reformulated and developed by Barnett (1990), that allows us to take a psychological as well as cultural perspective on children's play. Such a view is implicit in the work of other scholars. Elkind (1987), for example, has passages that clarify some of the confusion between psychological and cultural approaches to play while hinting at means for reconciling the two:

> If play is thought of as child's "work" then it must be translated into a lesson plan. A child playing store may be asked to put prices on his wares and total up the sales. And if play is though of as the expression of the child's creative impulse, she may be asked to say what her drawing or painting is and to make the sky and grass more conventional colors. Unfortunately, such treatments of child's play do not encourage the sense of competence but rather the reverse; they contribute to a sense of helplessness. (p.156)

Similarly, he presents another passage that complements the idea;

> We watched a group of four and five- year- olds playing with some plastic dinosaurs. "We are going to eat you up," said one little boy, moving his menacing looking beast close to his neighbor's. "You will have to catch us first, I'm faster than you," said the other boy as he ducked his smaller animal behind a wall of blocks. At the moment the teacher came over and decided to capitalize upon the children's interests (the so-called teaching moment) and to instruct them in some size concepts with the aid of the dinosaurs. "Which is larger?" she asked. But the boys clearly sniffing s teaching situation quickly ended their dinosaur play and went on to other projects (Elkind 1981. p.196).

Elkind (1981, 1987) draws our attention to two essential issues. When it comes to play, children become the adults. They use their own sense of industry to guide the play. This "adult" is one who is setting his or her developmentally appropriate goals. Thus, although a real adult may scoff at prices for bread at one million dollars, the child at play will not, and for that child there is no incongruity to be found in such a pricing system. Elkind's examples demonstrate clearly the dangers inherent in adult involvement. As in our example of preschoolers, once an adult decides to play and on seizing the teaching moment, fun leaves a playful child and routine sets in. If adults are involved, they frequently impose an educational element in play. They may ask the children which dinosaur is larger or how much a loaf of bread really costs rather than going with the flow and being playful themselves. The teacher could have asked which of those big dinosaurs was going to eat her or chosen a dinosaur of her own. When children set their own goals, they are developing and working through their own developmental tasks.

Such an approach makes irrelevant for our purpose the distinction between play and games. Meir (1986), for example, rightly indicated that the confusion between play and games has led to a great deal of confusion. We have indicated our general agreement with that position. Not all play is a game, although much play has game-like elements. We have provided an example of a game that is not. Moreover, we have provided a theoretical explanation for the difference. That explanation contradicts Sutton-Smith's (1972) contention that "We do not study the play element in our contexts" (p.xii). As Meir (1986, p.283) showed, Sutton-Smith's assertions grant at the start what he must demonstrate—namely, that not all acts under a child's violation on the playground are play and not at all adult-directed activity is wrong. Meir focuses our attention, as do Elkind (1981, 1987) and Barnett (1990), on the playful child. In our doing so, a great deal of clarity emerges from the confusion of much previous work, from arguments regarding the psychological or cultural aspects of play and games.

Sutton-Smith (1972) is correct in asserting that play is what we do when we have our choice to do whatever we want for enjoyment. He is wrong when he says it cannot have any purpose outside itself. The socialized and enculturated child *must* use the socio-cultural material at hand in order to construct play. It is impossible to think about nothing. But what the child does with the material of everyday life- how it plays with it, the joy it takes in this activity—is its concern as it constructs, deconstructs and reconstructs its environment. Brian and Shirley Sutton-Smith (1974, p. 243) and Brian Sutton-Smith and John Roberts (1967, 1980) have provided various descriptions of types of games, their hierarchy, and their play element. Along the way, they have also noted the cultural content as well as the function of those games. Therefore, it cannot be opposition to the relationship of play to culture and to learning about a child's culture that disturbs Sutton-Smith, though some of his writings may gave that impression.

What disturbs him most, it seems to us, is the position that fosters adult intrusion in play under the pretext that children do not know how to play. The preschool teacher in Ibadan who had her school children jumping up and down to the alphabet and saying "We are running," "We are jumping," was a murderer of the human spirit in common with her American, European, Japanese, Australian, and other counterparts. The children in the playground of the Staff School of the University of Ibadan were exercising under the direction of an adult. Their instructor, however, knew what games the children enjoyed. He listened to their playful requests. They looked forward to the release their hot, odoriferous classrooms. The social function, if you will, of exercise did not hinder the exercise of playfulness, except (and it is an important exception) that an adult ended the play.

The Marco Polo game is an example, we submit of "pure" play. As such, it supports our concentration that pure play has social and cultural functions as well as psychological functions posited for play. It is fun, allows for control, has repetition built into it., and the participants freely choose it and lose themselves in its performance. At the same time, the game itself reveals a great deal about the world in which the children at IITA live. It is a multi-ethnic world in which many of their parents have come to Nigeria from elsewhere and have "found" it just as Marco Polo himself discovered the mysterious Orient in his day. But the East keeps slipping away just as the culturally blind explorer thinks he has understood it. Obviously, the game is both psychological and culturological attempts to make sense of the marginal position the children know they have in the world. It is also great fun and, therefore, a chosen means to accomplish that task. One aspect complements the other; neither replaces the other.

In *Revolution in Learning,* Maya Pines (1967) addressed the issue of early learning and the failure of children who had forgotten how o play. She rightly chastised those educationalists who had banished play from Head Start and other curriculums in the name of academic achievement (Pines, 1967, 35, 40). Unfortunately, she praised those who wanted to create the conditions of play in the classroom, not understanding that if left to themselves children would create their own conditions of play. It is just this adult interference in play, which Pines herself condemns (1967, p. 114), that so upsets Sutton- Smith and that we put forward as dangerous in Elkind's (1981, 1987) examples and our own from Nigeria.

On the other hand, Elkind (1981, pp. 194-196) warns us of the inherent problems in moving from Montessori's approach to that of Freud – and back again. Montessori's approach has become characterized in the catch phrase "Play is the work of children." Its very phrasing denigrates play and reveals the middle- class bias, obvious in children's books such as *Pinocchio,* against childhood enjoyment for its own sake, an attitude parodied in *Alice in Wonderland,* for example. The Freudian, or neo- Freudian, perspective that replaced this position for a time emphasized the wild abandon and freedom of childhood, stating that anything they do freely is play. This position, on that Sutton- Smith (1972) appears to embrace, states that anything children want to do on the playground they should be allowed to do, short of mayhem. Elkind argues that Freud is ill served in such distorted reading, for Freud himself was not opposed to all self- repression or control. We would add that the current rise of Montessori schools does an equal disservice to Montessori and her original work.

Riley (1973) summed up the attitude against play that has, unfortunately, pervaded many preschools:

> "Play," in some quarter, has become almost a dirty word. The assumption seems to be that, though play a necessary activity of childhood that can't be eliminated entirely, it lures children off the path that leads most directly towards the kinds of intellectual growth and success our society wants of its you people. (p.183)

Elkind's (1981, 1987) point, with which we agree, is either extreme distorts. Play is not an either- or category. Rather, it belongs with other liminal activities to a category we term *creole* because it combines elements of two cultures in a dialectic fashion: it is both this and, at the same time, that (See Salamone, 1990, p.312, for a discussion). Robert Farris Thompson's (1989) powerful concept of creolization is especially apt for discussing play in Nigeria and, of course the rest of the Third World, but it is also appropriate for discussing children's play. Children are in a position of power disadvantage in their relationships with adults. Like others so placed, they must employ creative means to comment upon the world of the powerful and to learn to cope with it as well as reconstruct it for their advantage. Such a process is a limited one, at once psychological and cultural- in Robert Farris Thompson's works, "this" and "that too".

WILL SHE OR WON'T SHE? CHOICE AND DUKAWA WIDOWS

Empirically Observing how individuals solve the problems they perceive in everyday life, rather than speculating on what they probably do or ought to do, increases our understanding of the meaning of womanhood and of basic male-female relationships. Recent anthropological literature is still afflicted by ethnocentric views, despite the correctives that have been presented by such feminists as Paulme (1960), Sacks (1981), Leacock (1981), Etienne (1979a), Poewe (1980), and Mathieu (1977).

The ethnocentric perspectives, stemming largely from Lévi-Strauss' (1969) theory of "exogamous" marriage systems-whether properly understood by others or not—neglect female contributions to a social system of alliance and exchange. Prominent among the offending works are those of Harris (1977), Divale and Harris (1976), Fox (1972), Beidelman (1971), Goldschmidt (1959), Hammond and Jablow (1973), and Schneider (1962). Even so sympathetic a theoretician as Meillasoux is burdened by a view of the world as divided between active male dominators and passive females who are the victims of domination. Indeed, he writes (1981: 75, quoted in

Etienne 1979b: 242): "Women, despite their crucial role in reproduction, never appear as vectors of the social organization. They are hidden behind men, behind fathers, brothers and/or husbands."

In opposition to the above presumed universals of biology or psychology, the feminist challenge suggests that observers confound dominance with activity and acceptance of domination with passivity. In reality, the feminist view claims, women are not perceived by themselves or by the men within their system in many societies, at least, as passive objects that can be exchanged at whim. Perhaps Leacock states the position most succinctly (1981: 1, 4-5):

> Universal male dominance is a myth and not a fact. . . . And time and again, careful reexamination of the data and of the circumstances under which they were collected have proved me right: indications of male dominance turn out to be due to either (1) the effects of colonialism and/ or involvement in market relations in a previously egalitarian society; (2) the concomitant of developing inequality in a society, commonly referred to in anthropological writing as "ranking," when trade is encouraging specialization of labor, and production for exchange is accompanying production for use, thereby undercutting the collective economy on which egalitarian relations are based; (3) problems arising from interpretations of data in terms of Western concepts and assumptions.

In studying widowhood among the Dukawa of Nigeria, I contend that women do "not disappear behind their men," but only appear to do so when their men expect them to become invisible. One might argue that the dispute about male-female relations cross-culturally is addressed to the question of which hypothesis about dominance is the more problematic. The view I have characterized as ethnocentric is flawed not only because it fails empirical tests but because it is universalistic. Refuting such a universalistic statement about the domination of women everywhere requires only that examples of societies in which women are active be offered, not that their activity in every society be the same. It is not unusual to find societies in which women exert pressure and wield influence. Certainly, egalitarian societies offer example after example of women's participation in active decision making. Leacock's case, the Montagnais-Naskapi of Canada, provides an illustration of a system that, according to "accepted principles," should never have existed, namely, hunter gatherers with a matrilocal system. Her work established that colonial influences had led to the "traditional" picture of a patrilocal band (Leacock 1981: 4).

Similarly, my work depicts an egalitarian horticultural society in which men form the primary work team. Contrary to some accepted wisdom, however, and in spite of the value placed on patrilocality, most residence is neolocal because of women's pressure to structure situations so that they can better control them.

It is not unusual, then, to find places where women exercise very real power. This fact should not be any more of a challenge than the fact that men do. What should be at issue in both cases is the manner in which each gender does so, the sources of power, constraints on it, indeed all the ingredients of the social construction of reality.

In the following analysis of the Dukawa, I endeavor to present attitudes toward widows in the people's own terms. Women can and do use force to reassert their independence when cultural pressures are brought to bear. The key to understanding both female alliances and independence in this society is the institution of bride service (*gormu*). Widows are like unmarried women in that they have a variety of choices about their future. A number of factors influence widows' choices, and a minimax model helps analyze that matrix. Finally, much of the manipulative power of women comes from their linchpin function, and the symbolic elaboration of that function, resulting from their role in the alliance system, one far more active than envisioned in standard Lévi-Straussian thought. (See Lévi-Strauss 1969 and Rossi 1974.)

SETTING

The Dukawa, self-name Hune, live mainly in Rijau District, Kontagora Division, Niger State; and Shanga District, Yauri Division, Sokoto State, Nigeria. About 30,000 of the 34,000 Dukawa live in Rijau District; the remainder live in Shanga District. The Dukawa are a fiercely independent and egalitarian people who came to northwestern Nigeria from "the east" in order to maintain their independence from slave raiders. They continued their tradition of resistance to outside domination in struggles against the Fulani, the Hausa, and the British, earning a reputation as "truculent" troublemakers.

As defense against nineteenth-century slave raids, the Dukawa at first strengthened their two towns, Duku and Iri. Later they began to disperse, under pressure from the attacks of Ngwanache and his son, Ibrahim, two Fulani raiders from nearby Kontagora.

The Pax Britannica brought further dispersal, and abandonment of the towns of Duku and Iri. The names remain only as terms for the two sections of Dukawa. Today the Dukawa live in neighborhoods, albeit neighborhoods grouped into villages and towns by the ruling Hausa. Generally, each family composes a household, which cooperates with other nearby households. Average households consist of parents, unmarried children, and married sons and their children—about 25 people. Upon a father's death, however, the compound tends to fission. Each son moves in order to begin his own compound, impelled largely by pressure from his spouse, who sees greater advantage in independent action than in fraternal sharing.

Two factors facilitate such a move. First, women generally do not work on farms, except to help bring in the harvest. They have their own crops from locust and shea nut trees. They have the right to keep any money they make from those crops and from their control of brewing and selling guinea-corn beer (*giya*) or millet beer (*barukatu*). In order to maximize their profits, Dukawa women prefer to work in compatible surroundings. Generally, that does not mean compounds where their husbands' brothers and their wives are competing for scarce resources.

Although all adult Dukawa are expected to marry, some postmenopausal widows do not. They fit into the work system rather easily. They can perform the same work as other women and are generally welcomed by them as models. They have a number of options regarding residence, which are discussed in the following section. They will have little difficulty if any in obtaining accommodations or employment.

The struggle for survival takes place in a tropical savannah climate with essentially three seasons: rainy (June to October), harmattan (November to February), and *bazara* (March to May). The latter two are lumped together as the "dry season." The major climatological difference, however, is that the harmattan wind, a desiccating one, makes life extremely uncomfortable. The average diurnal temperature fluctuates about 40 degrees, from a mean maximum of 97 degrees Fahrenheit to a mean minimum of 58. The *bazara*, or hot season, sees little temperature variation; average maximum temperatures are over 100 degrees and minimum temperatures are not much lower.

The contrast between the dry and wet seasons, however, is more sociological than climatological. In the rainy season, most of the vital cultural activities occur, including marriage and bride service. Festivals, religious rituals, wrestling, hunting, farming—all the self-defining activities—occur then.

The Dukawa live in a setting of great ethnic heterogeneity. They came to northwestern Nigeria in order to escape slavery, and their stay there has been one of constant struggle to resist encroachments on their freedom. They have refused conversion to Islam, perceiving it as a surrender of their ethnic identity, and they have refused to allow *any* intermarriage, perceiving that with those of the wider society and complementary to them. The period of bride service serves as a rite of passage for the Dukawa, since it marks a transition from youth to adulthood. The friends, therefore, who perform bride service with a man, remain his closest friends throughout life, and they must support him in all disputes—those with kin and non-kin, Dukawa and strangers.

Similarly, women whose husbands have been *gormu*-mates retain lifelong close ties with one another, ties transcending their husbands' deaths. They have, in a sense, "come out" together, for their husbands have worked in communal service together for each of them. For women, as well as men, the *gormu* complex is a means of passing to adulthood. Just as their husbands support one another in disputes, so, too, do the women band together to protect their common interests.

Generational solidarity is an overriding principle of Dukawa culture. *Gormu* service, by fostering cooperation among men and women involved in it, promotes such solidarity. The period of bride service is one of testing the potential marriage by providing spouses with opportunities to discover whether they are sexually, temperamentally, and emotionally compatible. In turn, by working together from farm to farm for six or seven years, *gormu*-mates learn quite a bit about one another. They learn their moods, tastes, and reliability. They form an identity within Dukawa society and assume responsibilities for each other's actions.

After marriage, divorce is both difficult and distasteful. Spouses are therefore encouraged to learn as much about each other as possible before the final completion of *gormu*. On the other hand, children born during the *gormu* period are especially welcome, for they bode well for its successful completion. Since no husband wants his child to be lost to his lineage, the birth of a child almost compels him to complete his service, for if he fails to do so, or if his wife rejects him, then the child belongs to her patrilineage.

WIDOWS

It is clear, then, that in the light of the meaning of *gormu* women have a linchpin role in Dukawa culture. They are the repositories, or at least co-repositories, of key values; they are the juncture points of major alliances. By key values, I mean fidelity, stability, independence while cooperating, love, and chastity. The importance of completing *gormu*, moreover, in the sealing of an alliance is manifest where *gormu* has not been completed but children have been conceived. When death ends *gormu*—the time when Dukawa say they have a spouse but are not yet married—and the woman has conceived or borne the child of a man who died during *gormu*, then the man's younger brother will seek to marry the widow. Any children born before the completion of *gormu* belong to the woman's patrilineage unless she agrees to marry a man, preferably her husband's younger brother, from her husband's family. Such a marriage is a leviratic one. (See Salamone 1972 for a fuller discussion.)

Moreover, even if *gormu* has been completed, a widow with an unweaned child may take that child with her to her father's home. Although such a child is affiliated legally with the father's patrilineage, Dukawa fear that the child may never return once she or he accompanies the mother to her village. Therefore, widows with children find that their dead husbands' families urge them to remain and remarry into their group.

Especially sought-after are widows who were married by virtue of performing *gormu*. To the Dukawa such women have special meaning, for it is the *form* of Dukawa marriage that is particularly prized, requiring so much cooperative effort and symbolizing core values. In fact, even when an elderly man wishes to marry he will convert bride price marriage into *gormu* by hiring surrogates to perform a symbolic one-year *gormu* for him. (See P. Bohannan 1959 for comparable Tiv beliefs.)

The pressure of the junior levirate among the Dukawa by no means ensures that the widow will stay within her husband's family. The junior levirate, as found among the Dukawa, requires a man's younger brother to offer to marry his widow and raise up children for his name. He may, of course, also marry his own *gormu*-wife or any other wife he can afford. It does not, however, require the woman to accept the man's offer. Such a marriage would really be a continuation of the woman's former marriage. If *gormu* has not been completed, the arrangement conforms to what Evans-Pritchard terms "ghost marriage" among the Nuer. (See Evans-Pritchard 1951. In addition, D. K. Fiawoo, personal communication, points out the similarity of Dukawa and Nuer practices, as well as those in many other societies in West Africa with which he is personally familiar.)

A widow has the option of refusing the advances of her dead husband's younger brother, or, if there is no younger brother, his equivalent: a younger male cousin, for example. She can, and usually does, bargain for additional favors, for she is fully aware of her value. Such favors might include bride wealth to induce her to stay. That the bride wealth goes to her father does not deter her, for she gains prestige through its presentation. In addition, she will probably receive clothes for her child and herself. Anything that serves to highlight her value to her husband's family is welcome, for she is a person who has her proven worth.

Whether any further bride service or, most commonly, bride wealth is required depends upon a widow's bargaining power. Traditionally, such a marriage presented few problems if any for a man. Although monogamy is common, polygyny is not forbidden, and a leviratic union is not considered by Dukawa to constitute polygyny. A widow has the option of refusing any form of remarriage, leviratic or free-choice. No one will blame her for any choice she may make. Indeed, only a man's younger brother has no real choice, for he must seek to continue his brother's marriage and raise up children for his dead brother.

Dukawa do not have a "double standard" of morality. Extramarital affairs are equally condemned for men as well as women. Therefore, widows are not easy prey for men interested in comforting them during their period of mourning. Nor is the widow a rival to married women, pursuing their husbands' affections. No extramarital affairs are condoned by Dukawa. This does not mean that no adultery occurs. It does, and women as well as men initiate it. But the definitions vary. For a woman it consists of any extramarital liaison; for a man it consists of any liaison with a married woman. It should be noted that a man cannot simply dally with any free woman. His object must be marriage.

The only crime more grave than adultery is incest. Indeed, adultery is a more serious crime than murder, for it strikes at the cornerstone of Dukawa social structure and cultural identity, the family. In the case of a married woman, for example, the husband could kill an adulterer whom he caught in the act. He and his brothers could also attack the adulterer's home, destroying property and demanding compensation. No one will come to the adulterer's aid. There is more leeway in the treatment of the woman. Normally a wife would not be killed, but she might have her ear cut off, for "if she will act like a bitch," the husband will mark her for all to know her shame. Wives who admit their guilt and promise to reform may go unpunished; those who deny the act may be required to take an oath and undergo a poison ordeal at the home of the chief priest of *kurom njir*.

Neither do women sit by passively while their husbands engage in adultery. There have been cases of wives committing what Dukawa define as justifiable homicide against philandering husbands or the women with whom they are involved. (Salamone 1983 includes a discussion of Dukawa marriage law.)

Since celibacy among premenopausal woman is not a virtue, and is rare among postmenopausal ones, it is unlikely that a Dukawa widow will long remain unmarried. Therefore, it is pertinent to examine factors that will influence her choices regarding future actions. If a widow is happy with her husband's family, then she is likely to agree to a leviratic arrangement and remain with them. As noted above, a Dukawa compound ideally consists of a man and wife, their unmarried children of both sexes, and their married sons and the sons' wives and unmarried children. Upon the father's death, the eldest son should inherit his power. Centrifugal tendencies in Dukawa society, also noted above, tend to promote deviations from the ideal so that many Dukawa compounds are composed of men who have performed *gormu* service together—perhaps joined by some brothers, and by brothers-in-law. Variations occur and some compounds are composed of extended conjugal families.

For any given widow, happiness of course depends on subjective as well as more objective characteristics, but some common cultural traits do enter into her considerations. She will give serious thought to whether her prospective leviratic husband has treated her well before marriage. Their relationship has been one of privileged familiarity, so she will have had ample opportunity to know his moods. She will reflect on whether she has

found the women in his compound compatible in their mutual performance of farming and harvesting of women's crops—shea nuts, locust nuts,
and so forth. Moreover, she will put great store in whether her share of her
husband's property was given her ungrudgingly. She is entitled to furniture,
a share of any money, depending on how many children are alive, sufficient
food for her subsistence, and adequate woman's farm land and trees to care
for her needs.

She will also consider the sex and age of her children. If she has adult
males, she is assured of honor and protection among her dead husband's
group. If, however, she has only young daughters or no children at all, she
is in a weaker bargaining position. Young children can accompany her to
her father's home if they are unweaned. Their return to their father's compound is uncertain at best. Children therefore give a widow some bargaining power. If a woman finds that she and her children get along with her
dead husband's brothers, and if she discovers that her prospective levir appeals to her sexually, then there is good reason indeed to marry him.

Similarly, if her in-laws have found the widow to be an asset, to be a link
to a powerful and respectable family, to be pleasant, sharing, and a hard
worker—in sum, all that a Dukawa woman should be—then they will not
easily let her get away. They will appeal to her family to put pressure on
her to choose a spouse from among them. They will pay a good bride price,
even for a leviratic union, to ease her decision and increase her family's
pressure on her. Women of her dead husband's family will visit the widow
and as friends entice her to remain. If she has children past weaning, then
they will appeal to her to remain for the sake of her loved ones. Children
belong to their father's patrilineage, and a widow must leave weaned children behind. She can of course visit them, but upon their father's death
their uncle has the responsibility for raising them.

Rarely will a widow's in-laws not be eager to keep any woman still in
her childbearing years. A man's younger brother is obligated to raise up
children for his name, echoing both the Bible and Evans-Pritchard (1951).
Among traditional Dukawa, the father (*pater*) of any children resulting
from a leviratic relationship was the woman's first husband. Whoever the
biological father (*genitor*) may be, in fact, the children belong to the *pater*'s
patrilineage. The *genitor*, ideally the dead man's younger brother, is responsible for the upkeep of the children. Among Christian and Muslim Dukawa,
however, the children do not follow the leviratic rule but take their biological father's name. He then becomes, of course, their social father (*pater*) as
well.

A widow may, to reiterate, choose to marry outside her husband's family.
If she has produced children, particularly males, she is highly desired. If she
is still young, she may find men willing to perform at least a symbolic version of *gormu* for her on her father's lands. Such service, performed while

she resides in her father's compound, gives the suitor rights to her future children (rights *in genetricium*) as well as sexual rights (rights *in uxorum*). These rights supplant those of her dead husband, and no compensation is due his family, a further aid to her bargaining position.

A flattering offer to perform *gormu*—consisting, in the case of widows, of a year or so of service plus a bride price—underscores her social value. Old men often make such an offer because of the large property the widow controls and the cultural need to redistribute it lest she be accused of witchcraft. These old men further redistribute money by paying young men to stand in for them during any *gormu* service.

A woman may choose her husband's death as the occasion to marry an illicit lover. Because of the intimacy of Dukawa social life, it is unlikely that such a lover would be from her husband's compound or one close to it. She must be discreet enough to hide her affair in order to avoid any homicide or witchcraft charges. Dukawa women are not sexually shy, and although extramarital affairs are forbidden, they do occur with sufficient frequency as to be not unusual.

A woman's choices regarding remarriage could be summed up in a minimax manner: she chooses the best possibility given the alternatives. Among the factors taken into account are the following. First, compatibility with her in-laws. If a woman cannot get on with her father-in-law or, more importantly, with her mother-in-law, she has little incentive to remain in their compound. Her husband's brothers are also key figures in her decision. If she cannot work well with their wives, then her life is unbearable. Second, the sexual appeal of her dead husband's younger brother. Dukawa women make no attempt to hide their enjoyment of sex, and male sexual prowess is perceived as a key factor in marital happiness and stability. Third, the equitability of the inheritance and its distribution. As noted above, there is a subjective element involved. How much, after all, is sufficient? The spirit in which her husband's family doled out her share is important. Specifically, generosity of spiritcheerfulness in giving—is highly prized.

But other factors are important too. The presence of children and their age and sex, as noted above, play a key role in a woman's decision. Furthermore, quite simply, a woman may find that she is not marketable. If she has no other offers, or possibilities of any, then her choices are limited. Her own age and the length of time she was married are also important considerations. If she has spent many years in her husband's compound, she will be reluctant to leave. Indeed, she and her husband may be the grandparents of the compound. If she is quite young, however, her ties to the compound may be loose and her opportunities elsewhere may be great.

The alliances created by the marriage may be relevant too. If the alliance has worked out well, then her own family will exert its influence to have her remarry within the allied group. If it has proved worthless, then there will be no such urging. If a woman is young, family pressure may be hard to resist. I have, however, known even young women to resist parental pressure rather in the manner of modern romantic heroines. Indeed, such examples coupled with other data provide a strong case for the existence of true romantic love in a setting where modern sociologists tell us it cannot exist (e.g., Persell 1983). Perhaps they have forgotten that personal, idiosyncratic factors enter into a woman's decision, including the presence of a lover, personality, attachment to parents or brothers—in fact, anything, including the mood of the moment.

If a widow decides to remain unmarried, as is her right, she will normally return to her father's compound unless she is postmenopausal or has an adult son in her husband's compound. In the latter case, she has achieved great status in that compound and has more to gain by remaining. An unmarried widow will normally remain unmarried for a considerable time only if she is nursing a child, pregnant, or postmenopausal. If she returns to her father's compound, both she and her unweaned children have rights there. She is subject to him as head of the compound, and her father will gladly treat her children as members of his family, although technically they belong to their father's lineage. The children, upon weaning, should return to their father's compound.

If her *gormu* was not completed, then a woman will keep her children with her as members of her father's compound. It is quite difficult for her in-laws to take away children who would belong to them technically by virtue of the completion of *gormu*. They therefore endeavor to keep the widow in the family. If children are weaned before their father's death, then there is no difficulty. Problems occur when an unweaned child is taken by its mother to her father's compound. For the most part, only force can affect its return. The unweaned children will be considered members of their father's compound and will inherit through that lineage, male or female, but they normally reside with their mother's father. They may choose to return to their father's family, and do so if they have any grievances against their maternal relatives. In practice, any children a woman takes with her to her father's compound in her widowhood stay there and are treated as having full rights.

Postmenopausal women are not expected to remarry. They are quite outspoken, notable even among the far from reticent Dukawa for their opinions on every topic. Their sense of humor salted with scurrilous remarks is also one of their distinguishing characteristics. They are consulted in any important decisions of the compound and have full and equal rights with any other member.

No one has to care for a healthy widow who chooses to return to her father's compound. In fact, no one has to take care of any adult Dukawa woman. Dukawa women are perfectly capable of supporting themselves, or at least of contributing their share to family economic units. Women make alcoholic beverages, shea nut butter, and other products, which they sell in the open market and to their husbands. They raise their own crops, generally those introduced by colonialism, such as rice or wheat. They tend to household tasks, and when necessary work beside men in the fields. Generally they help men during the harvest time or in clearing fields.

Married women get land from their husbands. Widows obtain it from adult sons or fathers, or from the husband's group as a reward for years of service. Although Dukawa women, like others in Africa, are capable of working horticultural land on their own, they generally work only "kitchen" fields and economic trees in that manner. They work with the iron-tipped hoe when necessary, but in general they rely on men to work the fields. A widow will turn to a son, a brother, or another male, depending on where she has located. She will market any surplus for that man just as she has done for her husband. In sum, there is a clear division of labor. There are male and female crops just as there are male and female jobs. The Dukawa recognize the complementariness of the division and the need, at times, for distinctions to be forgotten.

In a leviratic relationship, the widow moves in with the levir. She has her own hut for herself and her children. Her children belong to her first husband but her new husband has full responsibility for her care and that of her children. For all practical purposes she is "his" wife, but her children are his brother's. Whether she is a junior or senior wife depends on her relationship with her new husband's previous wife, if any. Since the junior levirate prevails among the Dukawa, in most cases she is senior to her new husband and to any other wives he may have. Most Dukawa women, it is clear, are able to take care of themselves and base their choices accordingly. But widows who are ill do need care. In that case, it helps to have sons who will provide.

Dukawa say that no matter how much a daughter loves her mother, a daughter is mobile and a son is not. In other words, a woman's daughter has obligations that take her away to her own husband and children. A woman's son, however, has ties that draw him back to his own mother and her to him wherever he may be. In time of need she is most likely to turn to an adult son who is the guarantor of her rights in any situation of dispute.

If a woman has no surviving son and is in poor health, then once again *gormu* ties enter the picture. A widow may turn to her husband's *gormu*-mates for aid, and they are honor-bound to comply. If that is not adequate, then she must rely on her brothers, paternal uncles, affines, and so forth. No one in need will go unaided, provided there are sufficient resources. However, having to seek aid that a son would normally provide does cause embarrassment and a certain loss of prestige.

CONCLUSION

Dukawa perceive the family as the institution that best defines themselves and protects their cultural identity. Any attack on the family is a danger to Dukawa culture itself, for the Dukawa see themselves as a group of brothers and Sisters whose strength lies in maintaining family ties. The cultural position of widows underscores the point, for widows are treated as part of the family, not as cultural anomalies. They participate in decision making. Far from being liminal, they are quite tangible and active and make concrete choices regarding their marriage and subsequent residential considerations.

Of course, widows do not construct their social reality from whole cloth. Cultural considerations play a role in their decision making. Since land is readily available and currently plays no significant role, other cultural factors take on increasing importance. Those considerations become concrete when applied to a widow's phenomenological situation.

Significantly, an investigation of a widow's universe of choices reveals the manner in which the essentials of Dukawa culture refract in specific cultural situations, suggesting the profitability of investigating a set of values in various cultural scenes. Dukawa widows display individuality, independence, awareness of alliances, care for children, industriousness, and related cultural virtues. They form and represent alliances—past, present, and potential. In the widow's position is found the warp and woof of Dukawa culture: namely, independence and alliance, centripetal and centrifugal tendencies bound in a dynamic tension, for women link groups. Those groups represent forces of independence and alliance and a woman's choices can destroy delicately balanced principles.

Finally, it is necessary to be explicit about the nonpassivity of Dukawa women. Contrary to the prevailing wisdom of Lévi Strauss (1969), Harris (1977), Divale and Harris (1976), Meillasoux (1975), Hammond and Jablow (1972), and numerous others cited above, women are active shapers of their own destinies within the structural and cultural confines of their own situation. They are active members of a family unit, the basic unit of Dukawa society. They consciously make choices regarding the family with which they will affiliate. Those choices are based on a rational consideration of a number of factors, reducing to a minimax assessment. Widows form a continuum with other women, simply applying basic principles to their particular situation. Those principles serve to protect the cultural identity of the Dukawa and its members in the face of outside threats. It is interesting that the only Dukawa convert to Islam in Shanga District is a man who has openly violated Dukawa marriage sanctions on numerous occasions.

A study of Dukawa widows indicates that many facile statements regarding typical families need revision. Widows, for example, form up to 30 percent of the total adult female population. Dukawa have defined widows' positions in conformity with Dukawa principles and in a manner to incorporate them within Dukawa family life. Many Dukawa families, perhaps one third, include widows. Studies of the relationships of various types of widows—those who have chosen the levirate, those who have remained unmarried and formed a unit with their children, those who have remarried on principles other than leviratic—are required to discover specific consequences of such arrangements. Preliminary ethnographic impressions suggest, however, that no cultural distinctions result and few microlevel ones of any consequences are noted.

Such consequences, I argue, have more implications for the epistemology of anthropology than for the study of families. It provides yet another example of anthropology rushing to apply universal principles before empirical foundations are appropriately laid or of wrongly applying valid theories because of unconscious ethnocentrism regarding the institution being studied.

18

Dukawa Views on Death

The missionary felt quite proud of his new-found ability in Hausa, the *lingua franca* of Northern Nigeria. He had mastered its elements in but three months. Feeling confident, he stepped out among the Dukawa on a market day. Sweating from nervousness as well as heat, he began to deliver a sermon on the death of Jesus Christ. Dukawa sat silently and focused intently on his message, faces uplifted. Occasionally, they nodded at a striking passage, clucking their tongues to signify agreement. Now and then, they stuck their tongues out in amazement.

Emboldened by the Dukawa's unfettered response, the good father delved deeper into the mysteries of the faith. Tears welled in his eyes as he verbally painted a picture of the suffering and death of Jesus Christ. Gasps greeted his tale. Pausing first for effect, he then resumed his narrative of the passion climaxing with the Resurrection. Based on the response to that point, the missionary expected a warm response, perhaps even the equivalent of a standing ovation.

The response was notable, indeed, but not quite what he anticipated. The Dukawa bounded to their feet and went shrieking in fright and anger back to the bush, leaving the spiritual envoy of Western culture puzzled and chagrined. It not only forced him to begin his work anew, it taught him an object lesson in cultural relativity and the need to learn a culture before trying to teach those who live by its rules.

The incident, related to me by the missionary involved, provides a relevant and significant text for initial inquiry regarding the Dukawa understanding of death (Peter Ottilio, personal communication). Symbolic unpacking of the tale, helps sketch the general framework of their epistemology regarding dying, death, and the dead. Each Dukawa, then, can work out an individual variation of the theme appropriate to a personal context within the general cultural boundaries.

In common with many other groups in the world, the egalitarian Dukawa maintain that those who can most help you are the very ones who can most harm you. Dukawa ethos is strongly democratic and, in theory, a person should advance through personal efforts alone (Salamone 1988). Since, however, the good do not always prosper and the evil often do, something else must be at work. That something else, as with the equally egalitarian Tiv the Bohannans describe is some form of "extraprocessual" activity—witchcraft, sorcery, or the supernatural workings of a dead relative.

As the missionary cited above notes, "When the Dukawa bury a person, they want him to stay under ground." The only reason for returning to walk among the living would be to seek vengeance for an evil done before or after death. To prevent evils done after death, elaborate rituals are performed, including a send off party, bikin mutuwa (party for the dead), at which the dead person's exploits are recounted. Slights and other offenses committed before a person's death are uncovered through consultation with appropriate religious practitioners. Before describing these practices and analyzing their meaning, it is best to describe the setting in which the Dukawa operate.

THE SETTING

The Dukawa (Hune) and the closely allied Kamberi, with whom they have a joking relationship, inhabit an area of northwestern Nigeria best described as a tropical savanna. Each group is found in a number of states in what was under British colonialism ruled as Northern Nigeria. Their language belongs to the Niger-Congo language family, Benue-Congo branch, Plateau Division. The center of the Plateau Division is 10° North Latitude and 10° East Longitude.

The majority of the Dukawa's 30,000 population are in Shanga District of Yauri Division and Rijau District of Kontagora Division. Both districts were in the old Sokoto State and adjoin each other. I will concentrate on Dukawa practices in Shanga District, although practices in Rijau do not vary much. Neither do practices diverge greatly in new areas into which the Dukawa have moved within the last decade or so.

Although small, Yauri Emirate, coterminous with Yauri Division, is noted for its ethnic heterogeneity. Shangawa, Gungawa, Lopawa, as well as Kambari and Dukawa, consider themselves indigenous to the area. The ruling Hausa and Cattle Fulani are not considered indigenous. The ruling class is Hausa, not Hausa-Fulani as in many other areas of the North. The British, during their occupation, encouraged numerous other groups to migrate to Yauri, further increasing its ethnic diversity.

In such pluralistic situations, identity markers become quite significant. Given the Dukawa concern for equality, internally and externally, their resistance to Hausa and British control is quite understandable. A pivotal part of that resistance has been the preservation of religious practices in the face of pressure to convert to Islam. When armed resistance became impossible under British opposition, the Dukawa took to the bush and sought isolation from day-to-day contact. Such isolation has itself become increasingly difficult in the post-colonial world. Religion, therefore, is forming a last line of defense in the effort to sustain a separate ethnic and, consequently, political identity.

It is necessary to clarify what I mean by "tradition." I agree with Hobswam and Ranger (1983) that people "invent" traditions to suit their needs and that the search for a primordial collection of traditions in a living group is nonsense. Ethnic identities come and go according to their usefulness to a set of people engaged in a network of social interactions. Therefore, by tradition I mean an attitude of mind rather than a pristine chronological period somehow preceding any outside contact. This approach obviates the need to ascertain that a practice be of a certain age before it can somehow be considered "traditional," for if a people themselves have accepted a practice as an integral part of their "customary" way of life, then for them it is traditional. In conformity with Dukawa views, I have accepted the period just before the colonial period as their "traditional period."

During that period, and into the present, Dukawa social organization is acephalous, or multicentric, an organization in conformity with their high regard for egalitarianism. They live in extended family compounds in which property is freely shared. Each member of the extended family (dengi) is allowed sufficient free land to support his nuclear family.

Dukawa egalitarianism carries over into relationships between the sexes. Even though there is a sexual division of labor, women keep their earnings from their crops (shea nuts, for example) and from the indigenous alcoholic beverages they brew (*giya* and *barukatu*) and then sell to their husbands and their friends. Moreover, the culturally preferred form of marriage includes the performance of bride service (gormu) for a woman, whom a man has chosen, with her consent, to be his wife.

Indeed, gormu provides a royal road for understanding Dukawa core values. A man forms great ties with his age-mates during the seven year period of bride service. The team goes from farm to farm, working on their future fathers-in-law's farms. During its work, team members are allowed no conversation. They may sing only in Dukanci, their native tongue. Specifically, they sing the gormu song of the young man who is performing the bride service. These gormu songs identify the men throughout their lives. At each important event in a man's life, he and his mates sing his wakar gormu ("wedding song"). Finally, it is sung for the last time at his bikin mutuwa. No man is allowed to use another man's song, for each man must compose his own wakar gormu, expounding his own virtues to his father-in-law and wife (Salamone 1982 and 1978).

After the completion of gormu, divorce is rare, but possible. The most common motive for divorce is adultery. Both men and women are cautioned against the offense. The Dukawa, however, differentially define the practice for each sex. For women adultery consists of any extra-marital liaison. Because polygyny is allowed for Dukawa males, adultery is defined for them as sex with another's wife, including those who have begun gormu.

The Dukawa regard adultery as more serious than murder because it strikes at the very cornerstone of their social structure and cultural identity, the family. In fact, an adulterer's own family will abandon him. His actions have brought shame on the dengi, and they quickly pay the compensation due the aggrieved husband. They may parade the adulterer around naked in public, his ear cut like a dog's, whose behavior his sexual excess resembles.

The injured husband is left to deal with his wife. His treatment depends on a number of factors, including his love and affection, her remorse, the number of children she has produced and his own nature, among others. A husband could take an unrepentant woman to the kugom njir, a high priest who is head of the major religious cult. Here the Dukawa bring supernatural force to bear to right the imbalance in society. Men have poisoned their unrepentant wives here and attributed the death to God.

Similarly, incest strikes at the core of the family. It is defined as intercourse within the dengi. The dengi consists of all descendants, whether in the male, female, or mixed line, from the great-grandparents. Only God can punish those who commit incest because no dengi member may harm another one. The offense concerns only dengi members. There is a hint that, just as in "God's" punishment of an unrepentant wife, human agency may help "God" along. No Dukawa, however, would openly admit to that possibility.

Because the Dukawa perceive the family as the institution that best defines themselves and protects their cultural identity, any attack on the family is a danger to Dukawa culture itself. No one can defend the offenders, for the offense is literally beyond defense, it attacks the very concept of culture itself.

Finally, the entire complex of inheritance rules stresses the unity of the family. All full brothers, and sometimes even all dengi members, work their farms communally. It is a rare Dukawa who enjoys being alone. Both male and female work is conducted in teams. If a man dies without any living sons, land goes to the dengi and to his gormu-mates. With their consent, widows are inherited by one of the deceased's junior brothers. A woman has a shame-avoidance relationship with her father-in-law; therefore sexual relations with a man's senior brother would be the equivalent of incest because a wife regards a man's senior brothers as the equivalent of his father.

The entire complex of inheritance rules stresses the unity of the family, its cooperative nature, and the need to maintain alliances with other families. As in every other egalitarian system, there is a real danger of centrifugal forces. Thus, anything working against the family which is the very bedrock of alliances and values central to the maintenance and persistence of Dukawa identity is combated ferociously, including the use of supernatural means and the intervention of the dead.

DUKAWA, LIVING AND DEAD

The centrality of the family in Dukawa social and cultural life is beyond dispute. Anything that attacks the family is in itself bad and anything that protects the family is, conversely, good. All family members have an inherent obligation to defend the family, the dengi, and to punish those who work against its interests. When those interests endangered through the actions of family members, the family must work to guide those who endanger its core interests. They may not, however, kill an erring family member.

More specifically, no living family member may kill another living family member. It is essential to recall that the Dukawa family consists of the living, dead, and those yet to be born. The dead, truly, terrify the living for they can and must intervene in situations pertaining to the family. Some situation, such as incest, is beyond the power of the living to punish because death is the only punishment. Others may be too delicate for members to affect, such as internal feuding among family factions. Moreover, since Dukawa organization is really that of egocentric septs, each individual has his/her own egocentric network. Conflicts are, alas, natural to such a system of social organization. Additionally, since dengi exogamy and the junior levirate prevail spousal conflicts are virtually built into social relationships.

The dead dengi members have sufficient reason to walk the village paths, settling old scores and righting imbalances. The death of the dengi would mean their own cessation because there would be no one to perform the necessary rituals for them. They would be forgotten and cease to exist as individual entities.

Spiro (1952) has written eloquently about ghosts in Ifaluk. Without totally subscribing to his Freudian or functionalist orientation, it is possible to discern a great deal of similarity between the Dukawa dead and those whom he describes. Both act as the conscience of their people. They avenge

wrongs no one else can. Their appearance signals a social breakdown that
requires quick repair. Hidden thoughts become revealed as supernatural
practitioners are called into service. Internal aggressions are directed out-
ward and a solution provided.

Rifts between different segments of the family are common in egalitarian societies. Michael Mbabuike (1992, personal communication) notes
that among the Igbo of Nigeria's east and midwest, it is common from
time to time to have witchcraft and other accusations hurled at a branch
of the family that is prospering while another branch suffers undue losses
of personnel. These disputes, Mbabuike asserts, reach back to slavery when
one branch of the family would sell members of other branches to slave
traders. Ancestors are called upon to settle these disputes and bear witness
to the good will of surviving family members. The principle is, once again,
that in democratic societies people prosper only at the expense of others,
especially when merit does not emerge triumphant as the cultural ideal
states it should.

Similarly, among the Dukawa ancestors regulate the social world that has
gone askew. To neglect an ancestor is to tempt fate. It is also self-defeating
since an individual's good and that of his dengi are related. Of course, in the
day-to-day world interests do clash. Brothers quarrel. People are attracted
to those forbidden them. Younger brothers may not wish to marry older
widows. People do not always want to share or give away their prized possessions. Centrifugal forces are powerful in multicentric political systems.

As Spiro (1952) noted it is in just such situations that personified supernatural forces are most effective. Because personal independence became
not only a matter of pride, but also survival, for Dukawa after the civil wars
of the nineteenth century, supernatural forces have become indispensable
in maintaining their identity and cohesion. The Dukawa have had to maintain their identity in an extremely hostile environment. A brief diversion
clarifies the point.

The Hausa are the dominant group in Yauri. The Hausa-Dukawa history
is marked by bitterness and mutual hostility. The Dukawa, whom the Hausa
classify as "pagans" (*arna*), became victims of the internal slave trade which
Hausa and Fulani raiders organized. Yauri's relative isolation prompted the
Dukawa to choose it as a place of refuge. Because of Islam's association with
slave-raiding, the Dukawa resisted any attempts at Islamic conversion. They
interpreted any such pressure as hostile intrusion. Islam and its adherents,
especially the Hausa and Fulani, still remain the antithesis of the Dukawa
image of the good life.

In the various wars that mark Yauri's history over centuries, the Dukawa
allied themselves with the Kamberi against Hausa, Fulani, and other Islamic forces. They continued their resistance into the nineteenth century
against the most powerful threat posed to their continued existence, that of

Ngwamse and his son Ibrahim, Fulani slave raiders centered in the nearby Kontagora emirate. As a defense, the Dukawa first strengthened their major towns, Iri and Duku. Continued pressure from Ngwamse and his son, however, forced them to begin to disperse. Their Kamberi allies who chose to stand and fight rather than flee suffered terrible losses. These losses were such that they the Kamberi eventually sought refuge in marginal bush areas (daji). The losses were so great, moreover, that they led to significant social structural and adaptational changes (Adamu, personal communication).

In order to escape conversion or its alternative, enslavement, the Dukawa moved further into Yauri's frontier area, Shanga District. The independent Fulani raider, Sambo, further stimulated their dispersal through his conquest of Rijau District in Yauri and his removal of that district from Yauri's control. Sambo's actions served to intensify the Dukawa's self-definition as not only non-Muslim but also anti-Islamic.

Under the Pax Britannica, Dukawa-Hausa relationships deteriorated. The British were able to force the Dukawa to do things the Hausa and Fulani were not; namely, to pay taxes. Taxes, moreover, were to be paid in coin, forcing people to enter the money economy, strengthening the central government. Such strengthening made it virtually impossible for any group to escape its control through flight. Because the Dukawa continued to struggle against British control as they had Hausa suzerainty, the British deemed them "truculent" and barbarians (A.D.O. Yauri to Resident, Kontagora: NANK: K6099, Vol.II, letter dated Oct.6, 1917).

In 1913 the Dukawa were in armed rebellion against British tax collectors. In 1914, ninety-six Dukawa fled to the nearby town of Koko, but the British found them and arrested them for non-payment of taxes. Both armed resistance and flight proved useless against British power, and British power was allied with the ruling Hausa. This alliance further reinforced Dukawa self-perception as "outsiders" who must rely on themselves for survival. Their Kamberi allies had been forced to adapt an accommodating posture of apparent docility to survive. They reinforced their servility through supplying wives to other ethnic groups while receiving none in return. The Dukawa pitied and despised their friends for their behavior while resolving to distinguish themselves from it through independent action.

To strengthen their ability to act independently the Dukawa used the opportunities the Pax Britannica afforded to disperse even further than they had form their centralized settlements of Iri and Duku to decentralized dwellings. These independent, self-sufficient settlements consisted of isolated extended family compounds, usually established a mile or more from simller communities. Quite rightly, the British perceived these settlements as Dukawa attempts to avoid taxes and escape their "civilizing" influence as well as that of the British Muslim allies. Consequently, the British misunderstood the Dukawa as the following passage reveals.

... they had no chiefs of their own so have never recognized authority. . . . Their headmen are usually harmless old dotards left in the town apparently to look after the graves of their ancestors (A.D.O. Yauri to Resident, Kontagora: NANK: K6099, Vol.II, letter dated Oct.6, 1917).

These "harmless old dotards" were, in fact, the most powerful priests, the kugom njir, of the Dukawa.

British misperception of Dukawa authority patterns cost Yauri a large section of land and split the Dukawa population between Yauri and Kontagora. (See Salamone 1984: 49-51 and 64-67 and NANK: K6099, Vol. II.) Those Dukawa who remained in Yauri tended to be more conservative than those who came under Kontagora's domain. They believed that they would be better able to maintain their old way of life in Yauri's bush area. Indeed, the majority of the approximately 3,000 Dukawa who remained in Yauri were actually elders and, therefore, most in touch with tradition (Adamu, personal communication).

It was in the context of colonial control that the current Dukawa conception of "the good life" evolved, a life looked after by the ancestors. It has been in the context of Hausa post-colonial extension of colonial control that the current Dukawa conception has solidified, for if the colonial government was able to exert its authority and centralize the government in ways its Islamic predecessor had been incapable of doing, its various successor states have accelerated that process, perhaps, in ways repugnant event to the colonial government itself. In numerous ways, Nigerian independence has posed threats to Dukawa identity that British colonization did not. Among the weapons in Dukawa struggle to preserve self-identity is the Dukawa conception of the good life and the role of the ancestors in guarding it, a tasks which other African ancestors perform in similar circumstances. (See Middleton 1960, for example.)

THE GOOD LIFE

The ideal life for the Dukawa is one that best ensures Dukawa survival. Thus, the perfect Dukawa is one who follows the elders and their traditions. Those Dukawa, then who would turn their backs on tradition could not live the good life. A good Dukawa, however, does more than state his intentions to follow traditions. Certain specific acts are required. One informant states, he would "give his last penny to a person in need" (Bello, personal communication). Generosity is highly valued. Indeed, not to be generous often leads to witchcraft accusations. A good person displays other neighborly attributes. He does not fight, lie, or quarrel with others. At the same time, he controls his family and provides for it. He is a loving father to his children and a loyal spouse to his wife. The Dukawa punish male adulterers severely as we have seen above.

Since they disrespect outside law, they rely very strongly on internal controls, generally those based on family and friendship. The gormu-team epitomizes the intersection of the two principles for internal rule. As noted above, a man's gormu-mates become his closest friends, in many cases closer than even brothers. They hunt with him, drink with him, and, if need arises, bury him.

Hunting is central to Dukawa self-identity and a man generally hunts with his gormu-mates. To be a Dukawa is to be a hunter, and it is fitting that a man identifies his bride-service mates as an integral part of his ethnic identity. Many wakar gormu identify the singer and suitor as a great hunter.

Only good people can be successful hunters, therefore, harmony defined as good relationships among the dengi and friends, is essential. Without harmony people would be killed on the hunt either by other people or wild animals. Harmony, moreover, is essential to hunting because tracking is prized as highly as shooting, and without harmony there can be no successful tracking. In fact, given the problematic accuracy of Dukawa Dane guns, tracking is probably more valuable to the hunting process than shooting.

No one would consider taking a "bad person," a drunkard, womanizer, liar, cheat or quarrelsome person, on a hunt. Such people threaten Dukawa harmony and would spoil the hunt, the symbol of Dukawa values and identity. The Dukawa uses hunting rather consciously as a cultural metaphor for his independence and democratic way of life. Cooperation on equal terms with good people is essential to group preservation. Not surprisingly, hunting became essential to Dukawa self-identification only after they dispersed from their towns.

The present symbolic salience of hunting (Oh^obo) in Dukawa life is succinctly expressed in the following account.

> The reason why Dukawa hunt? A man must go hunting because they like to dance. You see, you must go hunting if you want to get a woman to get married. When your father or mother died, you could not get inside their funeral feat (bikin mutuwa). You would be ashamed, for everyone would laugh at you. Even when you die, they will laugh at you if you are not a hunter. The people will only beat the drum for one who has performed bride-service (gormu). Failure to perform bride-service means that you have never changed your life, even since you were born. You are not a real man. People will laugh at your wife, too. She will not be happy. Your brothers will not marry your widow. They will treat her as a stranger. A man cannot dance unless he has killed an animal. One who has killed four, or three, or two animals can dance. But if a man has killed only one animal, he cannot dance. A man who has never killed, cannot marry a woman --ever! If you have never killed animals, you can't come

to the hunters' lodge. They will laugh at you and will not feel happy (Matthew Bello, personal communication).

There is, therefore, a clear connection between hunting (oh^obo) and gormu. Unconsciously, Bello slips from talking about hunting to discussing the consequences for those who have not performed gormu. The reason is obvious: only those who have performed gormu can hunt, for without its performance one remains socially a child and children cannot hunt, a point Matthew makes dramatically clear.

> Small boys who follow hunters are killed if they kill an animal and the hunters do not. The hunters will tell their father a lion killed them.

Small boys are, of course, not adults. Therefore, they cannot hunt. Doing so jeopardizes an entire system that Dukawa have established to preserve their identity. At the very heart of that system is the gormu complex. Hunting is inextricably related to that complex and a key symbol in establishing and preserving Dukawa identity. In Yauri, to be a Dukawa is to be a hunter.

DEATH RITUALS

Unsurprisingly, then, death rituals incorporate aspects of hunting and bride-service. Connections between hunting and *gormu* underscore both the Dukawa idea of the Good Life and its function in preserving Dukawa ethnic identity. The fact that ultimately ancestors safeguard these complexes demonstrates their centrality to the Dukawa. The circularity and self-reinforcement of the two appears obvious. To be a Dukawa male is to be a hunter-warrior. But in order to be an adult male one must first perform gormu in conjunction with one's age-mates. Those age-mates are a man's hunting companions throughout life, further reinforcing the systemic nature of the gormu-orho^bo complex. Gormu is performed only for Dukawa women. The boundary-maintenance functions of the system are obvious. Significantly, in Yauri only Dukawa do not intermarry with any of the other ethnic groups there. They do, however, intermarry with a group in Niger State named the Dakkakari who are related to them and with whom they are often confused.

One more reflection pertinent on the interrelationship between hunting and bride-service comes from Matthew Bello.

> When a big animal is spotted and killed, the hunters begin blowing horns and hitting gongs. They start to shout, and they dance in bush. The animal is slaughtered in the bush. They come to the people to tell them to stay. They cut off its tail and throw it to the people. The elder gets the tail. Then with shouts

(eihoo!) they go to the slaughtering place and get meat. The hunter who killed the animal is given the head and tail by the elder. He doesn't worry about the meat. The meat is shared among all. But the hunters eat first. They distribute the meat to others. People are free to do with the meat what they wish. They can eat it when they want or give it away. The hunters used to have bracelets made from the skins. These were called wasaida; that is, "a witness for hunting." The hunters will not talk about an animal they have already killed. If they have killed an antelope, they will ask God to continue helping them by letting them kill a buffalo, and so on.

In Bello's vivid description, the communal nature of the hunt is quite clear as are the various themes I have delineated.

Not everyone, alas, lives up to society's image of the Good Life. People stray from that image, sometimes tragically. The problems people meet in so doing, however, tend to reinforce Dukawa values. Not the least of these problems come from the dead ancestors who, as Middleton (1960) reminds us for the Lugbara, remain an integral part of their society. The rituals associated with death clearly demonstrate the place of the dead within Dukawa society and their role in protecting that society.

One week after a person dies, people brew giya and barukata, mildly alcoholic beverages. The household head invites neighbors to come and drink together. Three goats and three chickens are sacrificed. Then the priest and mourners go to a crossroad and place three stones there. They pour the sacrificial blood over the stones. They may go to a kuka (baobob) or tsamiya tree, which they consider magical trees, and pour more blood. They also pour giya for the spirits to drink. Then elders begin to pray:

> We thank you and we ask you to help us as we are giving you drink and blood. We ask you to help us and help the survivor to get another spouse. . . <If the survivor is a man, they continue in this fashion.> to take care of him and give him water and food. Because we know everything is possible for you. May we reach home safely without any harm—through the power of magic and also of God. We ask this magic to give us strength to clear our farms and we pray that our farms are freed of all harm. We ask the dead person to pray for us to save us. We ask God to help us in this world to stay safely without trouble and to stay with all our family, through the power of magic. We drive you away, oh Spirit. We don't want you to come to us during the night. We give you a drink and honor you. Remember our actions and stay away from our farms.

At this point, they pour the drink on the ground. They put one broken pot to the North end of the stones at the crossroads that mark the grave. Until they have performed these rituals, they have dreamed that the dead has been following them. After the rituals are performed, they will try to forget the dead until the next death.

The Dukawa have a ritual termed "washing the house of death." They pour a drink in the courtyard to drive away bad things and the dead. It appears, nevertheless, that the dead do not go away. Therefore, the Dukawa leave a little food out in a room reserved for the dead. The dead, they believe, return in the form of a rabbit or cat to eat the food. Consequently, Dukawa, who hunt everything else, do not hunt rabbits and protect cats, for to kill a rabbit or cat is to kill a person a second time and risk reprisal from the ancestors.

In common with numerous African peoples, the Dukawa believe that a person has three souls. When a person dies, one soul is lost. The rabbit or cat represents the dead staying close to home. Some Kamberi and Dukawa maintain that if a child dies, it will enter a pregnant neighbor's womb and be born again near home. The old men, however, will come and remind people of the dead ones. They will sing songs appropriate to the work he has done in his life. The remaining *gormu* mates sing their friend's wakar gormu. They sing hunting songs to commemorate his kills.

The actual bikin mutuwa occurs anywhere from one month to one year after an adult's death. A husband is responsible for arranging his wife's biki, an eldest son his father's. Typically, however, all of the male children will provide for the feast. The bikin mutuwa is separate from the funeral. The funeral transpires very quickly, usually on the day of death itself. In common with the funeral practice, however, men shave their heads. If the dead person was a priest, then men and women shave their heads. There is a great deal of wailing for someone in the prime of life.

The mai-giro priest, who is in charge of the magical end of Dukawa spiritual life, chooses the actual grave site. The official grave diggers, nine or ten elders, dig a shallow grave. They dig one at a time in rotation. The grave is three feet deep and two-and-a-half to three feet wide. The length varies by the size of the person being buried. The grave diggers are paid in cash and kind by the family members. The donations are in recognition of the prestige of the elders.

The dead person is wrapped in a piece of cloth cut to his or her body shape. The wrapped body is placed on a mat (tabarma) so that the face shows. Men gather around the body to screen it from the family. No conversation is allowed with the body. The body is laid in the grave on an angle, lying on its right side as if asleep, facing east and the rising sun. Mourners place sticks and stone over the body, then dirt, and finally mud. The characteristic mound comes last with stones and the broken calabash on the northern end of the grave, over the head.

The widow's head remains shaved until the end of the bikin mutuwa. She many use red dye on her head. She is dressed in a leaf skirt, with Indian hemp cord (yagiya) around her waist. If the dead person is a woman, then her widower wears his loin cloth inside out, a *yagiya* around his waist, and refrains from wearing his hat.

A typical bikin mutuwa has about two-hundred people present. It lasts for three days and nights. Generally it takes place either in May at the end of the host season or in December or January before the hunters leave for their annual hunting expeditions. The crossroads grave is decorated during the feast. On the first day people arrive in order from those who live farthest to those who live most near the site of the party. Drummers continue to beat the appropriate rhythm according to gender, status, and so forth. Each group to which the dead person belonged dances in turn. Finally, the entire group dances together.

After the mourning is ceremonially ended, contemporary dances takes places. A man's wakar gormu is sung by his age-mates. They cut the yagiya. A procession follows. The woman who had shaved the appropriate heads is given donations. She disposes of the hair in appropriate ways in order to protect people from black magic. The cord is removed and burned after being placed in a calabash and hidden secretly in the bush.

A man's gormu-mates take care that at the feast, bikin mutuwa, commemorating his death young men come prepared to wrestle. Men from one Dukawa town wrestle those men from different Dukawa areas. Each side forms a line and kneels down. Each man shows his right hand, palm up. One champion will go to another. If they agree to wrestle they will shake hands. If one refuses, he will shake his head and withhold his hand. Then a large circle is formed and the men begin to wrestle by holding each other's waist. The first wrestler to knock the other off his feet wins. Drummers begin to beat the victory cadence as the victor's colleagues carry him to the drummers.

They leave him there as everyone dances around him. He is showered with money and flour is put on his head. If he wins his next bout, then he is truly praised. After this champion has proved his mettle, everyone fights. The bouts last for three days, the period of the bikin mutuwa. After that time, the head of the young men, their champion wrestler, lead them back. He sings in praise of himself. Those victorious wrestlers find themselves praised in good spirit by those whom they defeated. The winners are also appreciably richer and hear their praises proclaimed by drummers.

Other games occur at the bikin mutuwa. These also appear to be related to courtship and fertility, for it is at wrestling matches that marriage matches take place. The Dukawa fight with sticks, as do the Fulani. They do so to attract girls. When a man wants to have sex with a girl for whom someone is performing bride-service, the young man performing gormu calls his rival and challenges him to a stick fight. Each beats the other three times on the back in turn. At times, a contestant may die. The stronger of the two gets the girl.

There is no accident in the plentiful use of obvious fertility symbols and activities surrounding both the immediate death rituals and those encompassing the latter bikin mutuwa. In fact, there is a bikin mutuwa that marks the end of a man's bride service. The connection of life and death is clear. The refusal of the dead to leave home and the impossibility of forcing him or her to do so is both a warning and a source of hope for the future. (Much of the material on the gormu, and the bikin mutuwa is based on Prazan 1977 and interviews with Bello and Ottilio, as well as attendance at these ceremonies.)

CONCLUSION

In the beginning is the end. All that missionary needed to know about Dukawa life was revealed in their reaction to his sermon about the resurrection of Jesus. Indeed, they want their dead to stay buried, to remain underground, and not to haunt their dreams or pursue their footsteps in a determined manner.

The calabash that plays so prominent a role in the ceremonies is a sign of life for the Dukawa. The calabash holds seeds, giya and barukatu, and food. Hence, when it is broken and placed on the grave, it states that life itself is broken. The living must now give food and drink to the dead.

Burial at the crossroads and the use of "Y" symbols in the kuka tree, sticks for fighting, and on designs in general is such a well-known African and African-American symbol that it requires little exposition. The crossroads is a place of magic, a place of possibilities, where journeys cross and change. It symbolizes the merging of life and death.

The liberal use of fertility symbols and the frequent use of death symbols at times when fertility is being marked underscore the continuance of life in varied forms. The Dukawa consist of those not born, those living, and those to come. The belief in reincarnation tightens the circle and provides it with a dynamic rationale. The dead may not be welcome in appearances among the living. They cannot be made to go away, and they will protect the group even at the cost of hurting those who may have been close to them in their mortal form of life. They appear only at times of crisis and to re-emphasize core Dukawa values: the unity of the family, generosity, the role of gormu, and respect for tradition.

Thus, it is not amazing that the Dukawa view the dead with such marked ambivalence. On the one hand, they dread them. When they die, they want them to remain in their shallow graves. However, they cannot do without them. Among such necessarily fiercely independent people only the ancestors can punish many offenses. They do so automatically and without mercy. They are the conscience of the people and keep them on the correct road. Without the dead, there would be no Dukawa, for they have been invented in order to maintain a Dukawa identity in the multiethnic context in which these people live.

This study and those of other groups I have cited suggest that there is a cost to acting independently and living in decentralized households. Trust is difficult to develop in a hostile environment. Constant vigllence is required when the central power has historically attempted to either enslave or dominate your group in some manner or other. Although dispersal is necessary in such conditions, it makes ties to other members of one's group difficult, for each group must be the entire Dukawa people in microcosm. Less poetically each group must be relatively self-sufficient.

Some agency, however, must punish that which living people may not. The dead serve that function, among others, in life. Since Dukawa ideals, furthermore, are so difficult to meet day-to-day, each person dreads being the victim of the ancestors, for no one can be totally free of violation. Those who in life can most aid us can in death most harm us. Further research should continue comparison with other societies with egalitarian cultural values. Perhaps, then we could refine our hunches about the relationship between dread of the dead and democratic ideology more carefully.

Bibliography

ARCHIVAL MATERIAL

Aberdeen: Department of Religious Studies, King's College, University of Aberdeen.

AB/P12/1:14 Ajayi, William (n.d.) *Aspects* of *Protestant Mission World, Northern Nigeria.*

AB(f12j2:2 Crampton, E. P. T. (1967) *Christianity in the North* of *Nigeria.* Dublin: University of Dublin, B.D. Thesis.

Owoh, Aaron Chikwendis (1971) *C.M. Missions, Muslim Societies and European Trade in Northern Nigeria: 1857-1900.* Aberdeen: University of Aberdeen, Faculty of Divinity, M.A. Thesis.

AB/PI2/1:8 Trimingham, J. Spencer (1955) *Islam in West Africa.* Church Missionary Society

CMS: G5 Ag/07/1901l: Numbers 1-42. Red Number 214-The Hausaland Mission. Rhodes House.

MSS African S 783.

MSS British Empire S76.

Abdullah. (n.d.) The YauriDay Book.

Adamu, Mahdi. (1968) "A Hausa Government in Decline: Yawuri in the Nineteenth Century." M.A. Thesis, Department of History, Ahmadu Bello University.

Balogun, S.A. (1970) "Gwandu Emirates in the Nineteenth Century with Special Reference to Political Relations: 1817-1903." M.A. Thesis, Department of History, University of Ibadan.

Emir of Yelwa *(sic.)*. Complaint against attitude of, by the Gungawa River Tribe. National Archives of Nigeria at Kaduna Sokoto Proof 150/p/1918.

Kontagora Province, Portion of the Dukawa Tribe in Yauri Emirate. Transfer of to Rijau District. National Archives of Nigeria at Kaduna. Secretary to the Northern Provinces K6099,Volume I, II.

PUBLISHED MATERIAL

Abubakar, Imam. (1950) "Daura Sword Is the Symbol of the Seven States of Hausa-land," *West African Annual:* 114-15.- (1954) *Hausa Bakwai.* Zaria: Gaskiya.

Ajayi, J.F.A. (1965) *Christian Missions* in *Nigeria* (1841-1891). Evanston: Northwestern University Press. Asad, Talal. (1975) *Anthropology and the Colonial Encounter.* London: Ithaca Press.

Ajayi, J. F. Ade: "Political organizations in West African towns in the nineteenth century: The Lagos example." *Urbanization in African Social Change,* Edinburgh, 1963.

Aquina, Sister Mary, 1967 The people of the spirit: an independent church in Rhodesia. *Africa* 203-219.

Asad, Talal (ed.). *Anthropology and the Colonial Encounter.* London: Ithaca Press.

Atkinson, Jane Monnig. 1992. 'Shamanisms Today,' Annual Review of Anthropology, 21: 307-330.

Ayandele, E. A. (1970) *The Missionary Impact on Modem Nigeria.* New York: Humanities Press.

Baranowski, Shelley and Furlough, Ellen. *Culture, and Identity in Modern Europe and North America.* The University of Michigan Press.

Barkow, Jerome *(1970)* "Processes of Group Differentiation in a Rural Area of North Central State, Nigeria." Chicago: Ph.D. Dissertation, Department of Anthropology, University of Chicago.

Barth, Fredrik, editor 1970 *Ethnic groups and boundaries.* New York: Little, Brown.

Beidelman, T. O. (1974) "Social Theory and the Study of Christian Missions in Africa." *Africa,* 44, 8: 285-49.

Bello, Matthew. 1976. Field Notes and Interviews, Yauri, Nigeria.

Brooke, N. J. (1985) *Census* of *Nigeria, 1931 (Census* of *the Northern Provinces).* London: The Crown Agents for the Colonies.

Buchanan, Keith: "The northern region of Nigeria: The geographic background of its political duality." *The Geographic Review,* 1956, 43, 451-473.

Cohen, Abner. The Symbolic Construction of Community, London / New York: Tavistock Publications, 1985.

—— Two-Dimensional Man: An Essay on the Anthropology of Power and Symbolism in Complex Society. Berkeley: University of California Press, 1974.

—— Introduction" to Urban Ethnicity, ed. A. Cohen. London: Tavistock, 1974. 1981. The Politics of Elite Culture: Explorations in the Dramaturgy of Power in a Modern African Society. Berkeley: University of California Press.

——. 1993. Masquerade Politics: Explorations in the Structure of Urban Cultural Movements. Berkeley: University of California Press.

——. 1979. "Political symbolism". *Annual Review* of *Anthropology* 8: 87-113.

——. 1981. *The Politics* of *Elite Culture: Explorations in the Dramaturgy* of *Power in a Modern African Society.* Berkeley: University of California Press.

Cohen, Ronald, and John Middleton, eds. 1967. Comparative Political Systems: Studies in the Politics of Pre-Industrial Societies. Austin: University of Texas Press.

Condominus, Georges. (1978) *Ethnics and Comfort: An Ethnographer's View* of *His Profession.* Washington: American Anthropological Association: 1-17.

Dry, E. A.: "The social development of the Hausa child." *Proceedings of the III International West African Conference; Lagos,..1_56,* 158-63.

Durkheim, Emile and Marcel Mauss. (1965) *Primitive Classification,* Trans. with an Introduction by Rodney Needham. Chicago: University of Chicago Press.

Erikson, E. H.: *Childhood and Society, New York,* 1950.

Erikson, E. H.: "The problem of ego identity." *Journal American Psychoanalytic Association,* 1956, 4.

Evans-Pritchard, E. E. (1940) *The Nuer.* New York: Oxford University Press.

Fallers, Lloyd A. (1955) "The Predicament of the Modem African Chief: An Instance from Uganda," *American Anthropologist* 55 (2): 290-305.

Ferdnance, T., Colonialism and the economic demise and transformation of Northern 1998 Nigeria's slave fundamental extractors from 1903 to the 1920s, Journal of Asian and African studies, 33, 3 223-240.

Forde, Daryll and Karberry, P. M.: *West African Kingdoms in the Nineteenth Century.* New York, 1967.

Forde, Daryll and Kallberry, P. M.: "The influence of 'Islam on a Sudanese religion." *Monographs of the American Ethnological Society,* 1946, 10.

Gallaway, A. D. *(1960)* "Missionary Impact on Nigeria." *Nigeria,* 59-65.

Gertz, Clifford. 1968 *Islam observed: religious development in Morocco and Indonesia.* New Haven: Yale University Press.

Gluckman, Max. (1954) *Rituals of Rebellion* in *South-East Africa.* Manchester: University of Manchester Press.

Goffman, Erving. *Interaction Ritual.* Pantheon: New York, 1967.

—— *The Presentation* of *Self in Everyday Life.* Doubleday: Garden City, New York, 1959.

——. *Stigma.* Prentice-Hall: Englewood Cliffs, New Jersey, 1963.

Greenberg, Joseph H.: "Islam and clan organization among the Hausa." *Southwest Journal of Anthropology,* 1946, 3, 193-211.

—— "Somc aspects of Negro_Mooammedan culture contact among the Hausa." *American Anthropologist,* 1946, n.S., 43, 51-61.

Guiart, Jean 1970 "The millenarian aspect of Christianity in the South Pacific," in *Millennial dreams in action.* Edited by Sylvia Thrupp, 122-138. New York: Schoken Books.

Gunn, Harold D and F. P. Conant 1960 *Peoples* of *the middle Niger region in northern Nigeria.* London: International African Institute.

Hallam, W.K.R. (1966) "The Bayajida Legend in Hausa Folklore," *Journal* of *African History* 7 (1): 47-60.

Harris, P. G. (1930) "Notes of Yauri (Sokoto Province) Nigeria," *Journal* of *the Royal Anthropological Institute* 60 Ouly-December): 283-334. (1938) *Provincial Gazetteer* of *Sokoto Province.* London: Waterlow and Sons, Ltd.

Heiss, David R. 1970 Prefatory findings in the sociology of missions. *Journal* of *the Scientific Study* of *Religions* 6 (Spring, 1970), 49-63.

Hassan. Alhaji and Mallam Shuaibu Na'ibi: *A Chronicle of A buja.* Ibadan, 1952.

Hendrixson, Joyce (1981) The Changing Signiicance of Ethnicity and Power Relationships, Sokoto, Nigeria. *Studies in Third World Societies* 11: 51-83.

Heussler, Robert. (1968) *The British* in *Northern Nigeria.* London: Oxford University Press.

Herskovits, Melville 1943 The Negro in Bahia, Brazil: a problem in method. *American So Anthropological Review* 8: 394-402.

Hodgkin, Thomas (ed.): *Nigerian Perspectives-An Historical Anthology.* London, 1960.

Hogben, S. J. and Kirk-Grcene, A. H. M.: *The Emirates of Northern Nigeria.* London, 1966.

Johnston, H. A. S.: *The Fulani Empire of Sokoto.* London, 1967.

Jones, G. L "Social Anthropology in Nigeria during the Colonial Period." *Africa:* 4: 280-89.

Kardiner, Abram and Preble. Edward: *They Studied Man.* Cleveland, 1961.

Kuper, Leo and Smioth, M. G.(ed$.): *Pluralism in Africa.* Los Angeles. 1969.

Kuper, Leo. (1969) "Ethnic and Racial Pluralism: Some Aspects of Polarization and Depluralization " pp. 459487 in Leo Kuper and M. G. Smith (eds.) *Pluralism in Africa.* Berkeley: University of California Press.

Lewis, Diane. (1975) "Anthropology and Colonialism." *Current Anthropology* 14: 581-602. Matthews, Basil (1926) *The Clash of Colour.* London: Cargate Press.

Luzbetak, Louis 1970 *The church and cultures.* Techny: Divine Word Press.

MacBride, D.G.H. 1935. *Rijau Report.Rijau District, Kontagora Division. Niger Province.*

Middleton, John. 1960. *Lugbara Religion:Ritual and Authority among an East African People.* London: International African Institute.

Morris, H. S. (1968) *The Indians in Uganda.* Chicago: University of Chicago Press.

Oberg, Calvero. (1972) "Contrasts in Fieldwork," pp. 78.86 in S. Kimba11 and James Watson (eds.) *Crossing Cultural Boundaries.* San Francisco: Chandler Publishing Company.

Opler, M. K.: "Culture and child-rearing." *Modern Perspectives in International Child Psychiatry,* J. G. HoweHs (ed). Edinburgh_- London, 1969.

Ottenberg, Simon 1971 A Muslim Igbo village. *Cahiers d'Etudes Africaines* 11, Number 2.

Palmer, Sir Richmond. (1954) "Some Observations on Captain R. S. Rattray's Paper 'Present Tendencies of African Colonial Development'." *Journal of the Royal African Society* 55:57-48.

Parkin, David, Lionel Caplan, and Humphrey Fisher, Eds. *The Politics of Cultural Performance.* Providence, RI: Berghahn Books, 1996.

Pitt, David C. (1976) "Development from Below," pp; 7-19 in David C. Pitt (ed.) *Development from Below: Anthropologists and Development Situations.* The Hague: Mouton.

Prazan, Father Ceslaus 1977 "The Dukkawa." Pittsburgh : Duquesne University Press ; Atlantic Highlands [N.J.] : distributed by Humanities Press.

Rattray, R. S. (1954) "Present Tendencies of African Colonial Development." *Journal of the Royal African Society* 55: 22-56.

Reining, Conrad. (1966) *The Zande Scheme.* Evanston: Northwestern University Press.

Roder, Wolf 1970 *Kainji Lake research project, New Bussa, Nigeria.* FAD.

Roder, Wolf (1994) *Human Adjustment to Kainji Reservoir in Nigeria: an assessment of the economic and environmental consequences of a major man-made lake in Africa,* University Press of America, Lanham, MD.

Sahay, Keshari 1968 Impact of Christianity on the Uraon of the Raipur Belt in Chotanagpur: an analysis of its cultural processes. *American Anthropologist* 70: 923-942.

Salamone, Frank A.1972 Structural factors in Dukawa conversion. *Practical Anthropology* 219-225.

—— (1974) *Gods and Goods in Africa.* New Haven: HRAFlex.

—— 1975) "Becoming Hausa: Contributions to the Study of Cultural Pluralism," *Africa* 45 (4): 410-24.

——. (1977) "Missionaries and Anthropologists: Competition or Reciprocity?" *Human Organization* 36 (4): 407-12.

——. (1978) Early Expatriate Society in Northern Nigeria: Contributions to a Refinement of a Theory of Pluralism," *African Studies Review* 21 (2): 39-54.

——. (1974) *Gods and Goods in Africa.* New Haven: HRAFlex.

——. (1977a) "The Methodological Significance of the Lying Informant." *Anthropological Quarterly* 50(5): 117-124.

——. (1977b) "Missionaries and Anthropologists: Competition or Reciprocity?" *Human Organization* 56 (Winter).

Sanderson, Jimmy M.. Ethnic Boundaries and Identity in Plural Societies. *Annual Review* of *Sociology,* August 2002, Vol. 28: Pages 327-357.

Savishinsky, Joel S. (1972) "Coping with Feuding: The Missionary, the Fur Trader, and the Ethnographer." *Human Organization* 81, 5: 281-90.

Schapera, Isaac. (1958) "Christianity and the Tswana." *Journal* of *the Royal Anthropological Institute* 8: 1-10.

Smith, M. F. :..*Baba of Karo:.A. Woman of the Muslim Hausa.* New York, 1955.

Smith, M. G. (1969) "Some Developments in the Analytic Framework of Pluralism," pp. 415 58 in Leo Kuper and M.G. Smith (eds.) *Pluralism in Africa.* Berkeley: University of California Press.

——. *Government in Zazzau, 1800-1950.* London, 1960.

Sollors, Werner, Ed. *The Invention of Ethnicity.* New York: Oxford University Press, 1991.

Stavenhagen, Rodolfo. (1971) "Decolonizing Applied Social Sciences." *Human Organization* SO, 4: 854-48.

Tonkinson, Robert. (1974) *The Jigalong Mob.* Menlo Park, California: Cummings Publishing Company.

Turner, Victor W. *Schism and continuity in an African society: A study* of *Ndembu village life.* Manchester, England: Manchester University Press, 1957.

——. *The forest of symbols: Aspects of Ndembu ritual.* Ithaca, NY: Cornell University Press, 1967.

——. *The drums of affliction: a study* of *religious processes among the Ndembu of Zambia.* Oxford: Clarendon Press, 1968.

——. *The ritual process: structure and anti-structure.* Chicago: Aldine Publishing Co., 1969.

——. *Dramas, fields and metaphors: Symbolic action in human society.* Ithaca, NY: Cornell University Press, 1974.

——. *Revelation and divination in Ndembu ritual.* Ithaca, NY: Cornell University Press., 1975.

——. Variations of the theme of liminality. In *Secular ritual.* Ed. S. Moore & B. Myerhoff. Assen: Van Gorcum, 36-52, 1977.

——, and Schechner, Richard 1985.—*Between theater and anthropology* foreword by Victor W. Turner.—Phlledelphia: Univ. of Pennsylvania Press, cop. 1985.

——. *The Anthropology* of *Performance* / Victor Turner; pref. by Richard Schechner. New York: PAJ Publications, 1988.

Van Baal, Jan. (1972) "P ast Perfect," in Solon Kimball and James Watson (eds.) *Crossing Cultural Boundaries.* San Francisco: Chandler Publishing Company.

Van den Berghe, Pierre L. (1973) *Power and Privilege at an African University.* Cambridge: Schenkman.

Vengroff, Paul. (1975) "Traditional Political Structures in the Contemporary Context: The Chieftancy in the Kweneng," *African Studies* 34: 39-56.

Vincent, Joan. (197-7) "Colonial" Chiefs and the Making of Class: A Case Study from Teso, Eastern Uganda," *Africa* 47: 140-159.

——. (1978) "Political Anthropology: Manipulative Strategies," *Annual Review* of *Anthropology* 7: 175-94.

9 780761 847243